*Martyrs
of
Charity
Pt. 1.*

Christian and Jewish response to the Holocaust:
  A. Martyrs of Charity.
  B. Beasts of pray.

St. Maximilian Kolbe Foundation, originally known as Max Kolbe Foundation, is an interethnic and interfaith institution registered as a non-profit corporation: Religious – Educational – Charitable.

Dr. Wacław Zajączkowski

Martyrs of Charity

With a foreword by J.B. Sheerin, C.S.P.

A man can have no greater love than to lay down his life for his friends.

Matthew 26:40

... in so far as you did this to one of the least brothers of mine, you did it to me.

John 15:13

As one who in my home-land has shared the suffering of your brethern, I greet you with the word taken from the Heb-rew language: *Shalom*! Peace be with you."

John Paul II,
 Battery Park, New York,
Oct. 3, 1979.

Washington, D.C.
St. Maximilian Kolbe Foundation
1988

Cat. card:

Zajaczkowski, Waclaw, 1910—
    Martyrs of Charity. St. Maximilian Kolbe Foundation, Washington, D.C. 1988.
    336 p. illus. maps.
    (Christian and Jewish reponse to the Holocaust, 1. Martyrs of Charity, pts. 1-2)
    1. Holocaust, Jewish, 1939-1945. 2. Maximilian Kolbe, Saint. I. Title. II. Christian and Jewish response to the Holocaust.

ISBN 0-945281-00-5
First American edition 1988.
Copyright c. 1988. St. Maximilian Kolbe Foundation.

CONTENTS

ILLUSTRATIONS

MAPS

GERMAN CRIMES
IN POLAND, 1939–1945

Thousands of extermination places in Poland where millions of
Jews and Poles, with other Slavs were murdered in order to make
room for new Germanic Empire where Teutons (Germans,
Danes, Dutch etc.) were to be settled to create a hundred million
German Empire (Hitler's Third Reich)

NATIONAL CONFERENCE OF CATHOLIC BISHOPS
BISHOPS' COMMITTEE FOR ECUMENICAL AND INTERRELIGIOUS AFFAIRS
SECRETARIAT FOR CATHOLIC-JEWISH RELATIONS
1312 MASSACHUSETTS AVENUE, NORTHWEST
WASHINGTON, D. C. 20005   202 659-6857

" M A R T Y R S   O F   C H A R I T Y "

Since the end of World War II There has been a running controversy in ecumenical circles about the number of Jews saved by
Poles from a brutal death in the Nazi era. We were accustomed to
reading sweeping generalizations about Polish anti-semitism but
now the true picture is coming into focus due to the work of
painstaking researchers. Outstanding among these is Dr. Waclaw
Zajaczkowski who has compiled a book entitled Martyrs of Charity.
It is a painstakingly detailed account of hundreds of instances
in which Poles were murdered in World War II because they had
befriended Jews. It is a grim account of man's inhumanity to man
but also a glorious epic of Christian sacrifice for the sake of
the people of the Old Testament.

The author's account of the trials of the martyrs and the ago-
nies of the Jews is fascinating for its very diversity. I think
of two Polish rangers, Josef Zielinski and Stanislaw Lasota, shot
to death and their household burned for befriending Jews. There
is the tragic story of the farmers in the Krakow area who saved
150 Jews from extermination but 25 of these brave men paid with
their lives. Again, 25 Christians in the Warsaw area were murdered
when a Catholic farmer took in Jewish refugees and their children.
These martyrs knew full well the price they would have to pay:
posters nailed to trees served notice that death would be the
penalty for aiding Jews.

In December, 1942 a motorized detachment of select SS men
burned alive in a barn some 21 Poles along with the Jews they
had dared to shelter. A favorite form of Nazi slaughter seems to
have been that of burning victims alive. For sheltering about
100 Jews who had escaped from a concentration camp the Nazis
burned alive and exterminated the entire population of a village
inhabited by Catholic farmers. In Lukow county, December 10,
1942, Germans and their henchmen surrounded the farmhouse of the
Aftyka family, tossed grenades through the windows, ignored the
cries for mercy uttered by the victims in Polish and in Jewish,
set fire to the house and burned alive the farmer, his wife and
five children.

One particularly bizarre feature of the Nazi killings was that the killers, instead of murdering secretly, publicly announced their deviltry. On one occasion, they publicly hanged a Polish teacher and his wife for hiding a Jewish family, then proceeded to announce the killings through loudspeakers in the city hall square and to coerce the bystanders into witnessing the execution.

This book, Martyrs of Charity, is important in that it relies on no sweeping generalizations about Polish anti-semitism but presents the facts about time and place of Polish benevolence to Jews. In many places in Europe, the reaction of Christian Churches to large-scale murder of Jews was rather mild even though the mass murders were no secret. It is inspiring therefore to find so many Poles lived up to their Christian principles even to the point of martyrdom in saving Jews or at least, attempting to save them. Perhaps never before has this world encountered cruelty so monstrous as the brutal inhumanity of the Nazi holocaust but it can also be said that seldom has the world witnessed such a sense of brotherhood as that displayed by many Polish "good Samaritans" in befriending the long-suffering Jews. By reading these accounts of martyrdom Christians can come to realize that we are our brother's keeper even though we have to pay a high price in the process.

John B. Sheerin
C.S.P.
John B. Sheerin, C.S.P.

FORGOTTEN GRAVES OF POLISH
MARTYRS OF CHARITY

One of numerous visits by Dr. Wacław Zajaczkowski to the forgotten site of Christian martyrdom for giving aid to the persecuted Jews in Poland. Jewish diplomat and his wife saved with the sacrifice of life by Mrs. Banaszek and her children in Pustelnik never came back to pay respect to their rescuers. Their interest in the case was limited to the recovery of their valuables left in the attic and the exhumation of their daughter's body buried near their hide-out.

How mistaken was Emanuel Ringelblum who wrote in his Polish-Jewish relations: "There are more such hide-outs on the Polish side. In them are hidden the deathless friendship and gratitude of those rescued from the jaws of the Nazi monster. The people who do this should be decorated with the Order of Humanitarianism. Their name will remain precious for us forever. They are heroes who have fought against the greatest enemy of mankind... There are thousands of idealists like these in Warsaw and in the whole country, whether in the educated class or in the working class, who help Jews most devotedly at the risk of their lives. Every Jew snatched from the grip of the bloodthisty Nazi monster had to have a Christian idealist watching over him day after day like a guardian angel... This Polish gallery of heroes could provide subjects for wonderful novels about these noblest of idealists, who didn't fear the enemy's threats on his red posters..."

Twenty five years later, another Jewish historian, Szymon Datner, had to state with sadness in his Las sprawiedliwych: "How many Poles – young, old, and children – gave their lives in the fight against the extermination of Jews? They will never receive any medals, they will never hear words of gratitude. They are dead. They usually died with those they attempted to save. They frequently died with their loved ones – their wives, their children, their parents, end sometimes even their neighbors. In towns and in villages, their bodies were burned together with the houses in which they sheltered Jews. Sometimes, the opressors ordered that Polish Christians and Jews be buried together in the same mass grave..."

In Jerusalem, there is a square named after Konrad Adenauer, successor of Otto von Bismarck and Adolf Hitler in the office of a German Chancellor, there is at Yad Vashem denigratory exhibit on provocative Kielce affair, but here is no room for a monument to Christian Martyrs of Charity. This is a good reason for erecting such a monument in front of U.S. Holocaust Museum in Washington, D.C. as an answer to the vicious legend about the "bancruptcy of Christianity."

PUBLISHERS' PREFACE

This little contribution to Holocaust martyrology, as well as its announced companion volume, grew out of an urgent need to answer the unprecedented anti-Christian campaign conducted world–wide under the code name of the "holocaust". Its author, Dr Wacław Zajączkowski, as a theologian and church historian, in addition to having been born and raised in a typical "East-European shtetl" (Ghetto in Poland was a foreign, German, import), and having been previously involved as an editor of a Catholic monthly in the study of Jewish-Christian relations, seems to be uniquely qualified to write on this subject with a first-hand knowledge of recent events and their historical background.

At the beginning of the World War II he was attached to the former Apostolic Nuncio in Warsaw, Abp. Cortesi, then in Bucharest, in charge of Polish soldiers in Rumanian internment camps. He became editor of the first Catholic periodical for this nucleus of a Polish army-in-exile, collecting information on the fate of Poles and Jews in occupied Poland, first for the Apostolic Nuncio, then for the Primate of Poland, Cardinal August Hlond and the General Superior of the Society of Jesus, Wlodzimierz Ledochowski, in Rome.

Sent to the United States with the news about the horrors perpetrated by Germans in his native Poland, he created a Catholic Radio League in Chicago to support a radio program bringing to the attention of his fellow American Poles the terrible predicament of their mother country and became a director of the Chicago office of the *Catholic Press Agency* for English language periodicals, as well as an editor of a monthly periodical in the Polish language. His report about extermination of Jews in Poland and the deeply Christian attitude of Polish Catholics published in the *America* weekly of Feb. 13, 1943, provoked a favorable comment from the Editors as "a document which sheds great light upon the deeply human and Christian attitude of the Polish Catholics toward their tormented fellow countrymen of the Jewish faith. The facts reported, included precisely those incredibly horrible details which have appeared in the press of the United States – thus disposing of the notion that they were mere "propaganda" exaggerations: "Millions of helpless people are being massacred and a sinister silence prevails... This silence cannot be tolerated any longer... That is why we, Polish Catholics, are raising our voices... Our Christian conscience bids us to protest". It was also a call to the Western world not to wash its hands of Polish and Jewish tragedy "like Pontius Pilate". "Such sentiments, commented the Editors of *America*, correspond appropriately to the hospitable treatment which is reported as being given to Polish Catholic refugees by the authorities and populace of the Jewish colonies in Palestine".

Dr. Zajączkowski knew of numerous Polish Catholic families, among them his own family in Poland, which paid dearly for their rescue work for persecuted Jews with their lives. He was, therefore, greatly surprised to read one day, many years later, in the *Washington Star* daily a hateful comment by a Jewish refugee from Poland about the expression of public sympathy for a Hanafi Muslim leader whose entire family was wantonly murdered, asking excitedly: "Who stood up for us during the Holocaust?" It was a voice of person who owed her own rescue to a helping hand of a Christian Pole, but succumbed to the pernicious Holocaust myth that Jews in Poland suffered alone while the Christian world was "crucifying" Israel. Zajączkowski knew perfectly well of ineffective response to the Polish and Jewish tragedy on the part of Western world, even on the part of influential Western Jewry which was washing its hands of this crime like a Pontius Pilate. He recalled, therefore, the Polish aid to suffering Jews as an answer to the anguished question, "who stood for us?" by saying simply, "We did" (*The Washington Star*, Apr. 13, 1977).

"My church, my country of origin, my family did, by saving from certain death Irene Franziak and her daughter Anya, both living presently in Tel Aviv (an act of heroism honored later by a tree planted in the Yad Vashem Alley of the Righteous for the Zajączkowski family). And so did my in-laws by the name of Szwed, likewise decorated with a Yad Vashem Medal for the Righteous among the Nations, for saving the Wapniarski family, presently in Canada, and the Kac, Malcman and Szaja families who were never heard of afterwards. As a result of these acts of heroism – three persons from my family lost their lives as veritable Martyrs of Christian Charity". The letter pointed out countless other similar cases in Poland not listed on the Mount of Remembrance in Jerusalem. According to Emmanuel Ringelblum, Warsaw alone had at least 10,000 to 15,000 Polish families hiding the Jews in spite of a German law proclaimed on Nov. 10, 1941 that any form of aid to Jews would be punished by death, a law unknown in any Western part of occupied Europe*, a law defied in that part of Europe where the civilian victims

---

* Nechama Tec, her effort to belittle tremendous sacrifices of Polish Catholics in the rescue of Jews (see her recent book, *When light pierced the darkness*) attempts to cast doubt on the unquestionable fact that only in Poland and the adjoining Slavic countries a mandatory death sentence existed for any form of aid offered to Jews. Her suggestion that a death penalty existed in Vidkun Quisling's Norway is not only unfounded, but simply ridiculous.

Verordnungsblatt
für das Generalgouvernement

Dziennik Rozporządzeń
dla Generalnego Gubernatorstwa

1942	Ausgegeben zu Krakau, den 14. November 1942	Nr. 98
	Wydano w Krakau dnia 14 listopada 1942 r.	

Tag | **Inhalt / Treść** | **Seite**
dzień | | strona

10. 11. 42 Polizeiverordnung über die Bildung von Judenwohnbezirken in den Distrikten
Radom, Krakau und Galizien 683

Rozporządzenie policyjne o tworzeniu żydowskich dzielnic mieszkaniowych
w Okręgach Radom, Krakau i Galizien (Galicja) 683

*

§ 3

(1) Juden, die den Vorschriften des § 2 zuwiderhandeln, werden nach den bestehenden Bestimmungen mit dem Tode bestraft.

(2) Ebenso wird bestraft, wer einem solchen Juden wissentlich Unterschlupf gewährt, d. h. wer insbesondere den Juden außerhalb des Judenwohnbezirks unterbringt, beköstigt oder verbirgt.

(3) Gegen denjenigen, welcher davon Kenntnis erhält, daß ein Jude sich unbefugt außerhalb eines Judenwohnbezirks aufhält, und der Polizei nicht Meldung erstattet, werden sicherheitspolizeiliche Maßnahmen ergriffen.

(4) Nichtjüdische Personen, die den Vorschriften des § 2 zuwider den Judenwohnbezirk nicht rechtzeitig verlassen oder ihn ohne polizeiliche Erlaubnis betreten, werden im Verwaltungsstrafverfahren mit Geldstrafe bis zu 1000 Zloty ersatzweise mit Haft bis zu drei Monaten, bestraft. Den Strafbescheid erläßt der Kreishauptmann (Stadthauptmann).

§ 3

(1) Żydzi, wykraczający przeciwko przepisom § 2, podlegają według istniejących postanowień karze śmierci.

(2) Tej samej karze podlega, kto takiemu żydowi świadomie udziela schronienia, tzn. kto w szczególności umieszcza żyda poza obrębem żydowskiej dzielnicy mieszkaniowej, żywi go lub ukrywa.

(3) Wobec tego, kto uzyska wiadomość o tym, że jakiś żyd bezprawnie przebywa poza obrębem dzielnicy mieszkaniowej a nie zgłosi tego Policji, zastosowane będą policyjne środki bezpieczeństwa.

(4) Osoby nie będące żydami, które wbrew przepisom § 2 nie opuszczą na czas żydowskiej dzielnicy mieszkaniowej lub które wejdą do niej bez policyjnego zezwolenia, ulegną w postępowaniu karno-administracyjnym karze grzywny do 1000 złotych z zamianą na karę aresztu do trzech miesięcy. Orzeczenie karne wydaje starosta powiatowy (starosta miejski).

*

§ 6

Diese Polizeiverordnung tritt am 20. November 1942 in Kraft.

Krakau, den 10. November 1942.

Der Höhere SS und Polizeiführer
im Generalgouvernement
Der Staatssekretär für das Sicherheitswesen
Krüger

§ 6

Niniejsze rozporządzenie policyjne wchodzi w życie z dniem 20 listopada 1942 r.

Kraków, dnia 10 listopada 1942 r.

Wyższy Dowódca SS i Policji
w Generalnym Gubernatorstwie
Sekretarz Stanu dla Spraw Bezpieczeństwa
Krüger

Authoritative confirmation through the official journal of ordinances (*Verordnungsblatt*) by the German Nazi gouvernement in Kraków, of a videly accepted practice, announced also in the official posters by subordinate units in Warsaw, Częstochowa, etc. that any form of aid given to a Jew is being punished ba death – an ordinance unknown in any other country of German-occupied Europe – the historical fact which is being ignored or explained away by Judge Bejski and subjected to doubt by Nechama Tec in her pseudo-scholarly research.

amounted to 18 or even 26 million, mostly Christian (see *Enc. Brit.*). He ended with W. Broniewski's poem:

> In every Polish heart these words must be engraved as in stone:
> The blood shed unites us, the execution wall,
> Dachau and Auschwitz and our ravaged home,
> Every nameless grave and every prison cell unites us all!"

As it turned out the *Washington Star* letter was not only balm for a wounded Jewish heart but also for the feelings of many Christians who – in Harry J. Cargas' words – were "depressed, psychologically battered and starved for stories of Christian heroes during this period". A typical response came from a Lutheran American of Norvegian descent. who also enclosed a clipping of a denigrating press release:

"Dear Dr. Zajączkowski: Forgive me for writing to your home address which I found in the phone book of D.C. This is in response to your remarkable letter in the *Washington Star* of this evening. It pricked some thoughts on those matters that continue to plague, even though there are, from time to time, various comments about that period. In short, I am desperately searching for some authentic materials that tell of the real Christian persons during that time.

Having been born in the US in February 1942, like all others of similar age, there remain for us only stories of stories, and my situation of hearing frequently about this period from the Jewish point of view (note the attached item written by a very close older friend of mine – one whose family was a victim in Poland during that time) leaves me in a constant sad state of anxiety over what power real Christians had over what was going on.

In this emotionally-frought generation which follows, I must say, in some instances the black-white approach of "Christians participated, didn't they", absurd as it is, is difficult in words to explain away. To bridge this emotional gap, with persons too close to those events, may be impossible – yet, I feel a growing need to get some first-hand knowledge of the dilemmas that faced real Christians living at that period.

Since I was a child, there has been this constant question: "How would I have acted? What would I have done?" That, to me, seems to be the ultimate question for a human being. I am of Norwegian descent, am an editor in the World Bank, was raised in the Lutheran Church, attended the Norway-oriented, Church supported St. Olaf College in Minnesota and I believe in fully embracing the inherent truths and promises of Christianity, but hesitate to be too enthusiastic about man-made theology found in many places.

I have read some information, my place of work, being located very close to the B'nai B'rith library. The seeming inaction of the Pope, about which there has been a lot written, leaves a lot of questions too. If you have any time, I would kindly ask whether you know any materials I might read on the above mentioned statements. Thank you. (-) Carol W." (Original of the letter in the *Archives* of St. Maximilian Kolbe Foundation)

The text of Carol's enclosure merits being quoted in its entirety to fathom the depth of distorsion in presenting such a recent event as Nazi Germany's renewed attempt to gain what the Prussian General Staff already tried to accomplish in 1914 i.e. hegemony among the European powers and a territorial expansion toward the East – as sort of a religious war against the Jews in which both opponents were somehow lumped together, Poles and Germans, into one united "Christian" front – against the "innocent" Jews. Jewish innocence, or may we say, indifference or even a favorable disposition, toward the German Nazi war aims in the East, became the basis of their complaint that they were being killed only for "being Jews" in a religious sense of this word, as opposed to "Christians". In this phony version of the war, according to Dr. Josephine Z. Knopp, "Research Director" of the Philadelphia-based National Institute on the Holocaust, "thousands of Slavs... were caught up in the war against the Jews" (see *Sh'ma, a journal of Jewish responsibility*, April 29, 1977, p. 107) and, in the account of Michael Elkins in *Forged in fury*, New York, Ballantine Books, 1971, p. 125, Catholic Poles "who had thrown down their rifles picked up clubs and joined their erstwhile conquerors in beating the brains of nearly three thousand of their Jewish fellow citizens within the first three days of the war's beginning" – a pseudo-history, obviously "forged in fury" of a diseased mind.

The author of the enclosed press release, to gain greater credibility, is introduced with a phrase: „**A Catholic speaks up: Christianity died at Auschwitz death camp** – says Claire Huchet-Bishop. New York, (WJP) – Claire Huchet-Bishop, the noted Catholic scholar and devoted disciple of the late French-Jewish author, Jules Isaac, has charged that "traditional Christianity died at Auschwitz Death Camp."

"In a scathing exposition appearing in the April 1 issue of the *Miami Jewish Floridian*, Lady Huchet-Bishop, a former President of the International Conference of Christians and Jews, notes that "it has been said that "Christianity died at Auschwitz" ("discovery" made by Elie Wiesel, if we are not mistaken). "It did", she affirms: "the Christianity we have known, Constantinian Christianity, seventeen hundred years old, the Christianity allied to power, rendering unto Caesar what is due to God, culminating in the only instance in history of genocide carried out as a governmental policy, (Lady Bishop, obviously, never heard of Teutonic Knights' policy toward Prussians – U.P.) with the whole machinery of the state mobilized for the purpose and with the indifference of the institutional church to the fate of the Jews making it posible – an indifference directly due to the traditional anti-Semitism propagated for centuries".

"Not only did traditional Christianity die at Auschwitz", the well-known Catholic exponent of truth and justice avers, "Western civilization died, too."

"Had the Christian church cried out forty years ago, denouncing in not uncertain terms the extermination of the Jews at Auschwitz and other death factories", she emphasizes, "the world would not be what it is today. Had the Christian church taken an unequivocal stand against the Nazis, upholding the moral and spritual values Hitler flaunted, it might have suffered severe persecution, but it would have saved the respect due to those values, and thus it might have remained a beacon on earth, especially in the West."

"In capitulating to unspeakable evil through its indifference to the fate of the Jews, **the church as an institution not only signed its own moral death warrant**, but also unleashed in the world unrestrained reliance upon violence as a solution for all personal, interpersonal, national and international conflicts," she charges. "In the most critical hour of its history, **the church betrayed its mission**. Today, the whole world suffers the consequences."

Claire Huchet-Bishop concludes that "the very protean of anti-Semitism makes the fight against it a model for the worldwide fight against any minority hatred and oppression. However, the attitude toward the Jewish question remains the barometer which reveals the state of spiritual health of any human being, group, church or civilization..."

"Lady Huchet-Bishop is the author of numerous books, among which is *How Catholics look at Jews*".

This was the kind of historiography Philip Friedman was afraid of while speaking at a 1949 conference on *Problems of research in the study of Jewish catastrophe 1939-1945* where the following description of *"Khurbn* literature" was given:

"The bulk of it consists of personal records, memoirs, chronicles of events, pathetic accusations, etc. Few books have been written by scholarly or literarily trained writers... In effect, we have an incredible vulgarization and shallow banalization of the scholarly (or pseudo-scholarly) and pseudoliterary production in this field. The flood of inferior production is overshadowing the worthwhile material and is bringing much harm, causing miscredit and distrust to our whole *Khurbn* literature and to the results of serious research."

At the same time, Abraham Duker, wrote in his "Comments" (*Jewish Social Studies*, v. 12 (1950) no. 1, p. 80) in connection with the approaching rehabilitation of Nazi Germany and her Germanic allies, valiantly supported by the Jewish establishment:

"Unfortunately, at the present stage of the cold war, public taste in reading and research is not guided toward learning the truth about crimes which reflect adversely upon the status of the German people and their Quisling pogromist allies in many nations of Europe... (Vidkun Quisling in Norway, *Danish Waffen SS* in Denmark, A. A. Mussert's *S. S. Volunteer Panzer-Grenadier Brigade Nederland* in Holland, Léon Degrelle in Belgium, Pétain in France, etc. – U.P.)... the campaign to make the world forget, is waged by some presumably respectable people in most respectable quarters."

Originally, after the end of the War, respectable scholarly institutions arose in Poland which was the scene of a common, Polish and Jewish, martyrdom. An equivalent of the Israeli Yad Vashem which was organized in later years, the Polish Institute of National Memory (Instytut Pamięci Narodowej) started to collect historical materials (supressed in 1949), the separate Jewish Historical Institute was created with scholarly periodicals in Polish and in Yiddish supported by the Polish Academy of Sciences and the immensely rich materials of the YIVO institute were transferred from Wilno to New York. Quite soon, however, countries interested in reshaping history of recent events to their advantage started to pour money into a different kind of "research". The turning point occurred when billions of German Marks were poured into Israeli coffers on the basis of the so called Luxemburg Agreement between Ben Gurion and Chancellor Adenauer in 1952, and when the United States undertook massive transfer of funds to Israel.

During heated debates somebody hit upon the idea of giving the Jewish genocide a distinctive semi-sacral name of the "holocaust" to make it "unique". Some Jewish scholars protested in vain against what Prof. Henry Friedlander called "attempts to impose serious restrictions on discussions of the

Holocaust by those who wish to elevate the subject to the level of sacred history and who denounce opponents for sacrilege... you cannot treat the Holocaust as sacred history." (*ADL Bulletin*, Nov. 1977).

Others, like James Parkes, well-known author of *An enemy of the People: Antisemitism*, Penguin ed. "took pain to point out that there is evidence that **the Jews were less than thirty percent of Hitler's victims murdered in cold blood**" and was wondering at the practice of "omitting from a German translation passages suggesting a Jewish share of responsibility" (see his Preface to *AntiSemitism and the foundations of Christianity*, ed. by Alan T. Davies, Paulist Press, 1979, p. v, x). As to the number of victims, it was known that out of 18 millions of innocent civilians murdered away from battlefields in an attempt to exterminate unwanted populations in Central and Eastern Europe, 5,400,000 were killed in Poland and 10,300,000 in the Soviet Union, Poland with one fifth and Belorussia with one fourth populations lost. No German statistics of all the Jews killed were left, except for an affidavit of Dieter Wisliceny, dated Nov. 29, 1945 which quotes the only person who should have had an overall view, Adolf Eichmann, as follows: "I laugh when I jump into the grave because of feeling I have killed **5,000,000 Jews**. That gives me great satisfaction and gratification" (*Nazi conspiracy and aggression*, Washington, Government Printing Office, 1946). Cecil Roth, in *A history of the Jews*, Shocken books, 1966, p. 408) gave a cautious estimate, "perhaps as many as 6,000,000 – certainly well over 4,000,000" and Howard M. Sachar in *The course of modern Jewish history*, Delta Books, 1977, updated edition, gave his considered estimate "between 4,200,000 and 4,600,000", adding that "the figure of 6,000,000 released at the end of the war has since been discounted".

Max I. Dimond, in his *Jews, God and history*, New York, New American Library, 1962, p. 389, said: "The chilling reality is that when the Russians overran the concentration camps in Poland they found enough Zyklon B crystals to kill 20 million people. Yet there were no more than 3 milion Jews left in Europe. The ratio of contemplated mass killing was no longer 1.4 Christians for every Jew, but 5.3 Christians for every Jew. Nazi future plans called for the killing of 10 million non-Germanic people every year". He also cautioned: "If the Christian reader dismisses what happened in Germany as something which affected a few million Jews only, he has not merely shown his contempt for the 7 million murdered by the Nazis but has betrayed his Christian heritage as well. And if the Jewish reader forgets the 7 million Christians murdered by the Nazis, then he has not merely let 5 million Jews die in vain but has betrayed his Jewish heritage of compassion and justice."

Unfortunately, millions of German Marks and American dollars proved to be stronger than "Jewish heritage of compassion and justice". In the article on "The Holocaust: its use and abuse" in the *Yad Vashem Studies*, v. 14 (1981) p. 303, Leon A. Jick regretfully stated: "Twenty years later – at the beginning of the 1980's – the situation is radically altered. **"Holocaust" has become an instantly recognized code word.** It is the subject of scores of books, lectures, courses, television programs – even a children's game. Popular journals feature articles on various aspects of events related to the destruction of European Jewry. Politicians, whose acumen in recognizing, appropriating and exploiting popular issues is beyond question, respond by appointing highly publicized commissions, bestowing awards and punctuating their speeches to Jewish audiences with frequent references to "The Holocaust". Fund raisers exploit the interest in solliciting support for purposes which are often vague and undefined. Invoking the "holocaust" automatically guarantees a positive response".

People who used to say that "one cow in Palestine is worth more to us than a hundred Jewish corpses in Poland" suddenly discovered the value of these "corpses". Weizmann's "economic and moral dust" turned out to be more precious than golden dust attracting American prospectors to the brooks and rivers of early California.

"As the one weapon that will never let "them" forget how "we" suffered, the Holocaust continues to be immemorialized whenever Jews will it, and their multifold actions, exacted as many pounds of flesh", testifies a prominent Jewish writer. (Alfred M. Lilienthal, *The Zionist connection*, New Jork, Dodd Mead, 1978, p. 474) "Millions of people, he continues, other than Jews perished, and for these the bell does not seem to have been tolling. And it is not out of line to inquire of the cultists, these people so intent on keeping this issue of the "six million" alive, whether they have ever given any consideration to the Zionist role in the death of these "six million" victims" (op. cit. p. 483).

"When all else fails – says Lilienthal (p. 461) the "six million" Jews killed during the Nazi holocaust remain the ultimate silencer. These six million are quite literally pulled from the ovens, propped up and pushed forward to confront any who might raise the slightest question or smallest voice of dissent. Even the mere threat of this suffices to silence most people. But on many occasions, when the six million are ritually brought out, silence ensues. The line is maintained. Hitler has made reluctant Zionists out of many guilt-ridden Christians and assimilated Western Jews."

The judgment of the American Jewish educators is in agreement with the Jewish and Israeli scholars' observation. Prof. Byron L. Sherwin of the Spertus College of Judaica in Chicago, in his article "Teaching about the Holocaust – some guidelines" in *The Pedagogic Reporter, a forum for Jewish education*, v. 33 (1982) no. 2, p. 4, sadly confessed: "Except for fund-raising speeches, one heard very little about the Holocaust in the 1950s, 1960s and the early 1970s. But, now, in 1982 **there is a booming Holocaust industry**. In 1965 the Holocaust was given virtually no place in religious education – Jewish or Christian. College-level courses in Judaica were virtually devoid of offerings in Holocaust studies. Even Hebrew teachers' colleges largely avoided the subject in their classes. But, today, **"there is no business like *Shoah* business."** Self-proclaimed "experts" have emerged. Courses have exploded in secular and religious schools, in Jewish and Christian schools, in elementary schools and in universities, even in some nursery schools and in informal education programs. Curricula now abound. Conferences proliferate... Movie stars endorse "Remembering the Holocaust" like baseball players who endorse beer and shaving cream. Pop-psychology describes everyone as a "survivor". In England, for $ 60, one can spend a weekend at Camp Butlitz, a simulated Nazi concentration camp, replete with dirty camp uniforms, a diet of gruel, punishment drills, Nazi speeches and machine-gun nests... The earlier conspiracy of silence may have been preferable to the present commercialization of the Holocaust and **commercially promoted outbreak of "Holocaust fever"**... There are many historical, political, social, theological and psychological issues which are endemic to any study of the Holocaust. These cannot be glossed over by an appeal to raw emotions... To portray the Holocaust as an exclusively Jewish experience contradicts the historical fact that also millions of non-Jews were systematically murdered by the Nazis... Trying to capitalize upon the "popularity" of Jewish Holocaust constitutes an approach that attempts to reduce all of Judaism to the Holocaust. It tries to make the Holocaust a paradigm of Jewish history, the quintessence of the Jewish experience, the only possible catalyst for inculcating Jewish identity."

A similar warning comes from Judith S. Lewis, an Assistant Rabbi in Roslyn Heights, N.Y.: "If we stop at the terror, indoctrinating our students with only the evil, then, in effect, we complete the work of the Nazis. We allow the contributions of our people and heritage to disappear from this world. Rather, we must start with the survival of the Jews, looking back through our history to learn how – and why – we are here today... Our students should be made aware of the fact that not only Jews were affected by the Nazi movement... The Holocaust should be presented within the context of the total Jewish experience, rather than treating it in isolation and out of proportion to the rest of Jewish history and life." ("Integrating the Holocaust – a graded curriculum", in *The Pedagogic Reporter*, v. 33 (1982) no. 2, p. 7-10).

Finally, the Assistant Rabbi of Temple Israel in New Rochelle, William Lee Rothschild, in his article "New directions for Holocaust studies" in the same *"forum for Jewish education"* (p. 10-12) quotes the reactions of his students after his school "exploded in the past decade with Holocaust studies":

– "We're tired of the Holocaust. There is nothing more to learn. We've heard it every year since..."
– "People get really upset about it."
– "It's sickening to hear about. Why can't we hear about good things that happened to Jews?"
– It puts the Jews down. They were inferior if they allowed this to happen to them."
– "We always lose!"
– "Why can't we hear about something we do good (sic) as Jews?"

Then Rabbi Rothschild warns that "the students' comparison of the Holocaust with his or her American life drives a wedge between the student and Judaism. Judaism becomes a badge of failure, and foreign failure at that... We need not portray the entire spectrum of Jewish history as disaster after disaster."

Many years ago, Dr. Zajączkowski, invited to the headquarters of B'nai B'rith in Washington, D.C. for a presentation of Nathan J. Rapoport's monument of Jewish martyrdom to be erected in Jerusalem, pointed out the same sinister effect on Jewish youth and possibly, on future Israeli generations, of uniformly negative and black portaying of their past, even in such friendly and hospitable countries like Poland. He has received from the renown ed Polish-Jewish sculptor a request for relevant historical material and hearty thanks for a suggestion which he promised to follow in his future works. This letter is worth reviewing in its original Polish text.

NATHAN. J. RAPOPORT
54 WEST 174 STR.
NEW-YORK. 10023.

24 V. 1968

Drogi Panie Zajdlowski!

list Pana i wycinki z gazet
otrzymałem. Dziękuję z całego
serca za delikatność i szlachetność
Pana recenzji. Jestem do głębi wzruszony
dobrotliwością szlachetnym odruchem
i dobrą wolą.

To dobrze, że Pan się zgadza z
moim podejściem do budowania
pomnika dla Jerozolimy.

Dziękuję z góry za Pana pomoc —
nie jestem pewien czy będą mogły
mieć zmienić, ale to nie jest
wykluczone: — ponieważ jestem nią
tak wzruszony, że zrobię pewne
zmiany pracując nad ostatecznym
modelem.

Będę mógł w przyjaźni dać o
innych pracach wyraz Pana
sugestii.

Spotkanie Pana i Jego Świetlanej
Małżonki była świętem.

Życzę wszystkiego
Dobrego

Nathan Rapoport

Similar positive reactions among honest Jewish individuals were encountered by Zajączkowski's popularizing effort in form of exhibits at various American educational centers on college and university level. Principal Research Investigator at the Catholic University of America National Catholic School of Social Service, Dr. David Guttman, at this time involved in research on ethnic groups in the U.S.A. wrote, on September 20, 1978, with a carbon copy for University President Pellegrino:

"Dear Dr. Zajączkowski: I just came back from viewing the exhibit you set up in the Mullen Library of Catholic University. I am so deeply moved, it is hard to express my feelings in words. I have seen many exhibits about the Holocaust, but it was for me particularly meaningful and significant that this exhibit giving testimony to the heroic attempts of some Polish people to save the Jews while they themselves were under the threat of death is being shown at Catholic University. Being an Israeli and someone who personally witnessed and survived the atrocities of the Holocaust, I find it particularly important for an educational institution to present the truth and to contribute, hopefully, to people's enlightenment. I deeply appreciate your work on behalf of creating more human relationships among the ethnic groups and furthering the cause of peace and forgiveness. Your work is particularly meaningful for us who are engaged in the study of ethnic support systems, as I strongly believe that supports must exceed the physical world. Were those supports available to people at the time of World War II, perhaps much of the tragedy could have been avoided." (Orginal in *Archives* of St. Maximilian Kolbe Foundation).

The editor of the religious section in *The Washington Star*, William F. Willoughby, though himself "a WASP, "with an accent this time on the "P" (Protestant)", as he introduced himself, gave an enthusiastic endorsement for this kind of activity: "Zajączkowski does not want anyone to forget the Holocaust. Too many people paid the ultimate, horrible price to madmen. But he does not want anyone to forget, either, that the toll they exacted did not stop at the Jews. His fellow countrymen, most of them Catholic, fell too. "It is not fair to us Polish Christians, who suffered just as much under the Nazis, to give the impression that no one befriended the Jews in their terrible hour of need", Zajączkowski said. "We certainly did." He spent many visits to his native Poland, interviewing survivors of the Nazi rule and looking at pertinent documents wherever he could find them. He never began to exhaust the sources, but presented documentation to *The Star* of nearly 3,000 Polish Catholics who were burned alive, executed or died from torture because they befriended Jews. He believes that at least one million Polish Catholics helped the Jews under the ever-present threat of a Nazi-imposed law of Nov. 10, 1941, that spelled death for anyone caught or even suspected of being friendly to Jews... Those who gave their lives befriending Jews he calls Martyrs of Charity." (Who helped World War II Jews? We did!", *The Washington Star*, Sep. 28, 1978)

The only President of the National Conference of American Bishops who in recent years had the personal courage to contradict the Jewish offensive against the alleged "antisemitism" of Catholic Lenten Liturgy, Archbishop Quinn of San Francisco, gave his support for publishing the noble deeds of Christian Martyrs of Charity in a letter of Oct. 2, 1978, addressed to the author:

"Dear Dr. Zajaczkowksi: Thank you for sending me the information concerning the inspiring courage and charity of the Polish Catholics in caring for and saving the Jewish people. I feel that **this kind of information needs wider dissemination** and I was delighted to see it carried in our own *National Conference News Service* this week." (Original in Archives of St. Maximilian Kolbe Foundation).

Archbishop of Washington, William Cardinal Baum, personally opened an exhibit at the National Shrine of Immaculate Conception Memorial Hall in Summer 1976, where the aspect of Catholic heroic aid to the Jews was stressed, and out of his own pocket gave Dr. Zajączkowski $ 250 as his personal contribution to further his research. He also told of his visit to Auschwitz and to Kolbe's cell (a huge portrait of the holy Martyr being crowned with a red crown was featured at the exhibit) where, he said, "we saw the sign of evil, the manifestation of cruelty which is kept alive... I think it's good that the memory of such cruelty is being retained so that people do not forget. At the same time, however, we saw in this cell the sign of Triumph of Christ over evil and over death. That was a very profound experience for all of us." (*Catholic Standard*, Sep. 28, 1978).

Obliteration of this "sign of triumph of Christ over the evil" by the Holocaust fanatics suddenly emerged as their irresponsible goal just recently in the world-wide protest against the Carmelite Convent in a close vicinity of the Auschwitz death camp and the cell of St. Maximilian Kolbe, under the Jewish-atheist slogan formulated by Theo Klein, president of the Council Representing Jewish Institutions in France in a letter to Archbishop Angelo Felici, the papal nuncio in France: "It is too late, Your Excellency, for repentance on the places of the crime. (He implied it was "repentance" for Church's complicity – U.P.) The sky was empty then and it must remain so. Do not let a shadow be cast, be it that of the cross, on this immense field of our unappeasable sadness." (*NC News Service* story by Owen Williams of Meze, France, April 3, 1986) Unfortunately, some Catholic "eager-beavers" in places of influence in Rome like the Irish Superior General of Sisters of Sion, Katherine MacDonald, and a German-born "war refugee from Silesia" known as a "Jesuit Rabbi", Reinhard Neudecker of the Pontifical Biblical Institute who for seven years "prayed in the synagogue daily" joined the advocates of the "empty sky" over Auschwitz who went as far as to call on the Communist government of Poland to curtail Carmelite Sisters' prayers on the site of martyrdom of so many Catholic Poles – a truly depressing result of a mistaken "dialogue with Jews" based on distorted historical facts and years of Jewish brainwashing.*

The sky over Auschwitz was not "empty" for St. Maximilian Maria Kolbe. It was not empty for the Jewish convert, Edith Stein, a Carmelite nun like those who are being denied the privilege of prayer by some Jews*. It was not empty for hundreds of Catholic priests, many of them Jesuits, who died there. It was not empty for millions of believing Jews and Christians who were tortured and died there. Some of them could have had their moments of dispair, some perhaps lost their faith. But a "god" which may be dismissed when his worship does not pay off, is not the God of Jewish-Christian tradition although this may be suggested by title *When God and men failed*, a collection of essays with unfortunate contributions by Robert Drinan, S.J. and Richard McSorley, S.J. of Georgetown University.

Rabbi Richard Rubenstein made in *The Christian Century* a tragic statement about the "disconfirmation" of God's covenant with Jews which he calls "the most severe crisis faced by Jewish religious thought in almost 2,000 years. I expressed the conviction that the Holocaust was the disconfirming event par excellence for the classical Judeo-Christian theology of covenant and election. I argued that those believing Jews and Christians who affirm that God acts decisively in history, and most decisively in the history of Israel, **have no choice but to**

---

* Unfortunate threat of expulsion from their present site at Auschwitz suspended over the heads of Carmelite Sisters by the second Geneva meeting of Feb. 22, 1987, is only thinly veiled by the project of a new "center for prayers, encounters, dialogue and study" hopefully to be joined by the Jewish side, possibly also including the Carmelite Sisters dislodged from their existing convent (Card. Marcharski's interview with PAP). With a wholehearted wish for the success of these endeavors, let's hope there will be no bitter aftertaste of the noble Carmelite venture at Auschwitz as the one expressed by Rabbi A. James Rudin in an address to the Newman Alumni Association of the City College in New York attributing it... to the "pathology of anti-Semitism still existing" in the (Polish?) Catholic Church.

interpret the Holocaust as God's just chastisement of a sinful Israel or to regard that event as effectively disconfirming the theology of covenant and election... In view of the loss of faith experienced by those who could not regard the Holocaust as divine punishment... I turned to psychoanalysis, anthropology and the sociology of religion to defend the utility if not the sacrality of traditional Jewish religious practice."

Rabbi Rubenstein, eventually, found the difference between the Jews and Christians, which explains why so many Christians managed to save their faith even at the bottom of the Nazi hell, and most of the Jews did not: "Here is the difference, he says, between Christians and Jews: The Gospel ends beyond tragedy, on the note of hope. Resurrection is the final word. I wish it were so. But I believe my Pharisaic progenitors were essentially correct two thousand years ago when they sadly concluded that the promise of radical novelty in the human condition was a pathetic, although understandable, illusion, that the old world goes on today as it did yesterday and as it will tomorrow" (*After Auschwitz: radical theology and contemporary Judaism*, New York, Hobbs-Merrill, 1966, p. 264).

Zajączkowski, in his interview with the director of religious programs on the *Voice of America*, Fr. S. Filipowicz, S. J., expressed his discomfort if not horror, after having been invited by Yad Vashem to plant a tree in the Alley of the Righteous and to participate in the ceremonies at the Hall of Remembrance there. He didn't like the unrelieved blackness or rather hopelessness, of the place where no mention is made of the abundant blessings bestowed on Israel by God during the past two thousand years preceeding providential return to the Promised Land.

"It is, in the words of Sholem Asch, of the highest importance not only to record and recount, both for ourselves and for the future, the evidences of human degradation, but side by side with them to set forth the evidences of human exaltation and nobility. Let the epic of heroic deeds of love, as opposed by those of hatred, of rescue as oppposed to destruction, bear equal witness to unborn generations".

"On the flood of sin, hatred and blood let loose by Hitler upon the world, there swam a small ark which preserved intact the common heritage of a Judeo-Christian outlook, that outlook which is founded on double principle of love of God and love of one's fellow men. The demonism of Hitler had sought to overturn and overwhelm it in the flood of hate. It was saved by the heroism of a handful of saints." (Philip Friedman, *Their brothers' keepers*, New York, Crown, 1957, p. 13).

In an interview with *The Chicago Catholic* of March 2, 1984, entitled "Pole aims to enhance Jewish-Christian dialogue", Dr. Zajączkowski contradicted Fr. Drinan's unfounded remarks about the "sad record of the Catholic Church during the Holocaust": "I think, he stated, it was a glorious record... During his visit to Auschwitz, Pope John Paul II said that St. Maximilian Kolbe was not alone in his heroic sacrifice of love. John Paul also posed the question, "how many others did the same?" Well, my book is a partial answer to that question, taking into account only those who sacrificed their lives to save the Jews. These facts should be brought into the open to gain proper historical perspective in light of the current Jewish-Christian dialogue. The facts of the Holocaust need to be cleared up, especially when Catholics are singled out as antisemitic because of what the Nazis did to the Jews in Poland.... You constantly hear the misaccusation that Christianity crucified the Jewish nation during the Holocaust. That is a terrible accusation. My aim in writing this book is also to lift the spirits of Christians and Jews by indicating that there was no "bancruptcy of Christianity", of Judeo-Christian ethics, in Auschwitz. I want to reach all these people – ordinary Jews and Christians – so they know the historical facts and all dialogue can be improved... There is not much done in this field in America and there is even opposition on part of some professional participants of the "dialogue". I would be very grateful for any help which should have been forthcoming from those sources but has not. I try to do my best. It looks this will be the last thing I will do in my life".

Zajączkowski received lots of moral support from his native Poland: From the late Primate of Poland, Card. Wyszynski, from John Paul's successor in the Metropolitan see of Kraków, Card. Macharski, from the Executive Secretary of Polish Bishops Conference, Archbishop Bronisław Dąbrowski, from the Bishop of Tarnów Jerzy Ablewicz, from the Vice-Chairmen of Bishops Ecumenical Commission, Bishop Miziołek of Warsaw, und recenty, from present Primate of Poland, Cardinal Józef Glemp. These letters – leave, of course, the author solely responsible for the views expressed in this book which are based on his own research*.

The Secretariat for Catholic-Jewish Relations of the American Bishops Conference and its head Dr. Eugene Fisher, made the suggestion to give the book a shape of *Roman Martyrology* with the places, dates and the names of persons involved uniformly inserted. There was no lack of encouragement from Fr. Ronald Modras of St. Louis University, from Fr. Sheerin, a Paulist priest, the former head of Secretariat for Catholic-Jewish Relations, from Prof. Sloyan of Temple University, from Jerome Brentar of Cleveland and numerous other priests and laymen who care for the proper development of the Christian-Jewish dialogue.

What, however, personally touched Dr. Zajączkowski as an educator was the distress of the younger generation which

* The Director of the American Bishops' Secretariat for Catholic-Jewish Relations, Dr. Eugene Fisher was kind enough to recommend Zajączkowski's work for publication in little known *Polish American Journal*, excusing his own inaction in this important field by the "lack of funds" and Episcopal patron of the Secretariat, Bishop Mugavero of Brooklyn covered with silence Zajączkowski's appeal which evoked such cordial response from the President of the U.S. Catholic Conference, Archbishop Quinn of San Francisco. (See also *Wanderer's* article "Bishop and the Bureaucrat", followed by Msgr. Higgins's attack and the respected Catholic weekly's rejoinder of June 19, 1986: "Is "The Wanderer" Anti-Semitic?")

From the article in the *Jerusalem Post Magazine*, Jan. 16, 1987, in which Ernie Meyer attempts to explain curious practice adopted by Yad Washem in awarding the title of the Righteous to people who never "risked their lives" for Jews simply because there was no Nazi German law imposing in their countries a penalty of death for helping Jews as it was the case in Poland

Somewhat naive, but deeply realistic presentation of the death penalty from the German invader suspended over the heads of everybody, young or old, lay or religious, whoever dared to offer any form of aid and support to a persecuted Jew according to Christ's command in Matthew 25:40 that "anything you do for one of my brothers here, however humble, you do it for me".

– like Miss Carol W. of Washington, D.C. – hears only "stories of stories" distorted by vested interests; a younger generation of Christians and Jews who shouldn't be made to suffer for the mistakes of their ancestors. Such a terrible experience was for him Yad Vashem's invitation to plant a tree in the Alley of the Righteous to the honor of his family and the hostile reaction of Anya Franziak to the proposal of meeting the real granddaughter of Regina Zajączkowska, also named Anya, for the purpose of continuing Catholic Polish-Jewish brotherly ties on American and Israeli soil: Anya Franziak refused to meet and to attend the ceremony of planting a tree to honor her "dearest Grandma", as she called her guardian and educator for more then ten years, and her children who also risked their lives for her rescue.

It was a shock for him to hear a confession of a young Israeli soldier that the event of the "holocaust" as presented in Israeli schools shattered his belief in God Almighty and Just. He also added that sometimes he felt uncomfortable in the role assigned to him towards his fellow Israeli Arabs which closely resembled that of a Nazi soldier toward his fellow Jews in Poland. This trend shouldn't remain unchallenged. It's too dangerous for the young State of Israel and for the rest of the world. Only the unvarnished truth may stop this pernicious tendency.

Reb Moshe Shonfeld, in his book *The Holocaust victims accuse*, New York, B'nei Yeshivos, 1977, p. 2, violently protested the fact "that Jewish blood is the grease needed for the wheels of the Zionist state" and his findings are "hair-raising" as he says, with Jewish leaders "for the first time in history, hardening themselves against their refugee brothers, abandonning them and their children to starvation, disease and death". He quotes Rav Michael Ber Weissmandel's letter to Moshe Sharett: "I am convinced that in the years 1942–45, there was fateful negligence on the part of the authorized Jewish institutions. For decades our people strove toward one end – the Zionist goal, which was again and again aspired to – the gathering of all the Jews in a Jewish state. In the days of Hitler, another goal should have taken precedence – to save the lives of our people. However, our friends continued to go in the way dictated by the old goal, without discerning that the nation itself was dying in the interim... the Joint, the Jewish Agency, the Zionist administration and the Jewish parties in the democratic lands – did not recognize that the rescuing of Jewish lives was the central goal and that all other goals were to be subservient to it. You, comrade Sharett, and all the agencies, did not do a single thing – to alarm, without delay, the whole world... It is impossible to say that you did not receive information about what was occurring".

"At the time of the Kastner trial in Jerusalem, Shmuel Tamir, representing the defendant, addressed Judge Halevi as follows: "In Palestine, these facts remained almost unnewsworthy. Silence continued. Complete suppression... This was the battle of Ben Gurion at the time that the ovens were burning... Twenty years later, Dr. Nachum Goldmann, president of several Zionist organizations, confessed at an assembly commemorating the rebellion of the ghettoes on March 4, 1962: "There is no doubt that future Jewish history will judge the generation of the Holocaust which lived in the free lands as guilty. It will accuse it of failing to adequately prepare for the Nazi danger in its beginning stages, and of not daring to fight desperately the annihilation in this period... I will never forget the day on which a telegram from the Warsaw ghetto was delivered to me; it was a addressed to Rabbi Stephen Wise and to myself. We were asked why Jewish leaders of America do not protest day and night on the stairs of the White House until the President orders the bombing of the concetration camps and the railway tracks leading to them... Therefore we should not transfer the guilt to those who suffered and paid with their lives. If there is a basis to the historical "I' accuse", let us have the courage now to direct it against that part of the generation which was lucky enough to be outside of the Nazi domination and did not fulfill its obligation toward the millions killed".

Reb Moshe Shonfeld adds in the postscript the terrifying call from the Jews of Poland: **"Brothers – the remaining Jews in Poland live in awareness that in the most terrible days of our history you did not come to our aid."**

What, however, is most appalling in Reb Shonfeld's report, comes with the attitude of the "Chief Rabbi" of Sweden, Dr. Ehrenpreisz (since 1914), together with the leader of the Jewish community in Stockholm, who prevented acceptance of 10,000 Jewish refugees by the decision of the Riksdag (Swedish parliament) with the excuse that "10,000 additional Jews in Sweden could arouse a Jewish problem in this land that has never experienced anti-Semitism because of the small number of its Jewish citizens." "The efforts of these two wicked Jewish community leaders, says Reb Shonfeld on p. 111, succeeded in their goal... but the true motivation was typically Zionist, fitting in the principle that even if the death threatens the Jews,one should not find for them a refuge outside of Eretz Yisroel". He also quotes from the debate of Swedish Parliament members Moller and Kanut Peterson, the statement that "the representative of the government admits and agrees with the ideas of the oppostion, only asking that the matter be set down in the record, so that future generations would know who was to blame for the abandonment of tens of thousands of men, women and children to their slaughter".

The same cold, calculating approach toward the coming slaughter of undesirable Jews is evident in the answer the future President of the State of Israel, Dr. Chaim Weizmann, gave at the Zionist Congress in London in 1937, to the question from the audience: "The hopes of Eastern Europe's six million Jews are centered on emigration. Can you bring six million Jews to Palestine?" I replied "No"... from the depth of the tragedy I want to save two million young people... The old ones will pass. They will bear their fate or they will not. They were dust, economic and moral dust in a cruel world... Only the branch of the young shall survive... They have to accept it." (Reb Shonfeld, op. cit. p. 25)

It was a prophetic, though inhumanly cruel, statement. It was a verdict of death for those who were considered "economic and moral dust in the cruel world". Not only in the inhuman world of power-greedy Nazi Germany, but also of Nazi Germany's counterpart, the cold, calculating Zionist leaders.

"In January 1940, continues Reb Shonfeld terrifying story, a ship full of Jewish refugees stranded on the Danube River. The ship's captain demanded money to continue on the trip to Eretz Yisroel. Henry Montor, executive vice chairman of the United Jewish Appeal, replied to the request with the following: "Many of the passengers are old people and women... unable to endure the harsh conditions on this type of trip... to come to Palestine are needed young men and women who understand the obligations of a Jewish national home... **There could be no more deadly ammunition... than if Palestine were to be flooded with very old people or with undesirables...**" (Reb Shonfeld, op. cit. p. 25).

Some courageous writers like Eliezer Livneh, in his column, "The thoughts on the Holocaust" (*Yediot Achronot*,25 Nisan) frankly admitted this cruel calculation: "Our Zionist orientation educated us to see the growing land of Israel as the prime goal and the Jewish nation only in relation to its building the land. With each tragedy befalling the Jews in the diaspora, we saw the state as the evident solution. We continued employing this principle even during the Holocaust, saving only those who could be brought to Israel. The mandate's limitation on immigration served as a political factor in our battle to open the doors to *aliya* and to establishing the state. Our programs were geared to this aim and for this we were prepared to sacrifice or endanger lives. Everything outside of this goal, including the rescue of European Jewry for its own sake, was a secondary goal. If there can be no people without a country", Rabbi Weissmantel exclaimed, "then surely there can be no country without a people. And where are the living Jewish people, if not in Europe?" And, let us add, in East-Central Europe, in Poland, in Lithuania, in Ukraine – in this part of Europe which for almost a thousand years preserved the Jewish nation biologically, when it was expelled from Western Europe and from the East by Muscovy, and provided 80 percent of world Jewry congregated there with conditions favorable for the preservation of its spritual wealth and for the developement into a modern nation with its elective bodies, a nation within the confines of other nations federated in the old Polish-Lithuanian Commonwealth.

What in the eyes of Dr. Chaim Weizmann passed as "moral and economic dust", the exterminated Polish Jewry, became the object of nostagic memories for a handful of Polish Jews who survived the holocaust, due to sacrifices of their Christian neighbors: "When I say "we", wrote Bernard Goldstein in *The stars bear witness*, New York, Viking in 1949, p. 22, "I mean we living in Eastern Europe, the cradle of modern Jewish culture and, before Hitler, the greatest center of Jewish population in the world. In Poland, which was the focal point of this great Jewish community, there were many towns and cities in which the Jews were the majority. We were a nation within the nation, formed and tested in a thousand years of struggle, cherishing our heritage and our rights, cemented by our own language, culture, schools, trade and labor organizations".

As long as it was a traditional Jewish religious community, there were minor unavoidable frictions, but when the nature of Jewish society started to change in the direction of a world revolution which would give the Jews predominance over the the host nations, not without diplomatic and financial aid of Western Jewry, the situation drastically changed. For the host nations it was a question of "to be or not to be" when their national identity was threatened by ambitions of persons like Lev Bronstein-Trotski, Rose Luxemburg, and other prophets of the "world revolution" in which there would be no room for a free Poland, a free Lithuania, and a free Ukraine.

This fateful development is thus described in Abraham Shulman's *The old country, with foreword by Isaac Bashevis*

Singer, New York, Scribner, 1974, p. 27: "The first World War ended with the Bolshevik Revolution and the rebirth of an independent Poland. The Revolution brought an end to the Pale of Settlement; from then on Jews could live where they pleased. But the Revolution also brought an end to the socio-cultural structure of the *shtetl*. The new order realized some of the *shtetl's* old hopes, but it augmented its fears, too... Between the two world wars Jewish life went through a period of amazing renaissance in independent Poland, a period as never experienced before, except perhaps in Spain. Never before was the cultural life so rich. Yiddish literature flourished; for the first time Jewish political parties became a power in the political constellation of the country. Jewish life seemed to dig deeper roots than ever before. The Jewish masses achieved the highest standards of education. While the parents and grand-parents were still flocking to the "courts" of their Hasidic rabbis – to Kotzk, Ger, Kozhenitz, or Skernevitz – their children discovered a new kind of Zadikim. The books were no longer *Sefer Chasidim* (the book of the Righteous) of Rabaynu Hachasid, the *Shevet Musar* (Rod of Reproof) of Reb Eliyahu ben Abraham Hakohen, or *Likutei Mohoran* (Excerpts of Reb Nachman) by Reb Nachman Bratzlaver. The new books were *Das Kapital* of Marx, *Fields, Factories and Workshops* by Pyotr Aleksyevich Kropotkin, *Altneuland* by Theodor Herzl, and even *What is to be done?* by Lenin.... The young men and women had the same awe for these formidable-sounding books as their fathers had for theirs. For the first time the marketplace in the *shtetl* was not the sole meeting place between the Jews and-non-Jews... The streets in the larger cities saw tens of thousands of Jewish workers... displaying... red flags... Over the border, in the West, a man with a ridiculous mustache was preparing the *shtetl's* Final Solution."

"The man with a ridiculous mustache" smashed the Weimar German Republic's Communist Party which in the Polish-Soviet War of 1920 cut of delivery of Western aid to the embattled Poland with the aim of seeing Europe from the

Rhine to the Ural under Communist domination, over the prostrated body of the Polish Republic which was too stubborn and too firm im its Christian foundations to undergo a similar development to the one which took hold of the younger Jewish generation. This stubborn Republic proudly rejected on the other hand the offer of the "man with a ridiculous mustache" to join forces in the spurions "crusade" against the Communist East, thus signing her own death warrant, a "final solution" of her own. In the eyes of distant America, Poland of this time was an "inspiration" for the rest of the free world after the rest of Nordic Europe meekly surrendered like Denmark, Holland and Norway, or remained neutral like Sweden and Switzerland, not counting Czechoslovakia, Hungary, Yugoslavia, Rumania and Bulgaria which were, more or less, aligned with Nazi Germany.

The calamity of the Ribbentrop-Molotov agreement of Aug. 23, 1939 concerning the 4th partition of Poland didn't dash Zionist hopes of extracting their "two million" young and desirable Jews needed in Palestine while disposing of the rest in such a way as not to divert support and funds needed for building a state of Israel. The attitude of Orthodox Jews in Poland was rather aloof and far from united for the imminent "war against the Jews". Poland, however, without shrinking from the heroic task, was the first country to oppose Hitler.

In the capital of the doomed Polish Republic on September 1, 1939, Chaim A. Kaplan wrote in his *Warsaw diary* some astounding reflections: "We are witnessing the dawn of a new era in the history of the world. This war will indeed bring destruction upon human civilization. But this is a civilization which merits annihilation and destruction... Well, now the Poles themselves will receive our revenge through the hands of our cruel enemy". Then, on September 2nd: "The second day of the Polish-German war, which ultimately will turn into a world war and a slaughter of nations... My brain is full of chattering of radio from both sides... Each side considers itself to be righteous and the other murderous, destructive and bent on plunder. This time, as an exception to the general rule, both speak the truth. Verily it is so – both sides are murderers, destroyers and plunderers, ready to commit any abomination in the world." And so on, in the same vein: "Where is Poland's strength, its might?... And what will become of us?... This is not the Germany of 1914 – bad as it was, it had some conceptions of moral law and international law... You get impression from Breslau radio that the Polish army is not an equipped army led by officers trained for warfare, but a flock of sheep. Whoever saw or heard of such a thing in the history of the wars of nations – that a rich country with thirty-five million citizens, with an organized army, would become something to be stepped on by the German villain within five days?*... The unfortunate Jews are running for dear life... There is no bread... There are no policemen to keep order... One must admit that the bombs are not being dropped deliberately to harm the peaceful inhabitants. Hitler kept his word... The Supreme Commander has issued a proclamation that the capital is to defend itself... In his great anger the enemy would destroy every stone and every wall, and our homes would become our graves. Why? For what purpose are such precious sacrifices offered up... In two more days it will be Rosh Hashanah, our New Year. Our humanitarian and pacifist prayers will be in sharp dissonance to all that is going on around us: *Jacob goes his way and Esau goes his.*"

"A rumor had spread, wrote Kaplan, that Hitler had ordered the cessation of air attacks. He was forced to do this by Stalin "the merciful", who threatened to "void" their pact un-

---

* Contrary to Kaplan's hateful remarks, poorly equipped Poland resisted powerful Nazi war machine for 35 days and, after the Soviet invasion, her land and sea forces had to leave the country, continued to figh on all fronts till the victorious end, while Denmark "fought" 3 hours, Holland – 4 days, and powerful France, aided by the British expeditionary force of 250,000, collapsed in 30 days.

less attacks against the peaceful population ceased... Everything and everyone bears the stamp of war. Instead of Jews wearing prayer shawls and carrying prayer books rushing to the synagogue, one sees stretcher bearers carrying the dead and wounded dug out from the ruins of bombed buildings... the Supreme German command threatens the entire population of the city with dire consequences if any civilian groups try to stop the German army. Such cities will be wiped off the face of the earth... The incompetent and haughty Polish government has dug itself into a distant corner of the southeast border and must to be forced out. Never before in history has any people suffered a defeat as shameful as this... One ally – Poland – let down all the other allies. Who ever dreamed of this kind of military catastrophe... At their first contact with the Germans they melted like wax and proved that their valor was an empty disguise... There was a voice – from the German Breslau radio. The voice said: "The murderous Polish government is inciting the populace of Warsaw to fight against the German army..." If I want to know the truth, I must tune in Radio Breslau, which has tendency to exaggerate – or better yet, Radio Moscow... The Soviet army has crossed the Polish-Russian border... Now the cat is out of the bag... The other side (England and France) could not present Stalin with as meaningful a historical achievement as the annexation of the Ukraine and White Russia... The Soviet army is "conquering" (bloodlessly, of course) all of the western Ukraine and western White Russia, with Hitler's approval and aid. This is what is called a united front... The Soviets have come from the East, bearing "peace, order, and bread"... Stalin's government seems to be supported by strong public sympathy (by the Jews? – U.P.) in this move... Polish General Czuma, who is in charge of Warsaw's defense, and who doesn't know his right hand from his left, sent out a proclamation to the citizens... They are filled to overflowing with false patriotism... and the commanders regard thousands of lives as nothing when compared to a little military prestige... Beautiful Warsaw – city of royal glory, queen of cities – has been destroyed like Sodom and Gomorrah... And we are waiting for Hitler's army. After all the horrors that we have endured, we wait for Hitler's army as for the spring rains... Our only desire is to rest awhile, even if it is under Hitler's rule... The Polish General Rommel has shown his "heroism" by killing thousands of people and burning down the palaces in the capital; he has turned a bustling city into a desolate heap of ruins... all this has happened so that he may be able to announce to the world: Warsaw fights!"

"But in secret, among ourselves, wherever a small group of Jews gathered – even in the dark, cold cellar – we whispered our doubts to one another: These fools! These pompous idiots!... We spent most of our time hiding in cellars. I never knew that I was "fighting ferociously" in a knightly manner; I never knew that "the eyes of the whole world were upon me" and that people marvelled at my courage and wished me success. I was like a broken vessel – motivated by fear and genuine cowardice. I sat shrunken and shriveled, in dank cellar, overcome with fear and trembling at the horror of the bombs. Rommel and Starzyński suddenly made a "military hero" out of me... Now the French and British will come and smoke their pipes on Poland's ruin."

Such a defeatist attitude was not uncommon among the Jewish masses. When Polish boys were picking grenades, guns and munitions on the battlefields – and it was scattered everywhere, ready to be picked up by anybody – the Jews cautiously refrained to avoid severe punishment, mostly by death. But when the need arose they boldly demanded arms as if there were whole armories available to the Poles* when barely one out of ten in the Polish Warsaw uprising of 1944 had some sort of weapon since the Allied drop of arms for Poland was 40 times smaller than for Tito's Yugoslavia, even less than for tiny Albania.

---

* Hand grenades, for instance, had to be manufactured out of spray cans of "Sidol" filled with explosive material.

Chaim A. Kaplan, however, with all his scorn and contempt for his Polish neighbors, honestly acknowledged what later Jewish denigrators of Poland failed to say about the German antisemitic propaganda in Poland: "The oppressed and degraded Polish public, immersed in deeper depression under the influence of the national catastrophe, has not been particularly sensitive to this propaganda. It senses that the conquerors are its eternal enemy, and that they are not fighting the Jews for Poland's sake. Common suffering has drawn all hearts closer and the barbaric persecution of the Jews has even aroused feelings of sympathy toward them. Tacitly, wordlessly, the two former rivals sense that they are brothers in misfortune; that they have a common enemy who wishes to bring destruction upon both at the same time. Such a stand on the part of the Poles in relation to the Jews has endangered the entire strategy of the conquerors, and for this reason they approach the matter with greater efficiency. No nation lacks hooligan elements, and the conquerors have paved the way for them... The conquerors' eyes look on, but they are struck with blindness" (Chaim A. Kaplan. *Scroll of agony*. New York, Holocaust Library, 1981, p. 114).

The same unifying effect of common suffering of Christians and Jews was stressed by Emmanuel Ringelblum in his *Polish-Jewish relations*, Jerusalem, Yad Vashem 1974, p. 199: "Another very important factor uniting the Polish educated class with the Jews is their common suffering at the hands of the common oppressor. There is not one family of the Polish educated class that has not lost someone in Auschwitz, Dachau, Majdanek, or Oranienburg. Suffering purifies, suffering ennobles, suffering draws people closer together."

This unifying bond of common suffering between Jews and Christians in Slavic lands which groaned under the Nazi heel was certainly lacking between the oppressed Jews and their coreligionists in Western lands.

Szmul Zygielbojm, in his foreword to the brochure *It is true: Stop them now, German mass murder of Jews in Poland,* published in London, 1942, wrote: "I must mention here that Polish Christian population gives all possible help and sympathy to the Jews. The solidarity of the population in Poland has two aspects: first, it is expressed in the common suffering, and secondly, in the continued joint struggle against the inhuman occupying Power. The fight with the oppressors goes on steadily, stubbornly, secretly, even in the ghetto, under conditions so terrible and inhuman that they are hard to describe or imagine. Scores of newspapers appear in the ghettos and hundreds outside the ghetto walls. The Polish and the Jewish population keep in constant touch, exchanging newspapers, views and instructions. **The walls of the ghetto have not really separated the Jewish population from the Poles**. The Polish and the Jewish masses continue to fight together for common aims, just as they have fought for so many years in the past."

On the 12th of May, 1943, Zygielbojm committed suicide in London because he couldn't obtain from his fellow Jews in the West the kind of response which was given to Jews by Christian Poles. Elie Wiesel, upon arriving in America, was literally shocked. Seeing the powerlessness of their Christian companions in suffering, Jewish people in their ghettos and in the camps said to one another "If only the Allies knew... If only Roosevelt knew. If only Churchill knew. If only the American Jews knew, and the English, the Palestinian, the Swedish, the Swiss Jews, if only they knew... The victims steadfastly believed that when they knew, the situation would change immediately... If only the Allies were to know of Auschwitz, Auschwitz would cease to exist." These were the hopes of Jewish as well as Polish victims of Nazi horrors.

"They were wrong, says Wiesel. The proof is definite, irrefutable. People knew – and kept silent." Some of them had vested interests in remaining silent and in suppressing voices calling for help to Jewish as well as non-Jewish victims of Nazi Germany. They formed a pro-German America First Committee which pretended to advocate American interests but

"The wall didn't separate" Jews and Christian Poles (Zygielbojm). Contemporary illustration from Jewish underground paper *Yugnt Schtime*, December, 1940.

represented in fact those ethnic groups which, for various reasons, sided with the German aggressor.

As late as May 1942, the editor of Paulist Fathers' monthly, *The Catholic World*, James M. Gillis, pointed out that "if not under Hitler, Germans would fight under some other leader, with perhaps less *Schrecklichkeit* but with no less power and skill" (Editorial comment, p. 134). He even went as far as to accuse America of the same crimes as those committed by the Nazi Germans in Europe in relation to Slavs and Jews: "Sitting firmly on the spoils of successful land-grabbing in Texas, California and Panama, the United States, said Fr. Gillis, is in no position to "schoolmarm" another proud nation... there is reason to believe that ninety percent of the Catholic clergy and of the hierarchy were anti-interventionist". It was the Archbishop of New York, Cardinal Spellman who talked about "injustice" of the Versailles Conference to the American Veterans when Hitler pretended to correct this "injustice" by attacking Poland. One year after this attack, in *The Catholic World* of October 1940, p. 4, Fr. Gillis defended Adolf Hitler:

"If Hitler is crazy he is none the less the leader of many millions of sane people. At least as sane as you and I. At the present writing the most reliable informants out of Germany – at least those that I met – report that the people of the Reich are predominantly in support of Hitler, and as nearly unanimous as 80 million people ever are. Much more nearly unanimous than our 120 millions are in thinking him "crazy as a loon". Quoting the Jewish controlled *New York Times* of September 3, 1940, Fr. Gillis said that it was "the Poles who were too determined on armed arbitrament... for Germany did not intend and never has demanded that Poland be destroyed". On the other hand, he confessed, "England's predicament was Ireland's opportunity". "If the German people insist that... the old line politicians double-crossed them, I do not know any compelling facts that prove them wrong". When "Hitler talked about Germany's encirclement, there was encircle-

Leading U.S. Jews to Explore Painful Holocaust Questions

Associated Press; The New York Times

Arthur J. Goldberg, upper right, will be chairman of panel looking into the extermination of Jews in World War II; Seymour M. Finger will lead the research. At left: A Polish rabbi digging his own grave during a 1942 execution.

COMMISSION FOR THE INVESTIGATION OF THE BEHAVIOR OF AMERICAN JEWS DURING THE HOLOCAUST DISSOLVED UNDER THE PRESSURE.

It was a meeting of the most prominent Jewish personalities which assembled on Thursday, September 24, 1981 at the Cornell University Club on East 50th Street in New York City. Its sponsor Jack Eisner as a teen-age resident of Warsaw recalled watching the ghetto revolt of 1943 and thinking – about the Allies – "If they don't send warplanes to help, why don't they send at least some leaflets?" What was the powerful international Jewry doing at this crucial time? Why was the war time arms supply so meager in embattled Poland? Why was Gen. Sikorski who came to the U.S.A. with a request for long range planes met by American Jews with trumped-up accusation of "Polish anti-Semitism" instead of support? The Chairman of the panel Arthur J. Goldberg said at this occasion: "This has been a much mooted and argued proposition" concerning American Jewish responses to the Holocaust as the first news of it began to leak out of Europe in early 1942. He added that the study would "let the chips fall where they may". Hyman Bookbinder, a member of the President's Commission on the Holocaust, unconnected with Goldberg's group, said that the question, "Why wasn't more done?" remained an "agonizing" one for American Jews. Similiar opinion was obviously shared by other members of the group: Jacob K. Javits, Abraham A. Ribicoff, Morris B. Abram, Bruno Bettelheim, Sol Chaikin, Rabbi Arthur Hertzberg, Martin Mayerson, Jack Spitzer and Bernice S. Tannenbaum, to menttion just a few.

However, less than one and half years later, on Tueasday, Jan. 4, 1983, the group of such prestigious participants was forced to dissolve. Jack Eisner who funded the commission's work told the *New York Times* that "former Supreme Court justice Arthur Goldberg dissolved it because of pressure from Jewish groups." Eisner also said: "It would take the U.S. Jewish establishment 10 to 15 years before it could objectively look at its behaviour during the Holocaust." The panel's two-year study was to include an examination of what American Jewish groups did to reduce the number of European Jews annihilated by the Nazis between 1939 and 1945... Some members of of major American Jewish organizations criticized the commission's draft, concluded the news item entitled: PRIVATE COMMISSION ON HOLOCAUST DISSOLVES. With the abolition of an independent inquiry effort the vicious Holocaust propaganda regained free hand in accusing the Christian world and – in particular – the Catholic Poland of complicity in Nazi crimes.

ment... Germany was to be strangled. "Faithful fulfillment of the Versailles dictate", Fr. Gillis quoted Hitler, "would have exterminated sooner or later twenty million Germans". True, and I think that such was the purpose. Germans if not exactly exterminated, were to be rendered permanently helpless. It couldn't be done; any rational person with even a modicum of knowledge of history and psychology could see that it couldn't be done. When a people gets old, decrepit, degenerate, you may crush them. You can't crush them when they are in the prime of life. The Germans are in the prime of life. If Hitler is mad now, Clemenceau and Woodrow Wilson were mad in 1918. Perhaps their madness made him mad... The only reasonable and moral attitude for Americans to take is to stay out of it." Fr. Gillis shed a crocodile tear for Catholic Poles, massacred together with their priests and bishops in German concentration camps: "Poor Poland: she has been torn asunder three times before, and eaten up by wolfish powers to which she was thrown... but I cannot see that we are in conscience bound to fight in a war that is primarily for the maintenance of the *status quo* of 1918, or even of 1939. The *status quo* is not sacrosanct. In fact it is unjust. To fight for the maintenance of injustice would be inmoral."

Unfortunately, this line of reasoning Fr. Gillis was able to support because of the atmosphere prevailing in Rome. In his polemics against the statement of a well-known Catholic writer of Great Britain, Arnold Lunn who reminded the Paulist monthly of "Polish intervention which saved Vienna from the Turks" and was "both perplexed and hurt" by the the isolationist attitude of American Catholics: "We feel that you who are living in security and comfort should not choose this moment to reventilate all the old Irish grievances against England" (*The Catholic World*, June 1941, p. 332) Fr. Gillis invoked the authority of Pius XII: "Mr. Lunn is puzzled why American Catholics do not recognize that it is their duty to stop Hitler. It is significant that the Holy Father himself does not draw this conclusion."

Dr. Zajączkowski knew this line of reasoning from the literature he received during his stay at Curia Generalizia in Vatican from Fr. Brust, an Assistant representing Germanic provinces of the Society of Jesus, where Wilhelm Peuler, S.J. wrote under the "imprimatur" of Bp. Rarkowski, in the pamphlet entitled *Über die Ehre* (About the Honor of Germany): "It was not for material needs that present war was started. It was for higher values that we are fighting. The fact that God has elevated our nation above all nations of the world is not our merit and thus Germany's glory is God's glory (*Deutschlands Ehre ist Gottes Ehre*). Therefore, what ordinarily is a sin, to kill people, for us is no sin any more." – Such statement, distributed by military chaplains to Nazi soldiers in Poland, was a denial of Christian ethics, and Fr. Peuler was released from the Jesuit Order only to reappear after the war as an editor of *Klerus-Korrespondenz* and the director of Catholic radio programs in West Germany. But, with the entrance of Italy into the war, the connection between the Superior General, W. Ledochowski and American provinces was severed and the local Assistant, Fr. Maher took advantage of it to crack down on "war-mongering" as the awakening of American interest in German crimes against Poland was called.

The author of this book was ordered to leave his office at Lincoln Towers in Chicago from which the news of German massacres of Poles and Jews were distributed. War time programs from Gary, Ind. under the sponsorship of the Catholic Radio League had to be discontinued. Zajączkowski was personally lectured by Archbishop Stritch for his role in organizing a huge all-Slav Grunwald manifestation in Soldiers' Field on July 19, 1942 arguing that Teutonic Knights were "pious missionaries of Christian faith in Prussia", and not exterminators of the local population to accommodate German settlers, a program resumed by the Nazi Germany in the infamous *General-Plan Ost*, only this time directed against Poles and Jews. The Milwaukee diocesan paper denounced the calls for preventive bombings as "un-Christian". Even the rescuing of Polish and Jewish children, stranded in Teheran, was considered not advisable because the little children knew too much and their stories wouldn't be considered "atrocity propaganda" if they were allowed to come to the U.S.A. instead of Mexico.

"Who gave you permission to seek refuge in America for the Polish orphans?" asked furious Assistant Maher in his letter to the Author. The alternative ordered *in virtute sanctae oboedientiae* was – playing golf in West Baden, Ind. or *edere et orare!*

It is worth recalling these times today when the entire Catholic Church is accused of having a "sad record" of indifference and silence in front of a genocide. Certainly, 150, 000 demonstrators, with seventeen Catholic parishes participating in Chicago, can hardly be accused of remaining "silent" and compelled to recite a prayer about stepping over the "body of our brother Abel lying in blood" (see the alleged "prayer of John XXIII" which was proven to be a forgery of an Irish Jesuit).

"Brother Abel left lying in the pool of blood" by Catholic isolationists in America was – Catholic Poland. This accounts for such enthusiastic acceptance of Holocaust version of history by Fr. Drinan, S. J. and company.

If there was "indifference" in front of a wholesale extermination of people it was certainly not dictated by "Christian antisemitism". The dividing lines were somewhere else, not between Christians and Jews, as some Holocaust propagandists, Jewish and Christian, are attempting to suggest. The *New York Times* of September 27, 1981 carried an illustrated article about a Jewish committee composed of prestigious politicians, with an "initial grant, of 70,000" to explore some "painful Holocaust questions", but one and half years later, Jan. 4, 1983, the announcement came that "private commission on Holocaust dissolves... because of pressure from Jewish groups" to prevent "examination of what American Jewish groups did to reduce the number of European Jews annihilated by the Nazis between 1939 and 1945." These facts could be relevant for a Christian-Jewish dialogue concerning the genocide of Christians and Jews by the Nazi Germans. Maybe a committee of inquiry into the attitude of some Christian ethnic groups could better pinpoint the culprits than Claire Huchet-Bishop's and Prof. Littell's generic condemnation of "traditional Christianity". Calling Jewish genocide with a special name of "holocaust" – "uniquely unique", is misleading: What was really unique, was the fact that this time together with others, also the Jews were its object.

Immediately after the War, another "unique" event was discovered and branded as "crime unknown in the annals of human history": the removal of Germans from the old Slavic areas, into the Germany proper. The same people who did not take notice of millions being mercilessly slaughtered, not counting other millions driven into a slavery of forced labor in Germany, suddenly became alarmed, and still are, about the fact that this time the shoe was on the other foot. At the Catholic Academy of Munich there is a special section: *Martyrologium Germanicum*, and on one occasion the mayor of the city of Munich was talking about "two martyr nations: Germans and Jews".

Elie Wiesel, upon leaving the concentration camp, was shocked that "for the first time secure Jewish communities took no interest in their distressed brothers' plight. In Palestine, as in the United States, life continued as though Auschwitz did not exist. People celebrated Shabbat, the Holy Days. There was dancing in the kibbutzim in Galilee, there were elaborate affairs in New York. It was business as usual. Not one function was canceled, not one reception postponed. While Mordechai Anielewicz and his comrades fought their lonely battle in the blazing ghetto under siege, while Arthur Zygelbaum committed suicide in London to protest the complacency of the free world, a large New York synagogue invited its members to a banquet featuring a well-known comedian. The slaughterers were slaughtering, the mass graves were overflowing, the factories of Treblinka, Belzec, Maidanek and Auschwitz were operating at top capacity, while on the other side, Jewish social and intellectual life was flourishing" (Elie Wiesel, *A Jew today*, Bantam Books, 1979, p. 226).

There were, of course, empty gestures, as in the the case of "poor Poland" also among the American Jews: "Jewish leaders met, threw up their arms in gestures of helplessness, shed a pious tear or two, and went on with their lives: speeches, travels, quarrels, banquets, toasts, honors, as usual. Unquestionably, they were preoccupied by the fate of European Jews, perhaps even worried, but their lives were written off as lost anyhow; surely it was best not to undertake any action that was doomed from the start. Why waste the effort? Until August of 1943 they were not even able to agree on the need for enunciating a common policy. Finally, an "American Jewish Conference", supposedly representing almost all the major Jewish organizations, was born in the elegant halls of the Waldorf-Astoria. Many speeches were delivered, followed by many debates. And what did one speak about? Jewish objectives for... the postwar period. What to request, from whom, and who was to do the requesting. Still, one meeting was devoted to the fate of European Jewry. A few tears were shed, a few pathetic platitudes delivered. A few lines were uttered – for example, that certain young Jews had left the security of their homes – in Palestine? – to join the Warsaw ghetto rebels. After the usual resolutions were adopted, the participants came away with a soothed conscience, and that was it. There was no discussion of rescue plans, of emergency measures to influence public opinion and rouse the government into action."

While writing this "plea for the survivors" in 1975 (in his book *A Jew today*, p. 226-7) Elie Wiesel probably didn't know the American art of "public image making" from which he later profited as a beneficiary and as a literary expert learned that art as well. Only four years later he became the Chairman of the President's Commission on the Holocaust, and, in this capacity, reported from his visit to Poland that it was in Warsaw and Kiev and Krakow, not in Palestine or America, that "business was as usual" – similar to Weimar or Munich "a 2-hour bus or train ride": "Ten thousand human beings were being murdered and burned every day, and nearby, life went on as usual" (Elie Wiesel, *Report to the President,* September 27, 1979, p. 33). He and his Commission which included future "experts on the Holocaust" obviously didn't notice hundreds of execution sites in Warsaw alone where thousands of non-Jewish Poles were murdered daily, still marked with crosses, flickeering lights and freshly cut flowers. He never heard of Pawiak and Gestapo torture chambers at Aleja Szucha where thousands of Christians were martyred. He didn't see the huge Palmiry cemetery with thousands of crosses, only rarely mixed with King David stars, over the ashes of murdered victims and martyrs who were caught helping Jews. If these were for him not "human beings" then what were they? "Two-legged animals", not worth even mentioning? This artificial image, based on half-truths or on outright lies is already falling to pieces and its creators may, in the near future, provoke the wrath of the deceived public which can't be duped with a convenient explanation of "anti-semitism".

Belated Wiesel's mention of Polish rescuers of Jews is only a beginning of "light piercing the darkness" of Holecaust half-truths and outright lies.

Such an example of a "big lie" may be found in a collection of readings issued by the Anti(?)-Defamation League of B'nai B'rith, with the assistance of a grant from the National Conference of Christians and Jews, under the title *The Holocaust years: society on trial,* Bantam Books, 1978, p. 224: "At the end of the war, many Germans and Poles undoubtedly wished to see razed to the ground all vestiges of the infamous camps and crematoria. A number of camps were destroyed. At the insistence of the Allies, however, some camps were preserved, and designated as memorials or as places of historic interest. Many people felt, and still feel, that the people of Germany and Poland, where the camps were situated, should not be allowed to forget what took place in them".

One does not need even to go to Poland, to discover the "big lie", intended obviously to prove that only Jews were being killed there, but only to read the English version of the *"Guide to scenes of fighting and martyrdom in Poland, 1939-1945,* Warsaw, 1968, describing thousands of monuments, with photographs and maps, as well as listing numbers of Poles and Jews murdered there by the Germans, to realize fatuity of the authors who disseminate lies which can be so easily detected as an example of defamation performed by the Anti(?) – Defamation League with the unwitting cooperation of Christians. Huge collections of official German documents, posters and descriptions of eyewinesses prove what the Primate of Poland, Card. August Hlond wrote to Dr. Zajączkowski in a letter dated from Lourdes, April 7, 1941: "At present, we are holding the primacy of suffering. Let us profit from this martyrdom that whatever arises from ruins has also the primacy of faith, dignity and spiritual greatness". In the reports called *Relationes,* translated with the aid of multilingual staff of the Superior General of the Society of Jesus, Wlodzimierz Ledochowski, into four languages and wired from Rome to all parts of the world, terrible Polish Catholic losses were given in detail, and the Primate's account printed in the French clandestine series *Cahiers du témoignage chretien,* no. 13-14, under the title *Defi, l'ordre nouveau en Pologne,* which included also the Jewish martyrology, ended with a "litany" from the *Books of Polish pilgrimage* by Adam Mickiewicz, picturing the history of Polish martyrdom.

At the end of the war, Polish losses, submitted officially by Poland in 1946, were staggering. They included 6,028,000 killed outright, 530,000 physically injured as a result of torture, 60,000 psychically injured as a result of suffering, 1,140,000 increase in TB cases over and above the average level, 2,460,000 deported to forced labor in Germany with 32,000,000 working years without compensation adequate to support workers' families, 2,478,000 Poles expelled from their homes, and 1,215,000 population losses as result of fall of the expected increase due to the extermination policy of the occupiers. According to these data, of the total of about nine million people (8,908,000) who were prisoners of German concentration and extermination camps, 7,230,000 or 81.2% perished. This number included about three million European Jews (33.7% of the total) of which 1,950.000 were Polish citizens of Jewish origin. The number of ethnic Poles murdered in these camps was 1,077,000, the remaining losses by killings in prisons and Gestapo basements amounted to 1,286,000, with the ramainder of 521,000 Poles killed at various public executions in over 70 thousand execution places, not always marked with memorial plaques and monuments. Such were the "vestiges of crimes" which, according to the Anti(?) – Defamation League of the B'nai B'rith, "many Poles and Germans wanted to see razed from the ground" and were prevented from doing that under the pressure of international Jewry.

The well-known Polish hematologist of Jewish descent, Dr Ludwik Hirszfeld, book entitled *Historia jednego życia* (History of one life), Warsaw, 1957, posed the question:

"What are the Jews doing at the moment when the remnants of their tortured nation are being murdered? Only the protests of General Sikorski from London about the murder of Polish citizens are coming to us. But what are the Jews doing? Not those in occupied countries because they are being taken away for slaughter too. But those who are powerful in England and America. Don't they know? Or don't they believe? A terrible suspicion is downing on me, whether they haven't lost their conscience and dignity, or at least their pity; and whether at a time when the remnants of their near ones are being exterminated to the last they are not thinking in advance and calculating how those spared from slaughter are to settle themselves, how to do business with the hangman, and do everything about which we are not even allowed to think...!"

"The time will come, predicts Hirszfeld, when the Germans will conform. Somehow, millions of murders will be undone. The German Jews themselves can best do it. Those left may be satisfied that the Jewish question is finished with. The Germans will feel slight remorse. This remorse is valuable, it can be turned into cash and influence..."

What actually happened after the war was best described by the President of the West German Bundestag, Dr Eugen Gerstenmeier: "Germany found herself in a ghetto, the walls of which were created by reluctance and hatred; the aim of our agreement with Israel is to take the Germans out of the ghetto once and for all." Israel needed money and Germany needed rehabilitation, explained Chancellor Adenauer in his *Erinnerungen* (Memoirs). Israeli daily *Herut* wrote in 1964: "Relieving the Germans of the guilt towards the Jews constituted an element in the West German policy to obtain an "entry permit" to the circle of world nations..." Another Israeli daily *Haolam Haze* said in 1963: "The attitude of our government is based on a cynical transaction, perhaps the most cynical since Adolf Eichmann proposed a business deal to Brandt: goods for blood... We received money. We received help. We sold the GFR a certificate of morality which runs as follows: "We, the state of Israel, victims of Nazism, saved from Auschwitz, a recognized symbol of progress and socialism in the world, certify to all concerned that the holder of this certificate is no longer a fascist, but a completely new German who has right to be accepted in any circle". The ceriificate was sold on the same basis as the Catholic church once sold absolution... Ben Gurion whose effective aid to the murdered Jews was as insignificant as that of Manachem Begin and Golda Meir, had audacity to speak up in their name: "I am positive that if the six million murdered Jews could be asked for their opinion, they would certainly agree".

A publication of the Polish Association in Great Britain entitled *Jews in Poland* from which the above quotations are taken brings also a statement by Alef Bolkowiak: "In

Jerusalem there is the so-called Centre of National Memory where symbolic trees have been planted for the people who contributed towards the saving of Jews from murder by the Nazi Germans. Hundreds of these trees bear Polish names. But a whole forest was planted and named after Adenauer. How many forests have been planted to honor the Christian Poles who, according to the findings of responsible research workers of the Institute to the Memory of Martyrs and Heroes in Jerusalem, for instance Josef Kermish, saved the lives of over 110 thousand Jews in occupied Poland?"

Szymon Datner, a former colleague of Kermish, supplemented this statement, in the *Bulletin* of Jewish Historical Institute, with an estimate that probably another hundred ten thousand Jews hidden by Christians were caught and executed by the Germans. How many of their hosts were executed together with them – nobody will know. Prof. Franciszek Stopniak and Sister Teresa Frącek, in her dissertation at the Academy of Catholic Theology, talk in terms of fifty thousand. No Jewish research has tried to establish their number, since Jews don't acknowledge the value of what is being called "a noble failure". This is the reason why the Danes who, with a minimal danger to their lives, saved a few thousand Jews by transporting them, at 100 dollar per head, to nearby Sweden, are opposed to not so efficient Catholic Poles. It took an honest Danish historian, Poul Borschenius, to reduce undeserved and adulatory Jewish praise in his 5-volume work *The history of the Jews*, New York, Simon and Schuster, 1956, v. 5, p. 57:

"The Danes helped their Jewish fellow-citizens in 1943. But... it should be added that some Jews who returned after the liberation, to both these countries (Denmark and Holland) met with opposition and ill-feeling from those who had taken over their business."

In overcrowded Polish cities where one single room had to accommodate two or three families after the war, a reluctance to vacate the premises when they were claimed by the returning Jews was by Jewish historians branded as "antisemitism" but the same reluctance, in opulent and relatively little damaged countries which cooperated with Hitler was entirely overlooked for political purposes. While Stalin allegedly inquired about "how many divisions has the Pope", for Jews the most important question after the war was: "How many millions can a certain country contribute to Israel." For this reason, empoverished Poland didn't count much and was selected to play the role of a scapegoat for the Jewish disaster. Obvious manipulation of historical facts by recommended Holocaust historians was occasionally discovered by Hannah Arendt: "In my discussion of the situation in the Netherlands, I stated that "the prewar Dutch government had officially declared Jewish refugees to be "undesirable". Mr. Robinson declares categorically as usual: "This never happened", because he never heard of the circular letter issued by the Dutch goverment on May 7, 1938, in which refugees are declared to be "undesirable aliens"... the Dutch government was more outspoken than that of other European government" (*The Jew as a pariah*, ed. by Ron H. Feldman, New York, Grove Press, 1978, p. 268).

Chairman of the Yad Vashem Committee for the Designation of the "Righteous among the Nations", Judge Moshe Bejski, came out with the statement that "in Poland possibilities of rescue by individuals did not exist in a lesser degree than they did elesewhere", although he knew very well that only in Poland and nowhere else any form of aid to persecuted Jews was punished by death. To explain this contradiction, he created a peculiar theory of penal law, allegedly practiced by the Nazis: Where a criminal offense, and such was in their view aid to Jews, hardly ever took place – the penalty for it was escalated up to an automatic execution on the spot, but where this kind of "crime" was rampant as in Holland – the penalty was reduced. Also the effort to win informers which in Poland from material rewards was escalated to the penalty of death for a failure to inform, in Holland – as we know from

Philip Friedman (*Their brothers' keepers*, p. 184) – "dropped to only 7½ gulden (about 2 U.S. dollars) from the original price of "50 to 75 florin", which means that over there betrayals of Jews were, obviously, coming "cheaper by a dozen."

Another distorted approach in the entire Holocaust research is the comparison of willingness to help the Jews in various countires by stressing the proportion of Jewish population before the war to the number of Jews actually saved. Here, again, Catholic Poland is severely censored because the number of Jews saved by the Poles is unfavorably compared with the great number of Jews permitted since immemorable times to enjoy Polish tolerance and hospitality. This fallacy was noticed by Teresa Prekerowa in her book *Konspiracyjna Rada Pomocy Żydom w Warszawie 1942-45*, Warszawa, PIW, 1982, p. 325. The proportion of Jews saved to the number of Christian potential savers in Denmark was 0.12%, in Holland 0.3% and in Poland 0.4%. Huge numbers of Jews to be saved in Poland certainly did not make the job easier than did the minute number of Jews to be saved in Denmark. Jews in Denmark were not congregated in such accumulations as in German-made ghettos in Poland. There was also no penalty of death for aiding Jews and Denmark enjoyed much more liberal treatment by the Germans than Poland. There was no plan of extermination in any Western country, but on the contrary, they were considered as potential allies against the Slavic East. Also the geographical location made the escape much easier than in the land-locked occupied Poland. Thirty thousand Jews hiding in Warsaw alone at the outbreak of the uprising were much more difficult to keep in hiding than seven thousand Danish Jews. Emmanuel Ringelblum, to use one example, probably would survive in his hideout if not for the fact that 34 other Jews were hiding there. There was also an impossibility to move them to Sweden or any other neutral country. The intensity of murderous German activity in Poland compared with other occupied countries was per thousand inhabitants in Denmark less than 0.04 person, in Bel-

What Judge Bejski seems to have forgotten is that only in Poland Christians helping Jews were:

hunted like animals

herded in execution places

shot to death in public squares

hung on gallows in public

burned alive together with their families, and even with their household animals in some "accursed" villages like some ancient Canaanite cities at the times of Joshua.

Even teen-agers in Poland were executed, hung, shot or burned alive for helping Jews: This never happened in another country.

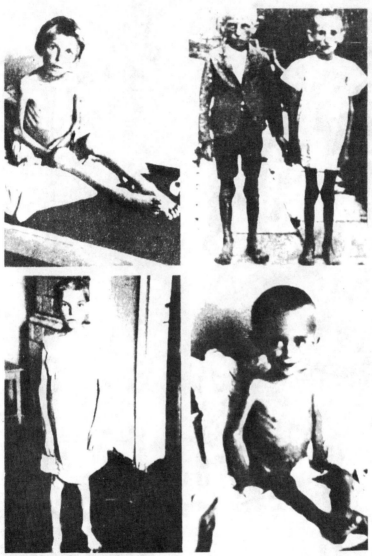

Cold-blooded extermination of twelve million of Christian Poles and other Slavs involved over two million innocent non-Jewish children, many of them killed only because their parents decided to risk their lives while harboring Jews. They are not being honored in the Israeli Children's Memorial Garden at Yad Vashem.

German Nazi deportations and executions in Poland in the eyes of Polish children.

gium 4 persons, in France 12 persons, in Jugoslavia 108, and in Poland 138 non-Jews killed per thousand.

When Max I. Dimond: (op. cit. p. 387) says: "Poland's action was the most shameful. Without a protest she handed over 2,800,000 of her 3,300,000 Jews to the Germans", one should ask whether it was not "more shameful" to "hand over to the Germans" over 3.000.000 of ethnic Poles, including prominent leaders: Bishops, priests, teachers and next to 1,000,000 Polish children.

Another Jewish author, Zygmunt Hauptman, published in Jerusalem in 1946 a hateful pamphlet in which he accused Catholic Poland of permitting huge Jewish immigration into the country "in order to have somebody to hate", and Harry Cargas in his *Christian response to the Holocaust*, asserted that Polish Catholics risked their lives by tossing pieces of bread to Jews carted away to concentration camps in order to enjoy the humiliation of the Jews fighting among themselves over each morsel. Such absurd accusation didn't even deserve an answer. But when at the Second Yad Vashem International Conference, *Rescue attempts during the Holocaust, April 8-11, 1974*, officially appointed lecturers went as far as to make suggestion that the only goverment-sponsored organization in Europe, under the name Żegota, was created in Poland just to cover up alleged "Polish antisemitism", the present, Jewish members of that organization protested.

Mrs. Miriam Peleg who under the name of Hochberg-Mariańska was known to have been a Jewish representative in the Kraków branch of the organization said "I would like to tell Mr. Krakowski that under no circumstances do I agree with his assertion that the work of Żegota was carried out in order to camouflage other activities. I make this statement as someone who was in contact with these people. As for Dr. Kermish's claim that the Poles boast about the Żegota group I can categorically state that even the announcement of Władysław Wójcik's death did not mention a single word about the fact that he was the Secretary of the *Żegota* branch in Kraków."

Abraham Berman was even more specific: "As Secretary-General of the underground Council for Aid to Jews (*Żegota*) and as a member of the underground Jewish National Committee... I am sorry that the lecture by my friend Yisrael Gutman was not objective and did not present an accurate picture of the Polish underground, and the attitude of a significant part of that underground to the Jewish tragedy, and the issue of extending aid to Jews... We must not, for political consideration, disregard the fact that thousands of Catholics, socialists, communists, Democrats, and Syndicalists, among them very simple people as well as Polish intellectuals, professors and students extended aid and helped us. We, the remnants of the Jewish underground, are alive today thanks to them. I therefore take exception to the tone used by my friend Mr. Gutman, as well as to the generalizations he and Mr. Krakowski made. The reality was incomparably more complex and tragic, and I obviously cannot make all the comments I would have liked to make about the two lectures.

I will confine myself to one issue – the number of Jews in Warsaw and its environs who were helped by the Poles from the categories I have previously mentioned... "Żegota" extended aid to more than 4,000 Jews in Warsaw... moreover it aided Jews... at branches in Cracow and Lwów, and had a special representative for Lublin and Zamość. Dr. Kermish, however, should have taken into account that the Jewish National Committee extended aid to 6,000 Jews. Who provided this help? We had more than one hundred cells involved in the relief and rescue of Jews, the majority of which were made up of Poles. Moreover... the third factor was the Bund, which helped aproximately 2,000 Jews. Once again, the active workers were members of the Bund and Poles affiliated with the Jewish National Committee, first and foremost, Polish socialists. In addition the fact that besides "Żegota" and the Poles affiliated with the Jewish National Committee and the

Bund, the members of the Polish Workers Party (P.P.R.) also helped the Jews. As Director of the Department of Jewish Affairs in the underground Polish parliament – the National Federal Council (K.R.N.), I know for a fact that hundreds of Jews, not only in Warsaw, but throughout Poland, were aided by the Communists. If we add up all these figures, it is not a matter of 4,000 Jews, but of at least 20,000 Jews".

"I therefore believe, stated Berman, that it is improper that in Yad Vashem, which is supposed to be a scientific institute, this help should be disregarded for political reasons. We must consider how matters were there and keep in mind that only in Poland was the situation that all those who helped Jews thereby endangered their lives."

Rachel Auerbach, who was a close collaborator of the Jewish historian Ringelblum in the Warsaw Ghetto, explained it more personally from her experience in Poland: "Those who were not there do not understand that reality; there were Poles who endangered their lives. I have already heard the opinion expressed that the entire Polish people was made up of murderers among whom were several good people, the "Righteous Among the Nations"... I believe that in passing historical judgment, one cannot judge people by their motives. One must also consider the reality in which things were done. The number of Jews saved was mentioned; there were also instances in which Poles were executed by the underground for handing over the Jews. I know of an incident which is not recorded in any book. Upon orders of a colonel of the Polish Home Army (A.K.) four people were executed. I was surprised that Sikorski's name was not mentioned and that the government-in-exile was referred to as if it were a homogeneous group. There were differences of opinion among its members as well. We know of hundreds of thousands of Jews who came back from Russia, and we cannot be certain that they would ever succeed in returning if not for the struggle waged by Sikorski so that Jews would also be released from the camps and be allowed to enlist in the Polish Army in the Soviet Union."

The last lecture by Judge Bejski didn't help much by a tendencious enumeration of seven rescuers, none of whom risked of his life by the hands of Germans: Raoul Wallerberg – a Swedish diplomat, Adelaide Hautval – a Frenchwoman, Elisabeth Abegg – a Prussian, Georg Duckwitz – a Nazi official, Oskar Schindler – an intelligence officer for the Nazis in Poland, Paul Grueninger – a Chief of Police in neutral Switzerland, and Aristides de Susa Mendes – a Portuguese Consul in Bordeaux. One of them, Oskar Schindler, lost in his flight a car loaded with gold and diamonds robbed from Jews. Not one person among those praised by Judge Bejski really risked his life – or sacrificed it – for a Jew.

There were hopes, expressed from the audience as the one by Mr. Beit-Zwi who thought that revelations of authentic witnesses like Berman and Auerbach "represent a turnabout or a breakthrough in the concept of Israel and the nations". They contradicted universally accepted myth of world-wide "anti-semitism", especially in Catholic Poland. His only question was "why was this revealed only now, after so many years elapsed!"

Joseph Litvak cautiously reminded the audience that Polish minister, Stanislaw Kot, "hinted, some time ago, that if the Jews did not stop portraying the Poles as anti-Semites, the latter who had information on the activities of the Jewish Police in the ghettos, would respond by publicizing information on the shameful behavior of the Jews."

No Catholic Pole ever did that, but the Jews themselves, Chaim A. Kaplan, Emmanuel Ringelblum, Bernard Goldstein, Reb Moshe Shonfeld, Alexander Donat, and dozens of other eye witnesses, left vivid descriptions of those scandalous events which overshadow everything that was written about Ukrainians, Lithuanians, Poles and others who were in fact dregs of their society, frequently punished by their own authorities as common criminals, while the "Jewish war criminals", as Reb Moshe Shonfeld calls them, were carefully selected and enjoyed lots of authority among their coreligionists.*

The Premier of Israel, Manachem Begin, attempted to cover this shameful chapter of his people's history by going on the Dutch television network (Television Radio Omroep Naardeweg 45-47, Hilversum) May 15, 1979, with an arrogant statement: "I am not going to visit the country of my birth, Poland. There were no traitors among the Poles in their struggle against the Nazis. But as the Jews were concerned, Poles collaborated with the Germans. Among 30 million Poles maybe one hundred were trying to help the Jews. Those tens of thousands of Catholic priests in Poland didn't save one Jewish life, although in the New Testament there is a Commandment of Love – copied from the Old Testament, of course, but it is still there."

No equal time was granted by the Dutch television network to a Christian denial of this bold lie. But uncommitted witnesses and students of history arrive at the same conclustion as the Associate Editor of the Daily Mail in London, Stewart Steven, who in his book *The Poles*, New York, Macmillan, 1982, p. 317, gave his judicious verdict:

"It was a disgraceful statement in which Begin dishonored himself and dishonored his own people: When the Germans completed their conquest of Poland, their first target for extermination was not the Jews at all, but the Polish intellectuals. Long before the ghettos had been set up, thousands of Polish university leaders, lawyers, and the like, the intellectual strength of the nation, were rounded up and sent to concentration camps. Contrary to what I imagine that 99.9 percent of the world believes, Auschwitz was originally built to house and murder Poles and not Jews. Reichsfuehrer-SS Himmler's "General Eastern Plan" allowed for the virtual extinction of

---

* More facts on this delicate subject await publication of our companion volume: "The beasts of prey".

the Polish nation once the war was won, and he began this policy the moment Poland was occupied, leaving the fate of European Jewry far less sharply defined, at least during those early stages. As the ghettos began to go up, the policy of unrestrained terror against the Polish population was still unabated. Whole districts suspected of being disloyal were razed to the ground, and their populations executed; constant blockades; street roundups and document checks leading to the arrests on the flimsiest of pretexts, reduced the population to a state of helpless despair... About that time the Nazis promulgated a law in Poland unique in all of Occupied Europe; it formally established that any Pole helping a Jew automatically receive the death penalty. Not only was that the law, but it was ruthlessly and unfailingly enforced to the letter by the Germans. A Pole who gave so much as a glass of water to a Jew outside the ghetto was liable to be shot. A Pole who failed to report to the authorities knowledge of a Jew in hiding was unfailingly deported to a concentration camp. But if Poland was the only country in Europe where helping of a Jew required the courage of men who are prepared to die for their fellows, it was also the only country in Europe where... a full-scale secret organization existed for the sole purpose of spiriting as many Jews as possible to safety.

And what is particularly impressive is that help came from every section of the population. The church behaved with extraordinary courage, even though nuns and priests were not immune from prosecution by the German authorities."

Dr. Zajączkowski's research was able to provide the Primate of Poland for his sermon at St. Augustin's during the celebration of the 40th anniversary of Warsaw Ghetto Uprising a documented list of 22 Catholic priests who were actually Martyrs of their Charity for the sons of Abraham having been killed for aiding Jews. Hundreds of obstacles placed in the path of the publication of his work in 1984 caused a serious delay and a need to look for a less expensive composition of its text outside of The United States, without impairing its final form.

Zajączkowski's efforts to bring his findings to international meetings on Lessons of the Holocaust in Philadelphia were thwarted by acrimonious attacks and violent denunciations, without anybody on the Christian side daring to take a more objective approach. It could not be done in a forum which invited the Judge of the Supreme Court of Israel, Honorable Binyamin Halevi, who stated that "millions of European non-Germans – Frenchmen and Poles and Russians and Lithuanians – **except perhaps for the Danes and Swedes?** – who were collaborators with Germany to exterminate the Jews... no people were annihilated according to plan... I asked witnesses time and again, "Did the Jews get any help?"... The answers were inconclusive: "We had the whole population against us. **Jews hidden by Christian families could be counted on the fingers of one hand".** But when the name of **a German,** Anton Schimidt was mentioned... **a hush settled over the courtroom.** It was as though the crowd had spontaneously decided to observe the usual two minutes of silence in honor of the man named Anton Schmidt. And in those few minutes, which were like a sudden burst of light in the midst of impenetrable and unfathomable darkness, a single thought stood out clearly, irrefutably, beyond question: How utterly different everything would be today in this courtroom, in Israel, in Germany, in all of Europe, and perhaps in the world, if only more such stories could have been told" (International Institute on the Holocaust: International Conference: *The lessons of the Holocaust,* October, 1978, p. 16-23).

This beautiful – but how fallacious in its hypocrisy – expression was followed by a refusal to listen to other, even more impressive stories of Christian heroism in attempting to save the Jewish companions of national disaster. Dr. Zajączkowski was at a special workshop for College and University Section "reminded (by its chairman, Dr. Yaffa Eliach) that our task was, after all, to discuss the teaching of the Holocaust and not historical questions." (op. cit. p. 204). Dr. Eliach oviously forgot that false premises lead to false conclusions and no proper "lessons" may be drawn from distorted historical facts.

"Honorable" Judges of Israel who arrange such meetings which on the surface radiate good will and impartiality, but in fact serve to bury the truth for obvious political reasons, indicated by Berman and Auerbach, and contrary to the hopes such as Beit-Zwi's for a "turnabout or a breakthrough in the concept of Israel and the nations", not only dishonor themselves and their court and their entire nation, but continue to keep their future generations in bondage of mistrust and hatred due to systematic misinformation and disinformation.

The well-known Catholic columnist, at one time head of American Bishops' Secretariat for Catholic-Jewish Relations, John B. Sheerin, C.S.P. wrote about this book in a draft for the preface: "Since the end of World War II there has been a running controversy in ecumenical circles about the number of Jews saved by Polish Catholics from a brutal death in the Nazi era. We were accustomed to reading sweeping generalizations about "Polish antisemitism" but now the true picture is coming into focus due to the work of painstaking researchers. Outstanding among these is Dr. Wacław Zajączkowski who has compiled a book entitled *Martyrs of Charity*. It is painstakingly detailed account of hundreds of instances in which Christian Poles were murdered in World War II because they befriended Jews. It is a grim account of man's inhumanity to man but also a glorious epic of Christian sacrifices for the sake of the people of the Old Testament".

One may wonder why these facts were concealed from the American public for such a long time. Even the editors of Paulist Press rejected recommendation of their one time expert on the subject of Catholic-Jewish dialogue that this book be published by them. In a burst of philosemitism, coming from a bad conscience, the title of the monthly *Catholic World*, known during the war for favoring the Germans and critical about the Jews, was changed into the *New Catholic World* and – as a result of this metamorphosis (from Saul into Paul or may be, vice versa) they have at their disposal ample funds to publish a special series of Stimulus Books under the direction of Helga Croner and the cooperation of many Rabbis.

Poland Was The Ally Of Nazi Germany? ? ?
The William J. Anderson Affair

All Polish Americans, all Poles, all those who pursue truth and honesty in government were insulted by the report issued by Mr. Anderson's General Accounting Office in which it was noted that Poland was the ally of Nazi Germany. It would appear that this statement was made on the basis of materials supplied by the office of special investigations of the Department of Justice. Efforts on the part of the *PERSPECTIVES* staff, as well as those of others to learn of the source of this statement have been futile.

We wish to know how this "error" was made. Also who checked the manuscript before and after it was sent to the printers. We cannot believe that Mr. Anderson doesn't really know who made the "error" nor do we know why he refuses to disclose this information. We have the right to know so that such lies will not be repeated. We will not rest until we smoke out the truth. Accordingly we ask our readers to write to William J. Anderson Director, General Accounting Office 441 G St., N.W., Washington, D.C. 20540, and to their representatives and senators, to demand an explanation. If this is not forthcoming, we ask our readers to demand Mr. Anderson's resignation. Each and everyone of us has been insulted. Mr. Anderson should remember that.

Stultification of American youth through so called Holocaust Studies in public and even in parochial schools has reached such proportion that some college students think that "Nazis" were Poles and recently a high official of Reagan administration, **William J. Anderson of the General Accounting Office publicly stated that in the Second World War Poland was an ally of Nazi Germany.**

In this vicious propaganda campaign a Pope was called "butcher" and St. Maximilian Kolbe, through his alleged "antisemitism", was "stoking the ovens of Treblinka and Auschwitz". For that reason we have reqested the publishers of *Sunday Visitor* for permission to reprint a chapter from their book *Anti-Catholic prejudice in America* by Michael Schwarz concerned with Jewish attacks against the Patron Saint of our Foundation, St. Maximilian Kolbe. It is supplemented by a few essays by various other Catholic writers in America and in the Great Britain which picture the background of Jewish prejudice against Christians setting obstacles against adequately presenting the whole truth. Anybody who fails to accuse Catholic church and Poland of "anti-semitism" is suspected to be an "antisemite" himself.

There was even a case of a "murdered book" *Dying we live*, of Eugene Kulski on the subject of the events in Warsaw during the Holocaust. His memoirs were accused of being "disquietly selective", avoiding "dark subject of Polish anti-Semitism" and "the church's silence". The book was printed but not distributed properly. This is the reason why the present book is financed by mostly private contributions.

INTRODUCTION

One of leading ideologists of the Holocaust, Yehuda Bauer, wrote in his "Trends in Holocaust research" (*Yad Vashem Studies*, v. 12 (1977) p. 34) that "after all, the testimony of the heroism of the Righteous Gentiles is of necessity also the testimony of the iniquity of others." If one adds to this statement the provision that only a Jewish testimony is being considered valid in determining "heroism" or "iniquity" of the Gentiles, then it becomes obvious that Yad Vashem Commission on the Righteous constitutes sort of a supreme tribunal judging Goyim on the sole testimony of the Jews which radically differs from medieval Christian provision that a Jew shouldn't be condemned without calling also on Jewish witnesses. It also a betrays lack of recognition that between "heroism" and "iniquity" there is a vast space for average people, not only Jews but also Gentiles, who are neither "heroes" nor "scoundrels" by simply not going beyond the call of duty.

For this reason, our book which extolls martyrdom for love and charity toward the persecuted Jews does not point an accusing finger at anybody for the sole reason that he hesitated to risk his own life and the lives of his beloved, his family and

his neighbors, to save a member of a nation which – with in-
finitesimal exceptions – did not respond with gratitude toward
its benefactors. Otherwise, the Polish Catholic share among
those recognized by Yad Vashem as the Righteous would be
not 2 thousand but 2 million of those who risked their lives by
stretching a helping hand to a Jew, or at least 2 or 3 hundred
thousand of those who were successful in actually saving a
Jewish life considering the fact that on the average 3 non-Jews
were executed in Poland for every Jew hiding with them
caught by German Nazis. Unsuccessful attempts to save
Jewish lives find no recognition in Yad Vashem which seems
to ignore the moral value of a "noble failure".

Beside Christians, we also brought together rare examples
of Jews who didn't follow Rabbi Isaac Nissenbaum's advice in
the Warsaw Ghetto that now is the time to protect the sanctity
of Jewish life – *kiddush ha-hayim*, and not to die for the
sanctification of the Name – *kiddush ha-shem*, confirmed by
rebbe of Żelechów who similarly counseled Jews to save their
"precious lives" at all cost (see Lucy Dawidowicz, *The war
against the Jews, 1933-1945*, Bantam Books, 1976, p. 291). We
have assembled examples of Jews who refused to die "only because they were Jews", but preferred to die for some higher
idea than preservation of their own lives, at least for the love of
their families or other members of Jewish community, although we didn't find one single example of a Jew dying to
save a Christian Gentile.

When Walter Lacquer in his book, *The terrible secret*, Penguin Books, 1982, wonders why the Jews in Poland – in spite
of sufficient knowledge of electronics – didn't construct one
single radio broadcasting station and preferred relying on
Polish underground for the transmittal of their messages, he
should have realized that a broadcasting station could be easily
detected by the Germans and the Jews preferred to leave this
risk to the Polish "goyim" whose lives were expendable and
not as "sacred" as their own. The same appplies to picking
arms on the battlefields or acquiring them from soldiers who

were eager to shed their military equipment in order to escape the fate of prisoners-of-war. Author's own family house in Włodzimierz was left by fireman to burn down when the munition gathered by his youngest ten-year-old brother in the attic started to explode after the house was hit by German artillery on the day of attack on USSR. If the Germans found the weapons in the house the whole family would be executed as it actually happened in hundreds of cases. The Jews in general were too cautious about their own lives and this was the reason why only a few hundred members of ZZW (Jewish Military Organization) in Warsaw accepted arms from Major Iwański long before the final slaughter of the Jews began. This handful of courageous Jews, mostly former members of the Polish Army, were the best armed and the best trained units in the Warsaw Ghetto according to the testimony of Emmanuel Ringelblum in *The Polish Jewish relations*, Jerusalem, Yad Vashem, 1974, p. 169.

In the Holocaust terminology one hears about "six millions of Martyrs and Heroes". But there is a basic difference between the "martyrs" and "victims". At the time of our common holocaust twice as many Christian Poles and other Slavs (well over 12 million) were killed by the Germans in cold blood away from battlefields as were the Jews. But they are simply called victims of the German *"Drang nach Osten"* – (push to the East). They died "only for being Poles, Slavs or other members of inferior races" similarly as Jews died "only for being Jews". There is nothing especially honorable in such death, although the tragedy is immense. Also the Palestinians who were killed in cold blood at Deir Yassin or in Sabra and Shatilla died "only for being Palestinians" and standing in the way of an invader. All of them were just "victims" of German or Jewish racism, and very rarely "martyrs" or "heroes". Simone de Beauvoir said in her preface to Jean-François Steiner's *Treblinka*, New York, New American Library, 1966, p. XXI, "heroism is not inherent in human nature" and "there are ethical limits to heroism" as Jerzy Mirewicz S. J. of London, England had to explain to Joseph Lichten who accused a Polish Catholic family of not keeping his child after a danger appeared that Nazi Germans will detect them (see his introduction to Iranek-Osmecki's *He who saves one life*, New York, Crown, 1971, about the heroism of Christian Poles).

When Chancellor Hitler issued the order "to kill without pity or mercy all men, women, and children of Polish race and language", only a handful of German heroes protested and the entire nation was singing *"Deutchland, Deutchland über alles"* (Germany above everything, even above the commandment not to kill) their church bells tolling at the fall of Warsaw, but it was to the credit of the Jewish people that thousands went to Israeli streets to protest against Sabra and Shatilla. They were reminded by John Paul II that they too "received", therefore should follow, "the commandment not to kill".

After the June 1985 *"Notes on the correct way to present the Jews and Judaism"* of the Vatican the American *NC News Service* reported: "The document immediately drew a sharp response from the International Jewish Committee on Interreligious Consultations. The agency, formed by five major Jewish organizations, said the new Vatican text suffered from a 'regressive spirit and formulations' and was 'totally inadequate" in its treatment of the two 'absolutely crucial aspects of contemporary Jewish existence', referring to the state of Israel and the extermination of six million Jews in World War II".

Franciscan Father Melchior (Malak), himself a survivor of concentration camps in Auschwitz and Dachau, produced a well documented indictment of the guilty who try to blame everything on the SS and Gestapo and members of the Nazi party, in his – already forgotten book *Man's inhumanity*, Detroit, Mich. 1949, p. 134: "If we admit that genocide was committed solely in concentration camps and that the only guilty ones were members of Hitler's party, the SS-men and Gestapo officials, we must remembert that the SS-men and Gestapo executioners were sons of German families. They were brought by German mothers. They were chosen from among

Germans who had not a drop of foreign blood. They were the ELITE, who enjoyed privileges because of their typically German background. The entire nation was proud of these boys, selected by "The *Fuehrer*" to represent the German spirit at its best."

"And they were not an insignificant group. Hundreds of thousands of German youngsters were trained as future SS-men. Every third family in Germany had a son, or a brother or a husband in the Gestapo or the SS-troops. Horror camps were not the only places where genocide was committed. In the East, millions of Russians and Jews were put to death in public executions."

"In the camps for labor workers, millions of kidnapped slaves were forced to build up the war potential of the Reich. Each village, each factory, had hundreds of slave workers, whose plight was often as heartrendering as that of the inmates of Dachau. They were also forced to perform dangerous and heavy tasks; they were also flogged and abused and starved by their overseers."

"Whenever a new transport of slave workers arrived at a village or in town, there was a stampede of prospective bosses, who rushed to market place to chose the strongest men and women. Who was it that compelled nine-year-old children to work in mines and forests? Who was it that depraved their souls and forced them to forget their native tongue? Who spied and shadowed and denounced thousands of men and women for the slightest misdemeanor? Who collaborated with SS-men in prisons and hospitals, where genocide was adopted as a daily routine? How can they say that all these moral sins were committed only by the party men?"

"When we were driven from the railway station of Halle to the prison, German passers-by's gathered on the sidewalks and laughed and sneered at us. I remember how we were abused and insulted by German women and how German children threw stones and mud at helpless victims."

"Were they all SS-men?"

"When Hitler waged the war and the Germans listened to loudspeakers which carried his boisterous and screaming voice, who was it that applauded and cheered the beloved *"Fuehrer"* frantically?"

"Twenty million human beings were murdered in cold blood by the Germans. They were not war victims; they were victims of a hatred cultivated by the German nation. One hundred million human beings were oppressed and subdued, not by the spirit of war but by the spirit of German pride... Without the support of the nation, the Nazi party would not have been in a position to realize its program of genocide. Atrocities were committed by the army, by the police, by the administration of the entire country, by the majority of industrialists and by thousands of farmers – in a word, by Germany. And that is why the German nation ought to atone for these unbelievably fiendish offenses. And that is why the world must not permit that those brutal and outrageous conditions be ever repeated in the future"

"The Germans should listen to the wise advice of the former Vicar General of Katowice diocesis in Silesia who was expelled, with many of his compatriots after the war, to Germany proper and wrote: "We will accept our plight. As a punishment for the sins of those who committed grave offenses against the Polish nation, against humanity and against the most sacred Laws. We will accept our sufferings as an atonement for our sins committed when we cowardly kept silent, as well as for all the crimes committed by the National Socialist rulers of which we are also guilty. Though we feel bitter, we will not cultivate in our hearts hatred towards other nations and particularly towards the Poles..."

"It is a lesson for all of us, says Father Melchior, for the entire world. Any nation that builds its future on the false foundations of egoism and pride, depriving others of liberty and of their welfare, sooner or later will crumble into the ruin."

It is a lesson also for the young Israeli nation.

Many centuries ago, Pope Gregory IX admonished the rapacious land-grabbing Teutonic Order using quotation from the Prophet Isaiah, 5:8:

"Shame on you! you who add house to house
and join field to field,
until not an acre remains,
and you are left to dwell alone in the land."

As the commandment "not to kill", also this prophetic warning was first issued to Israel and should be heeded to avoid the fate of the aggressive Prussia which simply disappeared from the face of the earth as Isaiah predicted for his own nation (Is. 9:13)

"The people of Israel have not repented;
even though the Lord Almighty has punished them,
they have not returned to Him."

With Israel angrily denying any fault on its side, two Christian nations, Germany and Poland, have stretched their arms in a mutual recognition of their mutual trespasses through the exchange of letters between the two Episcopates:

"You had the magnanimity to mention, wrote the German Bishops to the Poles, from all the centuries of our relations, first and foremost such examples as do honor to your own, as well as to our people – examples of work done together, of sincere esteem, of fruitful exchange, of mutual aid – even though all that could have receded behind the injustices and sufferings... We, no doubt have to thank our common Christian heritage for those brighter sides of Polish-German relations, in history... If we wish to be brethren in Christ, despite all the dissimilarities, then the cloud that howers, unfortunately, over our two peoples will have to vanish."

"Frightful things have been done, continued the German message, to the Polish people by the Germans in the name of the German people. We know the consequences of the war must be born by us; they are the consequences that are hard for our country too. We understand that the period of German occupation has left behind it a burning wound that even with the best will in the world is difficult to heal."

"All the more we are grateful that despite the millions of Polish victims during that time you recall the Germans who resisted the spirit of evil... In this we are all of one mind. We are children of the same heavenly Father. All human evil is first and foremost a guiltiness before God and the forgiveness must first and foremost be asked of Him. The request of the Lord's prayer – forgive us our trespasses – must first be directed to Him. Then with an honest heart we may also ask forgiveness of our neighbor. Asking forgiveness is an appeal to everyone wronged to see the wrong with the merciful eyes of God and to permit a new beginning."

"Christian love tries to identify with the anxieties and needs of others, thus overcoming tensions and barriers. It wants to extirpate the evils of hatred, enmity, revanchism, thus contributing towards overcoming the unhappy consequences of the war... We shall do all in our power to keep this link from breaking again... It is with brotherly reverence that we grasp the proferred hands. May the God of peace grant that these hands be never separated through the evil of hatred."

This magnificent display of Christian spirit met with violent disapproval on both sides from people who, as John Paul II said in his peace message of 1979, "judge everything on terms of relations of force, of group and class struggles, of friends and enemies an atmosphere conducive to social barriers, contempt, even hatred and terrorism", while "on the other hand, a heart devoted to the higher value of peace produces a desire to listen and to understand, respect for others, gentleness which is real strength , and trust. In this regard, the mass media of communication have great educational task". "Leaders of nations, concluded the Supreme Pontiff, and international organizations, learn to find a new language, a language of peace!" (*Origins*, Jan. 4, 1979, p. 455-460)

John Paul II as a pilgrim to Auschwitz-Treblinka in 1979, to "this Calvary of our Times" where he invoked the doctrine of "our old teacher", Paulus Vlodimiri of Cracow, that "at no time can one nation develop at the expense of another, at the price of the subjugation, conquest, develop at the price of the exploitation and at the price of death of another nation", thus proclaiming equal rights for all the sons, either of Japheth or Shem or an "accursed" Ham. He also spoke in the name of His Nation, Poland, which was deprived of freedom for such a long time and still suffers from prejudice and disrespect from the members of ethnic groups which until recently complained about the "teaching of contempt" and now themselves apply it to the alleged "sons of Ham" in the USA and in South Africa. Elie Wiesel at that time protested against the Papal visit and Mass at Auschwitz, in the same vein as today Theo Klein and others who wish to expel Polish Carmelite Sisters from their convent at Auschwitz to make room for themselves and nobody else.

John Paul II didn't omit an opportunity to speak in this spirit to Yasser Arafat of the hated PLO and drew upon himself a violent attack from the Zionist establishment which resulted in smearing yellow posters on the walls of Rome announcing canonization of St. Maximilian Kolbe with the Nazi emblem and the name of Arafat equated with a swastika, a provocation which, in turn, led to the bombing of a Rome synagogue and consequent torrent of vituperation accusing John Paul II of complicity in this act of terrorism and demanding an apology, not once but on every subsequent anniversary of this event.

Fortunately, however, also on the Jewish side there is a new trend to correct the biased perspective of Jewish history which originates in the hateful commemorations of various enemies of Israel like Haman or an Egyptian Pharaoh, expressed in stamping feet at the synagogue at the mention of their names or hiring a poor Christian fellow to allow himself to be beaten by Jewish children with sticks and stones in a hateful memory of Haman. This feeling of hatred at the most solemn celebration of Purim and Passover leads many Jews to attribute identical feelings to Christians at the celebration of such feasts as Christmas and Easter. This obvious misinformation was repeated by such Holocaust propagandists as Elie Wiesel. It was inculcated at a very tender age to Jewish children by their mothers who warned them that a Christian "goy" will kill them at the first occasion, and if he doesn't it is because he happened to be "too lazy". Israeli psychiatrist Jay Y. Gonen, talks about a Jewish child afraid to pass a horse and when mother quiets him down that this horse will not kick, expressing the fear that maybe the horse knows that we are Jewish".

The same vicious trend in education of children is being expressed in the Israeli version of the popular tv program called "Sesame Street" where the spectacular character of the soft "Big Bird" is being replaced by a porcupine with its spines and quills directed against the outside world.

Prominent Jewish social thinker, the first woman to teach as an ordinary professor at Yale Uniwersity, Hannah Arendt, pointed out the absurdity of seeking in the alleged universal hatred of Jews the bond uniting them into one nation. After the creation of the State of Israel there is no need for such an absurd bond of unity. Whence the growing tendency to break away from the *lachrimose* concept of Jewish history promoted by Solo Baron, Bernard Weinryb and a host of other, especially young Jewish historians. With the fall of the calamitous Jewish historiography falls also the myth of universal anti-semitism. But, for various reasons, some Christian writers like Franklin Littell, Edward Flannery, John T. Pawlikowski, insist on this device which keeps ignorant Christians "in bondage" as demonstrated in Lillienthal's book *Cover-over* in a special chapter entitled "Christians in bondage" while in the recent Jewish historiography, the opposite appears to be true.

"The tiny little group, the ten thousand Jewish souls, that lived in Catholic Europe in the year 800, says Solomon Rappaport, multiplied more than a thousand times in the following eleven centuries... More-over, throughout this period they maintained a higher standard of living than that of ninety-five percent of their neighbours. This constitutes great success in the group's struggle for existence – probably greater than any other national group in Europe". According to Rabbi I. A. Agus of Yeshiva University in New York... "the Jewish situation in the West of Europe was privileged until the end of the eleventh century". In the pre-crusade period, the Jews of Catholic Europe constituted a highly privileged class. Politically they were quite free; religiously they were uncontrolled and unrestrained; economically they were highly successful, and culturally they were by far the most progressive group in Europe. While their Christian neighbors huddled around the strongholds and castles of their lords and rarely dared venture abroad, the Jews were able to trade successfully in commercial centers located hundreds of miles away from their homes in Western Europe". (Solomon Rappaport: *Jew and Gentile*. N. Y. Philosophical Library, 1980).

Still during the second crusade St. Bernard of Clairveaux in France admonished the crusaders that "whosoever uses violence against the Jews commits a deadly sin." It was the same Saint who at the time of "Vendic crusade" in 1146 demanded that heathen Slavs between the Elbe and Oder rivers be either converted or exterminated. Here, again, Jews were much better off than heathen Slavs.

When the Church protection of Jews couldn't stem anti-Jewish violence in the European West and it seemed that the time of *akedah* arrived when the very existence of Jews was threatened there, binding of Isaac prefigurating his sacrificial death, the Holocaust was prevented by hospitable Poland throwing her gates open for Jewish mass immigration to the "new Canaan" in the contemporary rabbinical language or a "Po-lin" where the Jews could wait for the advent of their Messiah. How the Jews fared in Poland is a matter of record. Myer Law, in his book *The Jews of Poland*, London, Gold, 1944, p. 82, quotes *Responsa* of of the 16th century Jewish authority, Moses Isserles, saying: "In this country there is no fierce hatred against us as it obtains in Germany. **May it so continue until the advent of the Messiah**... Had not the Lord left us this land as a refuge, the fate of Israel would have been indeed unbearable. But by the grace of God, the King and his nobles are favorably disposed towards us. The Jews enjoy equal rights with their non-Jewish neighbors: **"The Jews pay taxes, wrote King Zygmunt August, and therefore are entitled to the same rights as others."**

"While Jews, says Myer Low, lived in their own quarter this did not preclude them from mixing freely with non-Jews. Isserles records that non-Jews frequented the Jewish quarter. Indeed we find them **living together on terms, not only of toleration, but of friendship and cordiality**... In the economy of the country Jews were well fitted to take the place of the middle class, then lacking, and were inevitably attracted by the opportunities open to them."

Jewish historian in Poland, Maurycy Horn, writes in the beautiful album *Polish Jewry: history and culture* published in Warsaw 1982, p. 13, that the chronicler of King Zygmunt Stary, Justus L. Decius, stated in 1521: "In this period Jews are gaining in importance; there is hardly any toll or tax for which they would be not responsible or at least to which they would not aspire. **Christians are generally subordinate to the Jews.** Among the rich and noble families of the Commonwealth you will not find one who would not favor the Jews on their estates and give them power over Christians." And another Jewish historian, Leon Poliakov, in his *History of anti-Semitism*, v. 1, New York, Vanguard, 1965, p. 249, quotes the papal legate in Poland, Card. Giovanni F. Commendone, who informed the Holy See about condition of Jews in the Polish-Lithuanian Commonwealth as follows: "**In these regions, masses of Jews are to be found, who are not subject to the scorn they meet with elsewhere. They own land, engage in commerce, study medicine and astronomy.** They possess great wealth and are not only **counted among the respectable people** but sometimes even dominate them. **They wear no distinctive insignia, and are even permitted to bear arms.** In short, they **have all the rights of citizens.**"

"Poland, says Rabbi Vinocour, had been one of Europe's first constitutional monarchies... The autonomy which Polish kings encouraged enabled Jews to build a communal structure which touched upon every aspect of life. Theirs was a world in which Talmudic law was not relegated, as in the West, merely to religious ritual, but operated in the marketplace and streets as well... **Privileges granted to Jews** were ratified by successive kings **throughout Polish history, creating a unique environment for the unparalleled growth and flourishing of Jewish heritage and culture**... Each separate Jewish community was administered by its *kahal*, a committee of scholars and oligarchs, and all the *kahals* were subject to a national legislative body known as the Council of Four lands, *Va'ad arba arazot* constituted at a congress in Lublin in 1581... Modelled after the *Sejm* (Polish national diet), the Council was **the only Jewish parliament that ever existed outside of Israel and was unparalleled in Jewish history for its duration and for the size of the territory its jurisdiction covered**.* The Council was backed by the authority of the Polish Crown and was officially referred to as the *Congressus Judaicus*. It had a decisive influence over every aspect of Polish-Jewish life from 1592 until its demise in 1764. The *kahals* and the Council maintained a complex system of synagogues, study houses, courts of law, hospitals, schools, welfare programs, and even tax collecting".

"But Poland had the misfortune of being squeezed by the predatory, expansionist neighbors – Russia in the East, Germany to the West, Austria to the South – each one engaging in repeated incursions of her borders... In 1648 a major disaster overwhelmed Poland and especially Jews in a rebellion of Cossacks... In the latter part of the eighteenth entury, Poland was partitioned by her neighbors. During that period, many Jews combined forces with Polish patriots to free their country from foreign domination. One of those Jews, Colonel Berek Joselewicz, **became a Polish national hero fighting with the legendary Tadeusz Kościuszko**, who later joined the revolutionary army of George Washington in America's struggle for independence. Of the Jewish participation in Poland's national struggle, Kościuszko wrote: "The Jews have proven to the world that when the welfare of humanity is at stake, they know not how to spare their lives".

During the 123 years of partitioned Poland Polish-Jewish relations deteriorated. Prof. Roman Dybowski in his study *Poland in world civilization*, New York, Barrett, 1940, pointed out elements of this deterioration **in gradual prevalence of Ashkenazim, or German, Jews over Sephardim** who originally constituted a sort of intellectual elite among the

---

* For the size of the Polish-Lithnanian Commonwealth before its partition see the map enclosed in the "Open letter" at the end of this book.

Polish Jewry. "These were the Jews from Spain and Portugal... They made their mark as teachers of Hebrew to the early humanists; also as medical men of repute, medicine having since Greek and Roman times a profesion widely practiced by gifted Jews. In Poland, the first Sephardim of eminence were doctors coming from Italy... They became **founders of medical dynasties, acquiring wealth and authority in the larger towns...** The first professor of the Hebrew language in the University of Krakow was a Jew of Italian origin, Leonardus David. The humanist learning and liberal views characteristic of the **Sephardim aroused violent antagonism among the Ashkenazim, who had brought to Poland the separatism and the esoteric rabbinical scholarship of the persecuted and secluded Central European ghettoes...** Among the Jews, the narrow-minded Orthodox bigotry of the Ashkenazim definitely got the upper hand over the enlightened humanist liberalism of the Sephardim. Classical secularist learning, which had still been combined with Jewish religious thought in the works of eminent Jewish teachers and writers in the 16th century Poland, now faded from the rabbinical schools; the esoteric doctrines of the Kabbala took the place of the bold rationalistic speculations of the preceeding period, and **the Jewish community shut itself up within the Chinese wall of strict religious dogma and intricate ritual observance.** The days when a baptized Jewish printer at Kraków, subsidized by the Bishop, published a New Testament in Jewish in 1540, were irrevocably over; there was **no longer any prospect of assimilation** of the Jews in the mass of their Polish surroundings through the medium of baptism".

Such narrow-mindedness is represented in America by Rabbi Eliezer Berkovits in his *Faith after the Holocaust*, New York, KTAV, 1973, concerning the Catholic-Jewish dialogue: "The strange reality of this "fraternal dialogue" is that whereas among Christians it is clerics, theologians, and the more committed and **knowledgeable Christians who propagate the idea of interreligious understanding, the Jewish "en-**

thusiasts" include the less committed Jews, the public-relations experts, the secularists".

"As to a dialogue in the purely theological sense, says Rabbi Berkovits, nothing could be less fruitless and more pointless. What is usually referrrred to as **the "Judeo-Christian tradition" exists only in Christian or secularist phantasy...** There are many who believe that Jews have at least the "Old Testament" in common. This is a serious misunderstanding. The Jews have no "Old Testament". The very fact that for the Christians it is the "Old Testament" indicates that it is not identical with the Hebrew Bible... The Christian interpretation of Biblical Judaism is not the Judaism of the Hebrew Bible... Nor does Judaism have a common sprirtiual patrimony with Christianity in the Patriarchs and Prophets; in Jewish understanding, the God of Abraham is not the triune deity of Christianity..."

"**This is the post-Christian era**... Having survived miraculously, the world-historic mystery of Israel is deepened ever more by Israel's return to the land of its origin... We are at the treshold of the new age. We who were there when the Christian era began; we in whose martyrdom Christianity suffered its worst moral debacle; we in whose blood the Christian era found its end[*] – we are here as this new era opens. And we shall be here when the new era reaches it's close – we, the *edim*, God's own witnesses, the *am olam*, the eternal witnesses of history."

"**Not for a single moment shall we entertain the idea that what happened to European Jewry was divine punishment** for any sins committed by them. It was injustice absolute... We have had innumerable Auschwitzes... but in the

---

[*] In 1974 at the cathedral of St. John the Divine in News York an international symposium of Christians and Jews announced the "beginning of a new, post-Christian, era", first provided with a question mark which was later removed, in the Holocaust propaganda, to proclaim the new, Jewish, era in the history of mankind.

magnitude of human suffering and degradation nothing equals the tragedy of the German death camps... The idea that all this has befallen us because of our sins, *mipnei hataeinu*, is an utterly unwarranted exaggeration... The idea that the Jewish martyrology through the ages can be explained as divine judgment is obscene. It was injustice absolute; **injustice countenanced by God.**"

"God's chosen ones suffer guiltlessly... **The Christian attempt to rob Israel of the dignity of Isaiah's suffering servant of God has been one of the saddest spritual embezzlements in human history**... Generation after genration Christians poured out their iniquities and inhumanity over the head of Israel... What is the weight of one sacrifice compared to the myriads of sacrifices of Israel? What is one crucifixion beside a whole people crucified through the centuries. But, it is maintained, the one crucified was a god, whereas the untold millions of Jewish men, women, and children were only human beings. Human beings only! As if the murder of an innocent human being were a lesser crime than the killing of a god. A god after all does not have to die. If he is killed, it is because he offers himself freely as a sacrifice. A god chooses to be killed; he knows what he is doing and why he is doing... To torture and to kill one innocent child is a crime infinitely more abominable that the killing of any god... Unfortunately, the teaching of deicide became an excuse, and often a license, for homicide. Pity any god thus caricatured by his devotees... Through Israel God tested Western man and found him wanting. **This gruesome failure of Christianity** has led the Western world **to the greatest moral debacle of any civilization – the Holocaust.**"

"The German crime of the ghettos and concentration camps stands out in all human history as the most abominable, the most sickening, and the most inhuman... The Nazi crime of the German people attempted to eradicate the last vestiges of a possible innate sense of humanity... The nemesis is not limited to Nazi Germany alone, it has overtaken Western civilization itself. The Holocaust is not exclusively the guilt of Germany; the entire West has a goodly share in it... **Had the nations and their churches not been silent and indifferent to** what was recognizably afoot in the early days of Nazism, world history would have taken an entirely different course... It is true the Jewish people had to pay a terrible price for the crimes of humanity... The state of Israel came at he moment in history when nothing else could have saved Israel from extinction through hopelessness... The less intense the Jewish involvement in the majority culture and economy, the greater the chance for the authentically Jewish deed of daily existence... Examining the world scene, a Jew can see nowhere the presence of God in history of Israel and only through it also in the history of man. **Eliminate Israel from history and there is no need for any reference to God".**

This megalomaniac concept of "chosenness" nursed behind self-imposed "Chinese walls" of spiritual ghetto results in unbelievable callousness for the suffering of other people. Rabbi **Berkovits scorns Catholic concern for the Israeli victims. He compares their removal from their native soil to the series of expulsions which were started in Europe by the Nazis as not even worth mentioning.** For him, they constitute "a renewal of biblical times... **We have been awakened to a messianic hour in our history"** (p. 154-5). "As no world conscience existed during the holocaust, neither is it anything to be reckoned with these days... Is it not ridiculous that Israel should be called the aggressor and accused of expansionist colonialism and imperialism...?" **Berkovits invokes the example of the Soviet Russia** which "concluded the infamous pact with Nazi Germany... incorporated part of Poland and Finland, swallowed up the Baltic states". These examples obviously are considered to be **an excuse for Israel's actions against the Palestinians, and the Catholic Church is singled out for ridicule in defending the rights of those "professional political refugees"....** Who are these people, he asks, **who dare to talk to Jews about humane treatment of re-**

fugees? The same that showed a murderous indifference toward the plight of millions of Jews as they were driven in cattle trucks all across Europe; the same people who witnessed the slaughter of one and half million (these numbers are thrown in without any attempt of documentation – W.Z.) Jewish children without moving a finger to help... If at all possible, the world conscience is sicker today than it was during the Nazi era... **Essentially, this is still the holocaust world**", says Rabbi Berkowvits. **Only this time, other innocent people are on the receiving end and the Jews are in the driver's seat**.

Such are the "**lessons of the Holocaust**" which don't allow for critical examination of historical events, as Dr. Yaffa Eliach reminded the author at the Philadelphia Conference in 1979. One **should not engage in "muddying the waters" by dealing with other victims of "man's inhumanity to men". What happened to the Jews is "uniquely unique", because they are chosen people**. The rest of the world, especially America, owes them support, even when they invade their neighbors and convert their cities in ruin. "American Jews, says Jay Y. Gonen, resent the hutzpah of Israelis who tell them how they ought to feel... It is because of this feeling that Israeli emotional claims have to be based on a blend of religious, ethnic, and also national ingredients... Hence, there is a strong intuitive reluctance in Israel to separate state from synagogue. Such an official separation would give American Jewry a final way out of the most central of all Zionist obligations... But if the Israeli appeal is based on the special circumstances of a hopeless entanglement of national religious and ethnic Jewish identity, then the appeal cannot be rejected out of hand."

The same "hopeless entanglement of national religious and ethnic Jewish identity" is being used to promote the support activities of the state of Israel among the Christians. And this is why in June 1985 Vatican "notes" the appeal to international law in appraising Israeli actions was branded as a "retrogression in Catholic-Jewish dialogue" and the omission of the statement that Holocaust is "a Christian problem" had to be corrected by the accompanying letter of Msgr. Jorge Mejía which – for this reason – had to be used together with the "notes". Vatican obviously is of the opinion that cruel Nazi practices were painful enough for the Christians who were killed together with the Jews to dispense with a phrase that implies that Holocaust was simply a Christian crime agaist the Jews. Such a distorsion of historical truth may be feasible in countries which were not affected by Nazi atrocities and didn't show much concern for suffering of Nazi victims during the war, not only Jewish victims, but also Christian as well.

Elie Wiesel's circuitous expression that Jews were "victims of the victims" should be corrected in the sense that so were the other victims and Jewish collaborators expedited more Jews to their deaths than any other. When even Jewish observers state that "there was no business like Shoah business", a publication of a special companion volume may be useful to demonstrate that "beasts of pray" are not limited to any nationality. At present let us concentrate on inspiring examples of "Martyrs of Charity" which will contribute to a correction of the biased Holocaust steamroller tactics. As Father John A. O'Brien said in his introduction to Philip Friedman's book *Their brothers' keepers*, "alongside of this depressing chronicle there is another which has been related only in fragments, and too seldom: it is the story of compassion, sympathy, bravery, and heroism of the thousands of men and women who shielded and befriended the victims at the risk of imprisonment, torture, and death. This is the story which needs to be told if we are to get a true picture of the moral caliber of the people whose homelands were used for the liquidation of the Jewish population."

"They were peasants, housewives, factory workers, teachers, professional men, and clergy of all faiths, who **fought with bare hands against the mightiest military juggernaut in modern times; they fought for the despised and persecuted Jew, and by their sacrifices and heroism they have enriched all humanity and strengthened the solidarity of human brotherhood. They make us proud of our comon humanity** and give ground for the hope that the ultimate victory will rest on the side of decency and honor. **These are the true heroes of our time and they will be enshrined in the hearts and minds of men as long as memory endures.**"

Our concern was to comb the chronicles of Jewish wartime tragedy through the entire Europe for the cases of punishment by death for helping Jews. The fact that 95 percent of these cases happened to be in Poland remains in consonance with the hospitable reception this country gave to the Jews since the Middle Ages till the recent time when 600,000 undocumented Jewish aliens were given Polish citizenship in 1926, inspite of overpopulation and general poverty.

"Now it must be stated, testified Wanda Grosman-Jedlicka in Bartoszewski and Lewin's collection *Righteous among the nations*, our survival would not have been possible but for the noble and unselfish assistance, sometimes bordering on sacrifice and heroism, on the part of many people who had not the slightest personal obligation towards myself and my family". Or Laura Kaufman's statement in the same collection: "As can be seen from what I had written, I was helped by people from various strata of society; nor was I privileged exception. Before the war I had been advised to go abroad in the event of war. This was still possible as late as 1940. I have never regretted not having done so. For five years I lived in the constant danger, **I experienced moments of horror, but all this had to be experienced among the Polish people in order fully to appreciate their true qualities.**"

Well-known hematologist almost fully assimilated into Polish society. Ludwik Hirszfeld, describes in his autobiog-

Prof. Ludwik Hirszfeld, a great scholar and a great Polish patriot of Jewish descent whose memoirs *Historia jednego życia* were prevented from being translated and published in the U.S.A. through vested Jewish interests.

Dr. Emmanuel Ringelblum, an unassimilated Polish Jew, rather unfriendly to his country of adoption, but so many times saved by Polish efforts that he couldn't conceal noble deeds of those who risked their lives for him and for other Jews.

Battered milk cans with a part of Ringelblum's "archives" (*Oneg Shabbat*) uncovered at 68 Nowolipki St. in 1946 and 1950, some of it stolen from the Jewish Institute in Warsaw and smuggled out of Poland to Yad Vashem where they are being edited with tendencious and biased annotations by Joseph Kermish, Shmuel Krakowski and other Jewish writers unfriendly to Poland and the Catholic Church.

raphy, unfortunately not yet translated into the English language, that when he was herded together with other Jews into the Warsaw Ghetto and heard from little Jewish urchins sneaking through the wall to beg for food on the Polish side, how lovingly were they received by the Catholics and provided with scarce food items, **his heart was swelling with the feeling of pride about "his" nation, the Christian Poles**.

"It is impossible to describe the attitude of Polish civilian population, wrote Samuel Bronowski in the above cited collection, outside the Jewish labor camp – **to say that it was friendly, would be too little. There was a marked compassion**. There has not been a single case in Poznań of a Pole who would betray a Jew escaping from the camp. There has not been a single case on the construction site of a Nazi foreman striking a Jew without an immediate reaction on the part of Polish co-workers. **Those Jews who survived did so only thanks to the help from Polish population** of Poznań". Poznań, may we add, was considered before the war an "antisemitic" city in Poland.

"It was much more difficult to help the Jews in Poland than in France, Holland, Belgium or Denmark, for instance, whose inhabitants had not been condemned in advance to a fate as tragic as that devised for the Poles. There is no evidence in German documents that the extermination of the peoples of Western Europe was part of the Nazi government's plans, or that it intended to turn the area west of the Rhine into a *Land ohne Volk* (land without people) to be flooded with German settlers", stated Tatiana Berenstein in the book *Assistance to the Jews in Poland, 1939-1945*, and added: **"The Nazis contrived in every way possible to provoke resentment and animosity between the various national groups**. For example... in Będzin they employed Jews in compiling the registers of Poles liable to deportation from the town. (In Płaszów Jews were employed in hanging the Polish inmates – W.Z.) Again in Spring 1942, five Jews were assigned to wholly clerical duties at the Treblinka labor camp... For several years a travelling exhibition called "The Jewish contagion" toured the General Governmernt with a display of the stock Nazi smears and scurrilities."

Vasily Grossman wrote in *The black book*, New York, Holocaust Library, 1980: "A secret order issued by Hitler before the invasion of Soviet territory permitted any and all punitive measures to be taken against the population... Looting, murder, arson, harassment and rape committed by German soldiers were not considered crimes, for such acts had the sanction and blessing of Hitler, his Field Marshals and his Generals. Hundreds and thousands of villages were put to torch. Entire regions were transformed into desert zones. The Germans levelled almost all the villages in the area between the Desna and Dnieper rivers. Vast areas in the Smoleńsk region and the Orłov oblast were turned into wasteland... Deprived of housing, millions of people took to the forests, living in earthen shelters and abandoned dugouts... The Germans viewed this murderous work as a preliminary stage in the preparation for settlement of the "eastern areas". Hitler was merely taking the first steps in his plan to destroy the Slavic people"

"One of the sections of *The black book* contains a number of documents, says Grossman, testifying as to how Russians, Byelorussians, and Lithuanians rendered fraternal aid to Jews in the worst days of racial terror... Old peasant women, young kolkhoz girls, workers, teachers, professors, priests often risked their lives and the lives of their families to save these innocent doomed people... Hundreds of Jewish children were saved by Russians, Byelorussians and Ukrainians who claimed that they were their own children and hid then for long months and even years... **Germans were unable to extinguish, to drown in the seas of blood the forces of good and reason which live in the souls of the people. Only the moral rabble, the scum of humanity, pitiful bands of criminals heeded the call of Hitler's propagandists.**"

"A Jewish girl, Rachel Rosenzweig, wrote to a Lithuanian Catholic priest, Bronius Paukštis, relates the book edited by two Communist writers, Ilya Ehrenburg and Vasily Grossman, a story by Girsh Osherovich: "Dear Father! Allow me to address you this way. Didn't you treat me the way a father would treat a daughter? Didn't you give me shelter when I came to you, so unhappy, after I have endured so much? Without questioning me or demanding anything of me, as if it were completely natural, you said: "You will calm down here, my child, and you will stay with me a while..." The letter is quite long. It is written with love and respect, and its entire content testifies to the fact that in the terrible conditions of the Nazi occupation in Lithuania there were kind, honest people who fulfilled their human duty calmly, as if this were only natural."

"The first time I went into the streets with my Jewish badge, tells R. Kovnator in the same *Black book*, a group of Germans was crossing the street... They rushed at me and began to shout out terrible curses. I leaned against the wall. Tears of anger and grief welled up in my eyes, and I was unable to utter a single word. Suddenly I felt someone put his hand on my shoulder; it was an elderly Pole. He said: 'My child, don't be upset and don't be offended. Let those who did this be ashamed.' He took me by the arm and led me away."

"A large number of Jews, says Naftali Nacht in *The black book*, hid among the Poles and Ukrainians. **No matter how the Germans endeavored to corrupt the hearts of the people with the fear of death, executions, treachery and greed, there were, nevertheless, courageous and honest people capable of heroism.** Educated Polish people saved many Jewish children from death, although for the most part they could take in only girls (for obvious reasons). Many Polish priests took in Jewish girls, hid them in the churches, and saved them from death. **More than one of these noble people paid with their own lives for saving Jewish children**".

Offices of B'nai B'rith occasionally show a film about the "righteous" Christians, but even Catholic nun, Carol Rittner, didn't dare to bring into her film on those "who dared to care" a truly heroic case of a Martyr of Love. This obviously would interfere with the stereotype of a Christian "Cain" standing beside the Jewish "Abel" in the "pool of blood". At the Department of State conference on the rescue of Jews every "survivor" had to insert into his story a remark about "general indifference" as if each rescue only confirmed the general rule of hostility to the Jews. Somewhere in Talmud there is a caution not to praise a "goy" too much, if he has to be praised, as not to make him appear "too beautiful". It is surprising how much professional precision guided the strategists of the Holocaust propaganda to attain its aims.

In Melbourne, Australia lives a Jewish survivor, Henryk Zelicki, who decided to put a lonely demonstration on the Remembrance Day in the City Square by setting up a menorah with **six candles burning in the memory of Jewish "six millions" and in the middle the tallest candle with red-white ribbon lit up to the memory of those heroic Poles who risked and actually gave their lives in attempting to save their fellow Jews.** On April 10, 1972 a crowd of 150 people listened to three national hymns, Israeli, Polish and Australian, looked at three flags, Israeli, Polish and Australian, a Polish priest prayed for the martyred Jews and Poles, because the Polish Rabbi Dr. Rappaport stated that in his books there is no convenient prayer for such an occasion. Invitations are issued avery year for this occasion to the Israeli Embassy, to the Jewish Council, to the Chief Rabbinate, but only Henryk Zelicki and his occasional listeners **celebrate the memory of Christian Holocaust heroes.** Is it not a beautiful idea, entirely in the spirit of genuine Christian-Jewish dialogue, **to introduce this custom into the celebration of the Remembrance Day in Catholic churches?** Also the American congressmen with large, Christian constituencies may find enough courage to **suggest for the Remembrance Day celebration in the Rotunda the practice of the Seventh Candle to honor heroic defenders of Jews** at the time of Holocaust.

Abhodah zarah 20'a. Toseph.

לו תתן להם חן שלא יאמר כמו
נוי זה נאה

Non attribues illis gratiam[1], ne forte dicatur: quam sit pulcher Goi iste[2]).

Ita ibi explicantur verba Deuteronomii VII, 2: ולא תנחם «et non misereberis eorum (Goim)», citata in Gemara.

Eodem modo explicat hunc S. Script. locum R. Szel. Iarchi:

לא תתן להם חן-אסור לו לאדם
לומר כמו נאה נוי זה

Non attribues illis gratiam; prohibitum est homini dicere: quam pulcher est iste Goi.

Iore dea 151, 14:

אסור לספר בשבחן אפילו לומר
כמה נאה עכ׳׳ום זה בצורתו קל
וחומר שיספר בשבח מעשיו או
שיחבב דבר מדבריו אבל אם
מכוין בשבחו להודות להק׳׳בה
שברא בריה נאה כזו מותר

Non est concessum aliquo profari in laudem eorum, nec etiam dicere: quam pulcher Akum iste. Quanto minus laudare (licet) opera eius, aut quid tale de eis narrare, quod eos claros reddere possit. Si tamen eum laudando intendatur dare gloriam Deo Benedicto, propterea videlicet, quod creaverit pulchras creaturas, tunc licet.

Original text from *Christianus in Talmude* by Prof. Justin Pranajtis, rendered only in Latin translation (to avoid spreading aversion to the Jews if translated in vernacular)

On September 18, 1978 the 95th Congress of the U.S.A. approved the Public Law 95-371 designating two days of April or May corresponding to the Jewish month of Nissan as the National Days of Remembrance of Victims of the Holocaust which involve "Jews and millions of other people", explicitly described as "Jews and Christians" in a statement of the National Conference of the Catholic Bishops. Forty years after the Nazi aggression against Poland President's Commission under the chairmanship of Elie Wesel recommended "that a living memorial be created to 'Jews and others' who perished in the Holocaust". In 1984 a cornerstone was laid in the area between the White House and the Capitol Hill for the Holocaust Memorial. **It is our hope that memory of our Martyrs of Charity be perpetuated there in front of the Museum as a monument to human solidarity** in the hour of need.

On July 4, 1946, after the local Jews were accused of ritual murder, the townspeople of Kielce, Poland, attacked the 200 Jews of the town, survivors of a community which numbered 25,000 before the Holocaust, cruelly murdering 47 men, women and children and wounding 50 others.

ב־ 4 ביולי 1946, לאחר עלילת דם על היהודים, פרעו המוני פולנים פרעות בכ־ 200 יהודים בעיר קילצה. שרידי הקהילה שמנתה לפני השואה 25,000 נפש. בפוגרום זה נרצחו באכזריות 47 ונפצעו 50 אנשים, נשים וטף.

The U.S.A. Holocaust Memorial Museum as an American institution may not be tarnished, under any circumstances to satisfy certain pressure groups, with scurilous propaganda pieces like the defamotory Kielce inscription in the Israeli Yad Vashem Museum (see the photo) according to which, it was a spontaneous attack of the "townspeople of Kielce" which left 47 Jews dead.

Former Warsaw government spokesman, a Jew himself, Gen. Victor Grosz blamed it on "General Anders' agents" allegedly bent on killing all Jews in "fulfillment of Hitler's testament" and Joseph Tenenbaum of the USA went to Warsaw demanding from Pres. Bierut that he requests an extradition of the commander of the victorious Polish 2nd Corps at Monte Cassino into Communist hands as a "war criminal".

No mention is being made at Yad Vashem exhibit of armed Communist militia men shooting Jews or two Catholic Poles killed in the defense of the attacked Jews who, anyhow, were getting ready to leave Poland for Israel. Since Stalin at this time was in favor of Jewish exodus to Palestine the obvious purpose of the Kielce provocation was to frighten Jews arriving from the Soviet Union by hundreds of thousands into joining a *briha* or a departure for Israel. It also diverted public attention from abuses committed in recent election which was anything but "free and unfettered". This sort of Stalino-Zionist provocation also was useful in accusing the Catholic Church and political opposition of vice-Premier Mikolajczyk of shameful crimes. No congressional investigation of shameful crimes demanded by Mikołajczyk was allowed and a local Catholic public prosecutor was replaced by a Jewish one who refrained from seeking the instigators of crime.

Such were suspicions of the American Ambassador in Warsaw, Arthur Lane expressed in his memoirs *I saw Poland betrayed*. They were later confirmed in the *Journal of Soviet Jewish Affairs* by Michael Checinski, former security officer and professor at the Military Political Academy in Warsaw.

At this juncture, one should expect, radical change ought to take place in the tone of Christian-Jewish dialogue. After the sholarly work of Richard S. Lucas, *The forgotten Holocaust*, University Press of Kentucky, 1986, we may notice, on the Jewish side, the beginning of light "piercing the darkness" in the work of Nechama Tec on *"Christian rescue of Jews in Nazi-occupied Poland"* at Oxford University Press, 1986, which criticizes "ambiguous criteria" employed by Yad Vashem in selecting "righteous" Christians without due respect for real danger of death in aiding a Jew, although she mistakenly casts doubt on non-existence of such penalty in the West and refers in her research to some thrashy "Holocaust literature" on "deeply-ingrained anti-Semitiam" of some countries, without an attempt to examine it more closely.

Simply ridiculous is her assumption that Catholic Poland which already at the Council of Constance (1414-18) defended "Jews and Saracens" and was called by the rest of the world a "paradise of Jews" had to wait for a hint from the Pope before performing acts of Christian charity which were simply dictated by a Christian conscience and incontrovertible teachings of the Gospel. She even goes in this gratuitous assumption as far as to attribute sort of a rebellious attitude towards the Church among those active in the rescue of Jews. Long list of acrimonious accusations was already laid to rest by a statement of Walter Laqueur in *The terrible secret, Bantam Books, 1980, that* **"there was nothing the Poles could possibly do more to save millions of Jews. They could, after all, not extend help to their own."**

At least, a beginning was made in recognizing Jewish debt toward the Catholic Church which saved more Jews from the death than the Red Cross or any other institution. Even Elie Wiesel finally brought himself tó express thanks to the "people of Poland" in his speech of April 30, 1984, at the site of the future Holocaust Memorial Museum in Washington, D.C. It remains **to see that this gratitude be expressed in the contents of its exhibits** which ahould avoid the pitfalls of the Yad Vashem Museum in Jerusalem. We sincerely hope that our "Martyrs of Charity" will serve as source of information which was suppressed for so many decades of hate-mongering against the Christian world.

Dr. Wacław Zajączkowski

CHRISTIAN AND JEWISH RESPONSE TO THE HOLOCAUST

Simon Cyrenean of the V Station on the Way of Cross helping Jesus to carry His cross gave an example to Christians how they should behave in the relation to their more disadvantaged Jewish companions of suffering under the oppression of Nazi Germans.

EXPLANATORY NOTES

Our survey covers the entire Europe. The scarcity of cases from Western Europe is due to the fact that rescuing Jews from the German hands was not punishable by death over there as it was in Poland. While in Holland the reward for the betrayal of a Jew dropped from 50 to 75 florin down to only 7½ gulden, in Poland the rewards and penalties escalated from a "bottle of vodka" as a reward to a mandatory death penalty for a failure to betray a hiding Jew. The pitiful attempt of Judge Moshe Bejski to blame Poles themselves for being punished so severely by the German legislator contradicts basic principles of a penal law which increases the penalty where the "crime" (of aiding Jews) is rampant and not vice versa. The fact that so many leading Polish "anti-Semites" died attempting to save the Jews would indicate a profound difference between Poland and the Western countries in this respect and its purely defensive character.

Due to a large number of cases of Christian heroism in Poland, an attempt was made to identify each case by place, date and names of people involved, as much as possible.

The administrative divisions and the geographical names conform to the *status quo* before the end of war and the areas taken over by the Soviet Union are, for all practical purposes, treated as Polish, though our resarch concerning these areas was very limited.

Numbers following the names of persons indicate their age whenever it was possible. It is terrifying to see how many little Christian babies had to pay with their lives for their parents' heroic attempts to save the Jews.

Most of our cases in the Jewish sections are concerned with persons who somehow elevated themselves over the urge to protect their own earthly lives and thus were not "led to the slaughterhouse like sheep", or dying only for being Jews, deprived of a chance to give their lives for the Sanctification of the Name (*kiddush ha-shem*).

While Holland as a free country was able to distribute after the War, 30,000 awards for aiding Jews among its own citizens, Poland's position, especially after the advent of the "Stalinist era" made it extremely difficult even to compile statistics of cases which were many times more numerous than those in Holland. Poland's equivalent of Yad Vashem was abolished in 1949 and its resources rendered practically inaccessible for an independent research, especially for non-Jews. Also the Israeli Yad Vashem is not very eager to open its resources to a non-Jew.

Our bibliographical references are, therefore, mostly based on second – hand sources which are listed, with appropriate abbreviations, immediately following the list of cases, in alphabetical order by authors.

Variants added in parentheses after some sources indicate different spellings of names or different dates found in those sources.

I. CHRISTIAN RESPONSE TO THE HOLOCAUST

AUSTRIA

1. September 1, 1944. **Oswald Bosko** from Vienna was murdered in Kraków. He was a member of the German military police in the local ghetto. He was executed for giving aid to Poles and Jews.

J.A. p.18. A.M.K. p. 28. T.Pa. p. 117 (Bousko).

2. Sergeant **Anton Schmidt** from Vienna, who during the war was assigned to the Wilno area, worked incessantly to save Jews. When discovered, he was executed for these activities, deemed unbefitting of a German officer.

F.H. p. 357. A.M.K. p. 129.

3. Baden, near Vienna. **Maria Fasching** gave shelter in her apartment to a Bohemian Jew named Jan Posiles. During an air raid she took him to seek safety in another building which was hit by a bomb. Jan was fatally wounded and Maria, also fatally wounded, died in a hospital.

A.M.K. p. 46.

BELGIUM

4. A **Catholic priest** was killed by the Germans for giving shelter to one hundred Jewish children.

P.L. p. 268.

BYELORUSSIA

5. Borysov, oblast Minsk. Nov. 10, 1941. An order was issued by the Germans to Byelorussians: "Upon meeting a Jew, cross to the other side of the street; greetings are forbidden, as is exchanging things". For violating this order, Byelorussians met the same fate as Jews. The Germans tried to find the Jews who were hiding under Russian names, and, when such people were found, they were executed along with the Byelorussians who were sheltering them.

Information supplied by P. Ausker-Łukiński in E.–G. p. 361, 364.

CROATIA

6. Cyril Kotnik who made successful efforts to save Jews in Rome, was arrested there, brutally interrogated and tortured by the German Gestapo. Released, thanks to Vatican intervention, he didn't recover from his wounds and died.

Ph.F. p. 204.

CZECHOSLOVAKIA

7. On July 22, 1943, the world learned from a press dispatch that **two Czechs** were killed by the Germans for trying to help Jews escape deportation to a concentration camp.

I.J.A. p. 61.

8. For aiding Jews who were persecuted by the Germans, **fourteen Czech gendarmes** were executed by the Gestapo.

Ph.F. p. 31-2.

9. Rudolf Masarek refused to part with his Jewish wife when she was being deported. He went with her to the Treblinka death camp and never came back.

Ph.F. p. 103-4 (Massaryk).

DENMARK

10. October 1943. **Mr. Heiteren,** son of a Danish Supreme Court attorney was killed during a fusillade which occurred in the course of the sea transfer to Sweden of seven thousand Jews destined for deportation to the Theresienstadt camp.

M.S. p. 111. R.H. p. 363.

FRANCE

11. Le Chambon–sur–Lignon, April 4, 1944. Local Protestant teacher, **Daniel Trocmé,** was arrested together with some Jewish youth during a raid by the Gestapo on his school. Suspected of being Jewish himself, he was deported to the Majdanek concentration camp and killed there. In 1976 Israel awarded him the Medal of the Righteous and a tree was planted in his honor. Also the Pastor André Trocmé was honored in the same way.

Ph.F. p. 352. Ph.H. p. 216-7.

12. Elizabeth Pilenko (Mother Eva) deported to KL Ravensbrück for her activities on behalf of Jews, she gave her "Aryan" card to a Jewish woman and was murdered in May 1945. Her son, **Yurii Pilenko,** died in the Compiègne concentration camp.

Ph.F. p. 47.

13. Several French policemen were executed for their refusal to round up and arrest foreign Jews who were being crowded into the Paris Vélodrome stadium, by the order of subservient French authorities, to be extradited for deportation.

Ph.F. p. 188.

14. A Catholic girl **Marianne Collin,** 23, was executed for giving aid to persecuted Jews.

Ph.F. p. 188.

15. An Orthodox priest, **Rev. Dimitri Klepnis,** was caught forging documents for Jews. He was dragged to the Compiègne, Buchenwald and Dora camps, was compelled to wear a special armband marked "friend of Jews" (*Judenfreund*), and was finally condemned to death.

Ph. F.R. p. 417.

GERMANY

16. Berlin (1) 1941. Two Protestant ministers, **Rev. Werner Sylten** and Rev. Martin Albert, who worked in the Büro Grüber at Berlin-Karlsdorf aiding Jews, were imprisoned and Rev. Sylten sent to the Dachau concentration camp from which he never returned.

R.-T. p. 125.

17. Berlin (2) November 3, 1943. Rector of St. Hedwig's Church **Msgr. Bernhard Lichtenberg,** in order to expiate for the crimes of his countrymen, volunteered for deportation to the Jewish Ghetto in Łódź (renamed Litzmannstadt), ruled by Chaim Rumkowski; but instead, died of tuberculosis on his way to Dachau.

Ph.F. p. 95. R.H. 299-300. P.L. p. 213.

18. Marburg. August 31, 1942. **Marie-Luise Hensel** attempted, together with her friend, Katherine Jung, to take the Jewish family of Dr. Herman Reis across the Swiss border; however, betrayed to the Gestapo by the owner of a hotel, was deported to Konstanz and committed suicide after 3 days of interrogation.

Account of Katherine Jung in A.M.C. p. 70.

19. An officer of the German Army in Holland, **Dr. Gerard Wander,** was executed for giving Jews false documents, baptismal certificates and saving them from deportation.

Account of Julia Heriquer in A.M.K. p. 149.

20. A German officer, stationed in Poland, unknown by name, befriended a Polish Catholic priest with a desire to become Catholic. He took good care of some Jewish girls who were provided with food in their hideout by the pastor and his parishioners. An SS unit, in reprisal for this behavior "unfit for a German officer", ordered a ditch to be dug and filled with quicklime. A long board was extended over the ditch and the Jewish girls were forced to walk over the ditch. They were knocked of the board, one after another, into the boiling fluid. The last to end his life in such way was the German officer who tolerated acts of Christian charity towards the Jews.

Account of Sister Janina Klonowska in the possession of Msgr. Kotowski in the Chancery of the Primate of Poland.

GREECE

21. Athens. Twelve Orthodox Greeks were publicly hanged by the Germans for having helped a group of Jews to escape deportation.

Ph.F. p. 18.

HUNGARY

22. Budapest. "Twenty five Jewish refugees hid in the home of the Social (Charitable) Sisters. They were denounced by an employee, a Nyilas sympathizer. One of the Sisters, **Sister Sarah Sarkhaz,** was taken away with a group of refugees and murdered".

Ph.F. p. 88.

ITALY

23. Dr. Giovanni Palatucci, A Fascist police chief of Fiume who helped many Jews, was deported to Dachau and died there.

Ph.F. p. 196.

24. Edoardo Focherini's seven children died in a German concentration camp because of their father's efforts on behalf of Jews. He was on the staff of the Catholic daily "L'Avvenire d'Italia".

Ph.F. p. 79.

25. Rev. Aldo Mai of Fiano, tortured to make him betray the whereabouts of six Jews he had helped to go underground, was forced to dig his own grave and shot to death by the Germans.

P.L. p. 213.

LATVIA

26. Riga. (1) August 24, 1941. The German police arrested the Latvian woman, **Anna Polis,** who hid Jews in her apartment and supplied them with food. In addition, all the residents of the house were arrested. On that day Germans killed Dr. Lipmanovich, Gruntman, Manke, Blum, Berkovich and other Jews. Anna Polis, who hid them, was executed two days later.

Account of Capt. Yefim Hechtan in E.-G. p. 322.

27. Riga (2) 1941. A Latvian girl, **Nina Gottschalk,** 19, rounded up together with Jews, probably for giving aid to them, was taken to an apartment on Elizabeth Street, where some drunken Germans, after having fun with her, decided to convert her into a being without bones. She was tied up inside a sack and methodically beaten with ramrods for two hours, until all her bones were broken. Then her body was wrapped into a bloody roll of flesh and thrown onto a boulevard near the opera theater.

E.-G. p. 304.

LITHUANIA

28. Pakalniskiai, near Gelgaudiskis. March 18, 1944. **Dr. Żakevicius** persuaded Christian farmers to hide Jews in their villages. He gave them a personal example of courage by hiding in his house four members of a Jewish doctor's family. Arrested by the Gestapo together with several farmers who helped him shelter the Jews, all were executed by the Germans for this offense.

S.N. p. 307.

29. A local Catolic priest from Vidukle, known as **Father Jonas,** gave shelter in his church to thirty Jewish children and confronted the German soldiers who tried to break into the church, shouting "If you want to kill the children, you have to kill me first". The Germans did just that and then massacred the children.

Ph.F. p. 140. P.L. p. 213.

30. Among those courageous Lithuanians who dared to oppose the German invaders was **Irena Gaużaskiene,** a laborer who tried to help a Jewish friend escape from the ghetto. She was shot to death by the Germans.

Sarah Neshamit in "Rescue Attempts during the Holocaust", Yad Vashem, 1977, p. 304.

31. In the Kaunas suburb of Sanciai lived a carpenter, **Juozas Paulavicius.** He decided to save Jewish doctors and succeeded in hiding two families, a total of ten people, plus two Russian prisoners of war in a hideout he build in his yard. After the war, he was murdered by nationalist bands.

S. Neshamit in "Rescue Attempts during the Holocaust", Yad Vashem, 1977, p. 304.

32. The Lithuanian clergy helped in providing birth and baptismal certificates for Jews hiding in the homes of Catholic Lithuanians. **Several priests** were killed for aiding Jews.

S. Neshamit in "Rescue Attempts during the Holocaust", Yad Vashem, 1977, p. 314.

NETHERLANDS

33. In February 1943, it was reported that **forty one Dutchmen** were hanged for harboring Jews and helping them to flee the country.

I.J.A. p. 245.

34. In March 1943, the Dutch poet, **Jan Kampert,** 40, who had been arrested for helping Jews to escape deportation, was reported to have died in a concentration camp.

I.J.A. p. 245.

35. Dionysius Bakker, who, with his wife Cornelia, secured hiding places for some eighty Jews and supplied them with food and other necessities, was caught and killed by the Germans.

P.L.. p. 203.

36. An **old Dutchman,** unknown by name, when told by the Gestapo to stop helping Jews, said: "Yet the Lord tells me to protect them. It is to Him that I shall listen". He was taken to a concentration camp with **his family** and died there in 1943.

Ph.F. p. 70.

37. Joop Westerweel, the Principal of Lundsrecht High School, was sent to the Vught concentration camp for rescuing two Jewish girls, and shot there.

Ph.F. p. 67 (Westerville) P.L. p. 203. H.A. p. 569.

POLAND

38. Adamów, Łuków county, voivodship of Lublin. August 1942. A partisan unit of Serafin Aleksiejew attacked a German military transport taking Jews to the Treblinka killing center. There were **losses in life,** but 200 prisoners were freed.
S.L. p. 273.

39. Albertyn, Słonim county, voivodship of Nowogródek. November 20, 1943. **Rev. Antoni Grzybowski, S.J.,** 39, was murdered by the Germans for helping Jews who were seeking refuge at the Jesuit Novitiate of the Byzantine rite.
Testimony of Rev. M. Michniak in B.L. p. 813. J.-W. v. 5, p. 76 (Oct. 20, 1943).

40. Aleksandrów, Biłgoraj county, voivodship of Lublin. February, June and July 1943. In five consecutive "actions" Germans raided the village, arresting and killing its inhabitans who were accused of sheltering Jews, Soviet prisoners of war and partisans. Entire peasant families were exterminated: seven from the Szwacha family: **Janina Szwacha,** 18, **Józef Szwacha,** 55, **Katarzyna Szwacha,** 50, **Mikołaj Szwacha,** 52, **Tomasz Szwacha,** 55, **Józef Szwacha,** 15, and **Szczepan Szwacha,** 24; fourteen from the Bździuch family: **Jan Bździuch,** 60, **Antoni Bździuch,** 55, **Franciszek Bździuch,** 37, **Michał Bździuch,** 53, **Stanisław Bździuch,** 32, **Antoni Bździuch,** 32, **Jan Bździuch,** 34, **Leon Bździuch,** 15, **Jan Bździuch,** 17, **Piotr Bździuch,** 54, **Stanisław Bździuch,** 29, **Wacław Bździuch,** 17, and **Tadeusz Bździuch,** only 11 years old; nine from the Psiuk family: **Agnieszka Psiuk,** 63, **Jan Psiuk,** 42, **Józef Psiuk,** 42, **Józef Psiuk,** 32, **Michał Psiuk,** 70, **Stanisław Psiuk,** 29, **Jan Psiuk,** 42, and **Michał Psiuk,** 52; **Kazimierz Banach** and **Stanisław Banach,** 38; four from the Szabat family: **Anastazja Szabat,** 58, **Stanisław Szabat,** 63, **Józef Szabat,** 34, and **Stanisław Szabat,** 20; **Kazimierz Bielak,** 22, and **Piotr Bielak,** 35; **Andrzej Borowiec,** 32, and Bronisław Borowiec, 19; Jan Gontarz, 36, and **Michał Gontarz, 32**; Jan Harasiuk, 23, and **Władysław Harasiuk, 22**; **Michał Kaman, 56**, and Jan Kaman, 43; Jan Komada, 44, and Józef Komada, 35; Antoni Łokaj, 19, and Franciszek Łokaj, 44; Aniela Mazur, 26, and Stefania Mazur, 18; Jan Mazurek, 26, Szczepan Mazurek, 45, and Tadeusz Mazurek, 31; Franciszek Brudzień, 36; Józef Budzyński, 36; Józef Bulicz, 56; Szczepan Dziura; Jan Rataj, 19, and Józef Rataj, 22; Maria Saweczka, 52, and Andrzej Saweczka, 58; Andrzej Solak, 82, Michał Solak, 62, and Andrzej Solak, 60; Mikołaj Szydełko, 57, and Roman Szydełko, 19; Katarzyna Zygmunt, 50, Michał Zygmunt, 52, and Stanisław Zygmunt, 55; also Stanisław Adamowicz, 40; Edward Bil, 19, and Jan Bil, 48; Jan Czernik, 40, Maria Czerwonka, 44, Paweł Droździel, 37, Władysław Gromek, 21, Jan Okoń, 20, Andrzej Kret, 50, Franciszek Kukiełka, the first to be murdered on Jan. 27, 1940; Michał Kosiak, 23, Józef Maciocha, 50, Franciszek Margol, 35, Józef Markowicz, 60, Józef Michoński, 25, Piotr Miechowski, 37, Józef Nizio, 26, Wojciech Nowak, 37, Józef Okoń, 36, Jan Ostasz, 19, Stanisław Otkała, 22, Stefania Pastuszek, 18, Katarzyna Pintal, 38, Magdalena Pisklak, 24, Michał Pokrywka, 47, Jan Potocki, 26, Wojciech Przytuła, 32, Anna Szkałuba, 43, Michał Watrak, 45, Jan Wrębiak, 50, Antoni Szupor, 31, Stanisław Świstek, 30, Stanisław Torba, 32, and Stanisław Tracz, 43. Most of the names, however, especially those of small children, remain unknown. Altogether, 446 persons were killed. In addition, Germans stationed in the village 500 Soviet Kalmyk prisoners of war who entered their service. Women were raped. Many households were burned down. Whatever remained standing was given to Ukrainian settlers in order to further aggravate ethnic antagonisms.

GKBZH 1082z/IML, p. 2-12. F.-R. p. 434-5 (290). S.K. p. 52.

41. Aleksandrówka (1) Biała Podlaska county, voivodship of Lublin. January 15, 1943. **Four Catholic Poles** were executed by the Germans for "keeping contacts with Jews".

PZPR KC DR Sign. 202/III, t. 8, 159.

42. Aleksandrówka (2) Biała Podlaska county, voivodship of Lublin, May 12, 1943. Germans shot **Bolesław Książek** to death for sheltering Mr. Idel, a Jew, who died together with his host.

GKBZH WB VI K. GKBZH Zh I/Ds/23/68.

43. Andrzejówka, near Chmielnik, voivodship of Kielce, December 1942. **Stanisław Trojan** was arrested and later executed by the Germans for sheltering two Jews, Ceal and Wehman, in his house.

W.-Z. p. 411.

44. Antonówka, Łuków county, voivodship of Lublin: May 22 to June 19, 1943. The entire **Puławski family** was exterminated by the Germans for giving shelter to a Jew.

GKBZH Egz. V. PZPR KC CA DR Sign. 202/I, t. 34, p. 19.

45. Antopol, Kobryń county, voivodship of Polesie. September 1943. **Albin Arciszewski,** 45, was beaten and shot to death for giving shelter to Dr. Piotr Czerniak, his wife and two daughters, to Izaak Elfensztein,to Lena Mazurska and to Itka Wołyniec. The Jews were murdered on the spot.

GKBZH WB V 157 (Orla, Cierniak) B.-L. p. 844. W.-Z. p. 425.

46. Bartosz-Kolonia, Sokołów Podlaski county, voivodship of Warsaw. June 1943. **Bronisława Wojewódzka** was shot to death for giving shelter to Jews. Her two sons, **Józef Wojewódzki** and **Marian Wojewódzki,** were arrested and sent to the Mauthausen concentration camp from which neither returned.

Testimony of K. Witt in J.K. p. 220.

Bełżec see **Lwów.**

Bemowo see **Boernerowo**.

47. Berecz, voivodship of Wołyń, 1942. Germans extermi-nated around **200 inhabitants** of Berecz and Podiwanówka for taking care of persecuted Jews.

Testimony of Maks Sobiesiak in W.-Z. p. 263, also 445.

48. Bereza Kartuska, Prużana county, voivodship of Brześć on Bug. Summer 1943. **Włodzimierz Chorew** and his parents from Mir, **Mr. Chorew** and **Mrs. Chorew,** were shot to death for hiding Leika Kaplan who excaped from the Ger-man-made ghetto. All were buried in a common grave near the local monastery.

Court deposition of K. Krycki in W.-Z. p. 401, also 445. GKBZH WB IX 43-45 (Mir).

49. Bereźno, voivodship of Wołyń. March 1943. **Three Polish farming families** numbering **ten persons,** were exter-minated together with the 12 Jews they were sheltering.

Court deposition of S. Dobraszklanka (a survivor) in W.-Z. p. 325.

50. Będzienica, Ropczyce county, voivodship of Rze-szów. October 27, 1942. Four Germans in civilian clothes en-tered the house at night and, under the threat of execution, de-manded to know the whereabouts of Jews hiding in the house-hold. The host, **Antoni Dziak,** was shot to death for his refu-sal to give this information. His wife managed to escape under the pretext of bringing a ladder. Meanwhile, three Jews, one by the name of Faust and two of the Pendys family, survived the search under a deep layer of hay.

Court deposition by Zofia Dziak in W.-Z. p. 396, also 427, 441. GKBZH WB IV 82 (two Jews, 3 Bendys brothers, Faust 30, Melers 40).

51. Będzin, voivodship of Katowice. **Paweł Ząbek** from Dąbrowa Górnicza was sent to KL Auschwitz and murdered there because of his activities on behalf of the Jewish commu-nity in Będzin, denounced by its Jewish leader, Moses Merin.

H.R. p. 188.

Biała see Tyczyn.

52. Białka near Parczew, Biała Podlaska county, voivodship of Lublin. December 1942. As a reprisal for hiding a Jewish woman and aiding Jewish partisans, the German SS men selected one hundred men from the population of that remote village and executed them near the local school; among others, **Karol Walęcki**, 17, who was voluntarily joined by his father, **Aleksander Walęcki**, 51. The Jewish woman was killed and, along with her, the following Christians: four brothers, **Bronisław Bartosiewicz**, 45, **Ignacy Bartosiewicz**, 48, **Kazimierz Bartosiewicz**, 35, and **Leon Bartosiewicz,**, 39; **Wacław Bielecki**, 30, as well as **Jan Bułtowicz**, 70, with his three youthful sons: **Bogusław Bułtowicz**, 19, **Jan Bułtowicz**, 17, and **Zygmunt Bułtowicz**, 19; **Antoni Bylina**, 47, **Jan Czernacki**, 41, **Józef Czeberak**, 34, **Feliks Drabik**, 50, **Aleksander Drogosz**, 15, **Karol Duda**, 53, **Bronisław Dutkowski**, 37, **Dionizy Dżyr**, 42, **Jan Giska**, 50; **Franciszek Gontarczyk**, 54, and **Stanisław Gontarczyk**, 31, **Bolesław Górski**, 32, **Czesław Grzywaczewski**, 15, along with his father **Szczepan Grzywaczewski**, 43, **Wacław Hernaś**, 26; four brothers: **Antoni Izdebski**, 34, **Jan Izdebski**, 48, **Stanisław Izdebski**, 43, the last one **Michał Izdebski**, 43, along with his son **Konstanty Izdebski**, 14; **Marian Jaskulski**, 18; three brothers: **Antoni Jędruszczak**, 19, **Stanisław Jędruszczak**, 31, and **Marian Jędruszczak**, 23; **Bronisław Kabat**, 39, **Bronisław Koperczuk**, 36, **Jan Borsuk**, 33, **Jan Kosznela**, 36, **Jan Kot**, 22, **Józef Krakowiak**, 38, **Jan Kubicki** with his son **Jan Kubicki**; two brothers: **Bolesław Kuszyk**, 21, and **Franciszek Kuszyk**, 28; **Józef Kunaszyk**, 35, and **Mieczysław Kunaszyk**, 17; family of **Aleksander Łukaszczuk**, 47, **Włodzimierz Łukaszczuk**, 37, **Jan Łukaszczuk**, 15, **Anastazy Łukaszczuk**, 16, **Józef Łukaszczuk**, 25, and **Piotr Łukaszczuk**, 35; family of **Emilian Majewski**, 50, **Edward Majewski**, 47, and **Konstanty Majewski**, 25; **Jan Makówka**, 51, with his sons: **Aleksander Makówka,** 16, and **Władysław Makówka,** 21; **Bolesław Malon,** 22, **Andrzej Mikulski,** 56, **Marcin Mioduchowski,** 43, **Stanisław Narusek,** 41, **Józef Niścioruk,** 61, **Czesław Panasiuk,** 24, **Kazimierz Pisańczuk,** 30, **Feliks Przystupa** with his father **Mikołaj Przystupa,** 53; **Stanisław Rojek,** 20, **Paweł Szlachta,** 23, two brothers: **Edward Szwaj,** 22 and **Władysław Szwaj,** 32; **Józef Wawer,** 61; three brothers: **Teofil Wałęcki,** 45, **Stanisław Wałęcki,** 41 and **Szymon Wałęcki,** 31; **Franciszek Zaczkowski,** 65, with his son **Franciszek Zaczkowski,** 15; **Nikita Zając,** 42, **Stanisław Zgierski,** 61; finally, a large family of **Bazyli Stelmaszczuk,** 43, **Jan Stelmaszczuk,** 43, **Józef Stelmaszczuk,** 32, **Karol Stelmaszczuk,** 27, **Marcin Stelmaszczuk, Władysław Stelmaszczuk,** 41, and **Zachariasz Stelmaszczuk,** 18. Antoni Stelmaszczuk managed to crawl out from under the bodies of his companions, as well as five other survivors of the massacre: Stanisław Prezździecki, Bonifacy Walenciuk, Jan Bloch, 43, Bronisław Suchorab, 20, and Michał Kondracki, 42.

F.-R. p. 22-23, supplemented by Mieczysław Jędrusiak in the weekly periodical „Za Wolność i Lud", March 26, 1983. Testimony of K. Sidor in. W.-Z. p. 268.

53. Białobrzegi, Opoczno county, voivodship of Kielce. July 1, 1942. German military police executed **Maksymilian Gruszczyński** for permitting some Jews to bake bread for themselves in his home kitchen.

GKBZH WB VI G 7.

54. Białystok (1) November 18, 1943. For helping Jews, German authorities exterminated the entire family Sawicki and other families related to them: Długołęckis, Szaszkos and Puchalskis; together with their children, **22 persons. Czesław Sawicki,** ps. Wytrwały in the Polish Home Army, was tortured and killed in jail. From among his family Germans executed: **Anna Sawicka,** 65, his mother and his father, **Wincenty Sawicki,** 70. His sister **Jadwiga Sawicka,** 20, also perished.

Their crime was providing helpless Jews with "Aryan" identification cards. Young wife of Czesław, Maria Sawicka, escaped with their son, Tadeusz Sawicki. **Regina Długołęcka** born Sawicka, died together with her husband and her two daughters, **Lucyna Długołęcka**, 4, and **Teresa Długołęcka**, 7, Brother of Czesław's wife, **Stanisław Szaszko,** his wife **Maria Szaszko** and **Antoni Szaszko** along with his 7-month pregnant wife, **Zofia Szaszko,** and their little son, **Wiesław Szaszko**, 3, shared the fate of their relatives. **Józefa Puchalska** born Szaszko, sister of Maria, along with her husband, **Antoni Puchalski,** his mother, **Stefania Puchalska,** 58, and his son, **Jerzy Puchalski,** 3, also gave their lives. Finally, Czesław's sister, **Maria Wasilewska,** was killed along with her **four sons.** Mr. Wasilewski was not there to share the holocaust.

GKBZH WB III 135, 134. W.-Z. p. 447.

55. Białystok (2) 1943. **Kazimierz Popławski,** 42, whose job was to smuggle Jews from the embattled ghetto, used to prepare himself for each trip in the house of Wanda Zarzecka, who served as a courier in the AK (Polish Home Army) in Starosielce. He used to lie fully clothed on a couch for days, awaiting a signal from her father that all the necessary arrangements were made. In spite of grim forebodings, he went on his last trip from which he did not return alive. His body was seen dangling from the walls of the ghetto, together with those of a dozen other Poles. This was done in order to frighten the rest of potential rescuers. Even the Soviet Jews, Ilya Ehrenburg and Vasyly Grosman, not particularly friendly to Catholic Poles, gave credit to the statement of Riva Shinder that "in general, it must be said that in those difficult days the friendship between the Polish and Jewish peoples burned particularly brightly..."

Testimony of Wanda Zarzecka-Klimek, related to the author in Warsaw on April 21, 1983. E.-G. p. 226-233.

56. Białystok (3) **Zenon Ignatowski, Jadwiga Dziekoń-ska** and **"Paprzyca" Niewiński,** a member of the Polish Home Army, were executed for giving aid and shelter to Jews escaping from the Białystok ghetto.

W.-Z. p. 447. GKBZH WB III 134, 135.

57. Białystok (4) For helping three Jews, Paweł Kores and Szulim Kores accompanied by the wife of one of them, to escape from the ghetto and leave the city, German authorities executed **Aleksander Sawicki,** not related to the martyred family of the same name, mentioned above.

GKBZH WB III 70.

58. Białystok (5), There was **a group of Germans** from Austria, Sudetenland and Germany who provided the underground Jewish organization with all kind of assistance by obtaining jobs, forged papers and shelter. They provided arms and informed of impending German moves. Two of these Germans were discovered by the Gestapo and sentenced to death.

Ph. F. R. p. 449.

59. Białystok (6), "A forester named **Markiewicz** from the forest preserve of Three Pillars, his wife and three daughters were stripped naked and tortured, but they did not reveal the hiding place of Jewish partisans".

Stenogram and letter of Riva Shinder-Voyskovska in E.-G. p. 233.

' **60. Bidaczów Nowy** (1) Biłgoraj county, voivodship of Lublin. October 6, 1942. Germans murdered **twenty two Catholic farmers** for sheltering Jews. Their bodies were buried at the site of the massacre.

W.-Z. p. 407.

61. Bidaczów Nowy (2) Biłgoraj county, voivodship of Lublin. **Jan Wróbel,** a Polish farmer, and his wife **Maria Wró-**

bel suffered the penalty of death for sheltering a Jew. Their farm was put to torch and their bodies were thrown into the flames by the Germans.

GKBZH WB V 114-115. OKBZH in Lublin Ds 12/1/BLNDP v. 1, p. 67. W.-Z. p. 445.

62. Biecz, Gorlice county, voivodship of Rzeszów. **Józef Pruchniewicz** was shot to death for sheltering from 1942 to 1944 the Blum family of four which survived the ordeal. The executioners were from the Gestapo headquarters in Jasło.

GKBZH WB IV 432. W.-Z. p. 441. T. Bi. p. 5.

Bielin see **Włodzimierz.**

63. Bieniakonie, Lida county, voivodship of Wilno. **Józef Olbrycht**, together with Izaak Reich whom he was sheltering, was shot to death by the Germans.

GKBZH WB II 81.

Bilcza see **Kielce.**

64. Bircza, Przemyśl county, voivodship of Rzeszów. 1943. **Roman Sigielin,** a Catholic, was executed by the Germans for keeping Jews in his house.

W.-Z. p. 443. GKBZH WB IV 447.

65. Bobowa, Gorlice county, voivodship of Rzeszów. Spring 1943. **Dr. Józef Pietrzykowski** was killed for sheltering a Jewish child.

W.-Z. p. 443. GKBZH WB II 186. Account of Bro. Stanisław Wojtarowicz, S.J. given to the author in Chicago, III. Feb. 20, 1984.

66. Bobowiska, Puławy, voivodship of Lublin. June 31, 1943. **Kazimierz Hołaj,** 35, **Michał Podolski,** 32, **Feliks Pęcuła,** 45, and **Stanisław Pęcuła,** 30, were shot to death for giving refuge to Jews persecuted by the Germans.

GKBZH ASG Sign. 16, p. 791. OKBZH in Lublin Ds 88/67.

67. Boernerowo, suburb of Warsaw. February 1, 1944. Informed by a *Volksdeutsch* (a Polish citizen declaring German nationality) that a Polish streetcar technician, **Bronisław Przybysz,** 40, was sheltering a Jewish family of four in his apartment on POW Street 4, the German Gestapo arrested all five, forced them to dig their own grave, riddled them with bullets from a machine gun and shoved their bodies into the common grave, with Bronisław Przybysz still giving signs of life. A Catholic parish employee, Ławniczak, who witnessed this gruesome sight, lost his speech for two weeks. Aniela Siemianowska, who provided the Jews with false identification cards, remained in hiding and was able to give her testimony to a Jewish investigator, Dr. Szymon Datner, after the war.

Archives of the Jewish Historical Institute, dep. no. 6445. Also see its "Bulletin" no. 73 (1970) p. 135.

68. Boiska-Kolonia, Lipsko county, voivodship of Kielce. January 2, 1943. German military police from Lipsko exterminated **two Catholic peasant families** for aiding Jews. Their households were looted and burned to the ground. Thus perished: **Stanisław Borycki,** 44, his wife **Zofia Borycka,** 38, and their eight month old baby, **Zbigniew Borycki,** as well as **Józef Krawczyk,** 36, **Zofia Krawczyk,** 33, and their son, **Adam Krawczyk,** 8.

F.-R. p. 307. OKBZH in Kielce, Ds 7/69.

69. Bordziłówka, Biała Podlaska county, voivodship of Lublin. Summer 1943. Two Polish children, **Zofia Zając,** 4, and **Stefan Zając,** 1, were killed by the Germans in reprisal for sheltering Jews by their parents who were momentarily absent and managed to escape.

GKBZH Zh 1183/79.

70. Borki, Kielce county, voivodship of Kielce. **Maria Biciańska** was shot to death by the Germans for hiding three Jewish refugees from Warsaw, two of them women.

GKBZH WB I 33.

71. Borszczów (1) Borszczów county, voivodship of Tarnopol. March 17, 1943. For sheltering 11 Jews, among them Maria Moszko with her three children, Józef Zusko, his wife Sara and their three sons, and Józef Mendel, also with three children, two Polish forest rangers, **Józef Zieliński** and **Stanisław Lasota,** along with **Mrs. Lasota** and their son, **Jerzy Lasota,** 4, were shot to death and thrown into their house which was set on fire. All the Jews managed to escape the holocaust with the aid of their saviors, before the Germans arrived.

Testimony of Stanisława Korzeniowska in GKBZH KO 69/70. GKBZH WB IX 17, X 16-7.

72. Borszczów (2) Borszczów county, voivodship of Tarnopol. May or June 1943. For ignoring official posters which imposed the penalty of death in retribution for sheltering Jews, **Mrs. Bogucka,** wife of the late Karol Bogucki and mother of three children, was arrested. Severely beaten and taken to the town of Czortków, she was never seen again. The corpses of eleven Jews who had been hiding in her cellar were left scattered around their household in the hamlet of Pastewnik. Three little orphans were saved by the neighbors.

Court deposition of A. Kusznier in W.-Z. p. 388, also 421. GKBZH WB XI 30.

73. Borysław (1) Drohobycz county, voivodship of Lwów. Accused of providing shelter to Syda Turschein, **Jan Olszewski,** 17, was deported to the Reich and hung there in the city of Bremen without disclosing her whereabouts. Meantime, the Jewish woman, hidden by Jan's mother in Warsaw, survived to tell the story.

Testimony of S. Turschein in W.-Z. p. 338-9, also 448. GKBZH WB VI C.

74. Borysław (2) Drohobycz county, voivodship of Lwów. December 29, 1943. The Pastor of the local Roman Catholic parish, **Rev. Andrzej Osikowicz,** 43, died in KL

Majdanek, deported there for encouraging his parishioners to give aid to the persecuted Jews.

W.-J. v. 4, p. 299. GKBZH WB VIII 18.

75. Bór Kunowski, Starachowice county, voivodship of Kielce. July 4, 1943. In order to punish villagers instrumental in helping Jews in their forest shelters, SS Oberleutnant Krüger selected one village for total destruction. At 1:30 after midnight, German military police chased all villagers from their houses into an open space where 23 names were read from a prepared list. Selected men were locked in a barn while their wives and sons were forced to bring bundles of straw to be used to burn their husbands and fathers alive. Thus perished: **Jan Ćwiek,** 31, **Jan Karwacki,** 24, **Stefan Kita,** 23, **Edward Klepacz,** 21, **Jan Klepacz,** 61, **Jan Klepacz Jr.,** 37, **Stanisław Klepacz,** 36, **Stanisław Król,** 31, **Wojciech Libor,** 41, **Józef Listek,** 54, **Aleksander Madaj,** 39, **Władysław Pasieka,** 30, **Jan Pasternak,** 37, **Józef Pasternak,** 49, **Stanisław Płatek,** 41, **Mieczysław Sajur,** 23, and **Tadeusz Sajur,** 22. **Piotr Pasternak,** 23, succeeded in escaping through a hole dug under the walls of the barn, but was thrown back into the raging flames. Another group of twenty persons, mostly women and children, were killed with pistols: **Anna Górecka,** 31, **Apolonia Górecka,** 20, **Bronisława Górecka,** 43, **Helena Górecka,** 40, **Joanna Górecka,** 15, **Andrzej Górecki,** 3, **Henryk Górecki,** 49, **Władysław Górecki,** 14, **Jan Kita,** 16, **Adam Klepacz,** 17, **Józefa Skrzydło,** 54, **Natalia Skrzydło,** 20, **Stanisław Skrzydło,** 13, **Władysław Skrzydło,** 18, **Piotr Standowicz,** 21, and one person whose name remains unknown. Their bodies were buried with the charred remnants of the other group in one common grave.

Testimony of A. Kantowicz in B.-L. p. 283-4. W.-Z. p. 277, 432. F.-R. p. 135. E.F. p. 409-14 (47 victims). OKBZH in Kielce Ds 67/69. GKBZH WB I 160.

Borzęcin see **Brzesko.**

76. Brańsk, Biała Podlaska county, voivodship of Biały-stok. July 15, 1943. **Rev. Henryk Opiatowski,** formerly a chaplain in the Polish Army and a native of Landwarowo of the same county, was arrested for providing shelter to Jewish refugees from the local ghetto. He was shot to death by the Germans.

J.-W. v. 4, p. 214.

77. Brasław, Brasław county, voivodship of Wilno. Summer 1942. Rev. **Mieczysław Akrejć,** 56, while interceding with the Germans on behalf of the innocent Jewish population brought to slaughter, was killed together with the Jews.

J.-W. v. 4, p. 204.

78. Bratnik, Lubartów county, voivodship of Lublin. December 6, 1943. The German Wehrmacht (armed forces) shot to death **Franciszek Obara,** 32, for sheltering Jews.

GKBZH Egz. V. Bratnik.

79. Brody (1), voivodship of Tarnopol. May 8, 1943. Polish partisans from a nearby forest decided to bring a group of Jews headed by a well-known Jewish poet Shudryk from the Lwów ghetto. Suddenly, their truck, heading for Zyblikiewicz St., was surrounded by the German SS. Its occupants sold their lives dearly, killing several Germans. The next day, May 9th, the forest near Brody was combed by a battalion of German infantry. The partisan struggle with the German force three times their strength continued for three days. Only a few partisans survived.

E.-G. p. 121.

80. Brody (2), voivodship of Tarnopol. May 1943. Two Jewish freedom fighters pursued by the Germans, found shelter in a house which was soon surrounded by the German military police. Its **Polish inhabitants,** though cruelly beaten, refused to show the hideout of the escapees and were shot to death. The two Jews committed suicide.

R. P. p. 162.

81. Broszków, Siedlce county, voivodship of Warsaw. January 9, 1944. **Wiesław Walczewski,** arrested June 28, 1943 in the village of Ciesie for helping Jews, was executed in the Pawiak prison.

S.D. p. 99,115. GKBZH WB VI 99.

82. Brzesko (1), voivodship of Kraków. 1942. **Stanisław Czarnecki** and **Józef Chudy,** 20, were shot to death by the Germans for giving aid to persecuted Jews.

Testimony of W. Myśliński in B.-L. p. 853. GKBZH WB II 153, 158.

83. Brzesko (2), voivodship of Kraków. Because of the massive aid to the Jews from the local Catholic population, close to 150 Jews were saved from extermination, but **25 farmers** of the area paid for this with their own lives: four from Okocim, five from Dębno, two from Brzesko, one from Iwkowa, two from Borzęcin, one from Szczurowa, one from Radłow, and three from Szczepanów. Altogether, twenty persons were shot to death on the spot and the remaining five were deported to Auschwitz from which they never returned.

Testimony of W. Myśliński in B.-L. p. 851.

84. Brześć on Bug (1), voivodship of Polesie. June 1943. The Dean and Pastor of the local Roman Catholic parish, **Rev. Jan Urbanowicz,** 48, was shot by the Germans for giving aid to Jews.

Ph.F. p. 126. J.-W. v. 1, p. 167. W.-Z. p. 353. B.-L. p. 95. GKBZH WB VI 4.

85. Brześć on Bug (2), voivodship of Polesie. Summer 1943. **Stanisław Podgórski,** a member of the "Wachlarz" (Fan) team of the Polish Home Army which operated as deep into Soviet territory as Mińsk, capital of Byelorussia, was murdered in the Brześć jail for sheltering a Jewish family.

A.P. p. 219.

86. Brześć on Bug (3), voivodship of Polesie. For sheltering two Jewish families in his house at Krótka Street a man named **Barczak,** together with one of the Jews, was killed by the Germans. The other Jewish family, with the aid of Mrs. Paulina Barczak, was saved by Władysław Słoniewski who took them to a nearby forest.

GKBZH WB XI 11.

87. Brzezie, Radom county, voivodship of Kielce. **Antoni Kuczmera** was executed in Jedlnia for giving aid to three Jews, one of them the wife of Abram Mendel.

GKBZH WB I 6.

88 Brzeźnica Książęca, Lubartów county, voivodship of Lublin. **November 4, 1943. Four Catholic Poles** were executed by the Germans for sheltering Jews.

GKBZH Egz. V. Brz. K.

89. Brzostówka, Lubartów county, voivodship of Lublin. November 1943. German authorities executed **a Catholic farmer** for giving aid to the persecuted Jews.

GKBZH Egz. V Brz.

Brzoza see Zarzetka.

90. Brzoza Królewska, Leżajsk county, voivodship of Rzeszów. 1942 or 1943. **Sebastian Kozak,** 70, his wife **Katarzyna Kozak,** 65, and **Tomasz Wach,** 41, were shot to death together with sixty two Jews sheltered by them, among them Lea Krzeszower with her three children, and Izaak Szwanenfeld with his wife and two children, Pinkas Wachs with his wife Gitla and four children. This ocurred sometime between June 1942 and May 1943.

B.-L. p. 834, 849. S.D. P. 87. W.-Z. p. 443. GKBZH WB IV 350-1, 401. GKBZH./B v. X, p. 162.

REICHSKRIEG.
Reichshof, den 2 7 APR 194

JUSTIZANGESTELLTER
als Urkundsbeamter der Geschäftsstelle
des Sondergerichts beim Deutschen Gericht.

G.13/44

18/44 **Im Namen des Deutschen Volkes!**

Strafsache gegen 1. die Sophie Gargasz, geb.am 27.3.1900 in
Jablonka Krs.Krosno, Tochter des Winzent Mycka
und der Pauline geb.Kozicki, Landwirtin, verheiratet, wohnhaft in Brzozow, Podlesie Nr.373,
Krs.Krosno,

2. den Jakob Gargasz, geb. am 25.7.1881 in Wola Ja-
sienicka, Krs.Krosno, Sohn des Stanislaus und der
Marianne geb.Sawik, Landwirt, verheiratet, wohnhaft in Brzozow, Podlesie Nr.373, Kreis Krosno,

wegen Judenbegünstigung.

Das Sondergericht Reichshof

hat in der Sitzung vom   19.April   1944 an der teilgenommen haben:

Landgerichtsdirektor Pooth

als Vorsitzender,

Amtsgerichtsrat Stumpel

Amtsgerichtsrat Dr. Aldenhoff

als Richter, beisitzende Richter

Oberstaatsanwalt Dr.Naumann

als Beamter der Staatsanwaltschaft,

Gerichtsvollzieher Hagelstein

als Urkundsbeamter der Geschäftsstelle,

für Recht erkannt:

*die Angeklagten Sophie und Jakob Gargasz müssen,
weil sie der Jüdin Katz Unterschlupf gewährt haben, zum
Tode verurteilt*

The death sentence for harboring a Jewish woman, Mrs. Katz, as stated
in the above court decree in the name of German people, was mandatory, even
for witnesses. There was no valid excuse based on ignorance of the fact by Mr.
Gargasz.

91. Brzozów, Krosno county, voivodship of Rzeszów. April 19, 1944. **Zofia Gargasz,** 44, and her husband **Jakub Gargasz,** 62, were sentenced to death "in the name of the German People" by a court of three judges, Dr. Aldenhoff, Dr. Naumann and Dr. Stumpel, presided by Judge Pooth with court reporter Hagelstein. After carefully considering the case of unlawfully sheltering a Jewess, Mrs. Katz, the German court rejected the defense that the accused acted in a situation of conflict between the German law and their religious convictions as Seventh Day Adventists. All mitigating circumstances, especially in the case of Mr. Gargasz, initially unaware that his wife was harboring Mrs. Katz, were put aside since there was only one penalty for helping a Jew, the penalty of death. The German judges, therefore, were unable to pass any other sentence – even in case of an American citizen (Mr. Gargasz) – except the sentence of death.

B.-R. p. 44. W.-Z. p. 447. Testimony of T. Seweryn in B.-L. p. 849. GKBZH WB IV 221, 222. Also the enclosed facsimile of the death sentence.

92. Budzów, Sucha Podbeskidzka county, voivodship of Kraków. June 4, 1944. Under suspicion of "aiding Jews and partisans" a local farmer named **Krupa** was murdered together with his son. Many other inhabitants of adjoining villages were sent to various concentration camps for the same reason.

F.-R. p. 53. OKBZH in Kraków, Ds 6/70.

93. Busko-Zdrój, voivodship of Kielce. Winter 1943. German military police executed **Jan Witkoś** for giving refuge to a Jewish girl in his apartment. This fact was revealed to the Germans by a frightened Jewish boy who was seeking safety in another apartment of the same building.

Court deposition of S. Kwiecień in W.-Z. p. 370, also 429. GKBZH WB I 197.

94. Bużek, Złoczów county, voivodship of Tarnopol. March 21, 1944. In reprisal for hiding Jews in a cellar, Germans exterminated the entire **Łeńczuk family of four.**

W.-Z. p. 433. GKBZH WB IV 444.

95. Cezaryn (1) Puławy county, voivodship of Lublin. July 3, 1943. **Jan Machul,** 42, was shot to death for giving shelter to three Jews, one of them a woman.

GKBZH Egz. V Ds 95/67. GKBZH WB V 85.

96. Cezaryn (2) Puławy county, voivodship of Lublin. October 1943. A **Catholic farmer** was murdered by the Germans for hiding two Jews.

B.-L. p. 833. GKBZH Egz. V Ds 40/71/Pl.

97. Chełmno on Ner, Konin county, voivodship of Łodz. 1942. For having transmitted to the Swiss Consulate in Berlin the first news about the death camp for Jews in that locality, **Stanisław Kaszyński,** secretary of the village, was executed in the Rzuchów forest after a subsequent message was intercepted.

L.B. p. 156.

98. Chmielnik (1), Stopnica county, voivodship of Kielce. Autumn 1942. During the deportation of Jews, **Antoni Szczygielski** from the village of Szyszczyce and **Witold Jędrusik,** 25, were arrested and shot to death for aiding Jews confined in the ghetto. Both were betrayed by Szaje Fastak, a Jewish Gestapo agent, who was executed by the Polish underground for this crime.

W.-Z. p. 409. GKBZH WB I 146.

99. Chmielnik (2), Stopnica county, voivodship of Kielce. 1942. A Polish **Christian woman,** unknown by name, was killed by the Germans for entering the ghetto area in order to bring aid to its Jewish inmates.

W.-Z. p. 413.

100. Chodnów, Skierniewice county, voivodship of Warsaw. December 29, 1943. **Władysław Rutkowski,** 31, and his wife, **Genowefa Rutkowska,** 30, were executed by the Germans for sheltering a Jewish couple by the name of Helcberg. They were denounced by a *Volksdeutsch* (a Polish citizen claiming German nationality) named Lentz and sentenced to death by a special German tribunal (Sondergericht) of Piotrków.

GKBZH WB 101-2. Also, facsimile of the court decree in GKBZH Ds XL III.

101. Chominne, Biała Podlaska county, voivodship of Lublin. November 7, 1943. For aiding the Jews, the German military police from Wisznica executed the entire Olesiuk family: **Wojciech Olesiuk,** 43, and **Stefania Olesiuk,** 40, with their three children: **Piotr Olesiuk,** 14, **Stefan Olesiuk,** 9, and **Szymon Olesiuk,** 3. Children were buried next to their parents in the place of execution.

S.D. 102. B.-L. p. 841. W.-Z. p. 427. GKBZH WB V 64.

102. Chotel Czerwony, Busko-Zdrój county, voivodship of Kielce. Spring 1943. **Piotr Kupisz** and **Bronisława Kupisz** were shot to death near their house for sheltering three Jews. The murder was perpetrated by the German military policemen from Nowy Korczyn, Randtke and Gawenda, who obtained the necessary information from a Jewish woman sheltered by Kupisz but later caught and recognized as a Jewess.

Court deposition of. S. Kwiecień in W.-Z. p. 370. GKBZH WB I 153-4 (Kupis).

103. Chotówka, Stołpce county, voivodship of Nowogródek. In the absence of a farmer, named **Lipnicki, his entire family** was exterminated and the farm burned to the ground because Germans had discovered that Jews were hiding there. When he returned he found only smoldering ashes.

W.-Z. p. 445.

104. Ciecierze, near Chmielnik, voivodship of Kielce. December 24, 1942. On Christmas Eve, German military police surrounded the house of **Feliks Stradowski,** 57, who was sheltering a Jewish woman, Gaul, and her daughter. Mrs Gaul was shot to death while the girl remained in hiding. Stradowski was taken to Chmielnik, beaten there for not disclosing the girl's whereabouts and sent to KL Auschwitz. He never came back.

W.-Z. p. 411.

105. Cielechowizna (1), Mińsk Mazowiecki county, voivodship of Warsaw. July 1943. **Kazimierz Przekora** was shot to death by the Germans for sheltering Jews in his house.

W.-Z. p. 423. GKBZH WB VI 1313.

106. Cielechowizna (2), Mińsk Mazowiecki county, voivodship of Warsaw. July 1943. German military police from Mińsk Mazowiecki executed **Zygmunt Dziurkowski** for giving refuge to Jews in his household.

GKBZH WB VI 1313.

107. Ciepielów (1), Lipsko county, voivodship of Kielce. December 6, 1942. **Szczepan Sułecki** was arrested, taken behind a farm building and shot there for giving aid to Jews.

GKBZH WB I 182.

108. Ciepielów (2), Lipsko county, voivodship of Kielce. Winter 1942/43. **Antoni Mrożkowski** was shot to death in the vicinity of Ciepielów heights for aiding Jews.

GKBZH WB I 183.

109. Ciepielów (3), Lipsko county, voivodship of Kielce. A **Polish peasant woman**, unknown today by name, was raising a Jewish child together with five children of her own. Denounced to the Germans and interrogated by them as to which child is Jewish, she was forced to watch her children be shot one by one while refusing to give this information. The sixth child to be shot happened to be Jewish. This heroic mother was executed at the end.

Testimony of Barbara Natus in "Tygodnik Kulturalny" weekly, no. 2, Jan. 9, 1983.

110 **Ciepielów Stary**, Lipsko county, voivodship of Kielce. December 6, 1942. A motorized detachment of the SS, under the command of Officer Berner, burned alive **twenty one persons** from the Kosior, Kowalski and Obuchiewicz families, known to harbor persecuted Jews in their houses. In this act of officially-approved terrorism intended to frighten the Catholic population, the following Polish Catholics gave their lives: **Władysław Kosior**, 42, **Karolina Kosior**, 40, with their six children: **Aleksander Kosior**, 18, **Mieczysław Kosior**, 12, **Irena Kosior**, 10, **Tadeusz Kosior**, 16, **Adam Kosior**, 6, and **Władysława Kosior**, 4; **Adam Kowalski**, 47, and **Bronisława Kowalska**, 40, with their five children: **Janina Kowalska**, 16, **Zofia Kowalska**, 12, **Stefan Kowalski**, 6, **Henryk Kowalski**, 4, and **Tadeusz Kowalski**, 1; one of Kowalski's daughters jumped from the flaming inferno through the window, but was shot and thrown back into the flames; the Obuchiewicz family, **Piotr Obuchiewicz**, 58, and **Helena Obuchiewicz**, 35, with their four children: **Władysław Obuchiewicz**, 6, **Zofia Obuchiewicz**, 3, **Janina Obuchiewicz**, 2, and a 7-month old **Obuchiewicz baby** with no baptismal name mentioned. This cruel punishment did not deter Stanisława Lewandowska, a neighbor of Kowalskis and Obuchiewicz, from keeping Dawid Semkowicz, who survived and, after the war, moved to Haifa, Israel.

Testimony of M. Bielecka in B.-L. p. 862-5. R.-R. p. 48. Testimony of J. Mirowski and a court deposition of J. Bielecki in W.-Z. p. 372-3 (Obuchniewicz) GKBZH WB 82-3, 98-104.

111. Ciesie (1), Mińsk Mazowiecki county, voivodship of Warsaw. June 28, 1943. On Sunday morning when the villagers came back from the High Mass in a nearby church of Cegłow, the German Gestapo, SS and military police made a raid on their houses suspected of sheltering many Jews. The tragedy originated early in 1942, when a farmer named Kieliszczyk had taken in Jewish refugees from Cegłow: Freja Goldsztein and Fatima, along with her three children. In a neighboring farm, a Jewish girl by the name of Jabłonka found refuge, though the penalty of death for such a transgression of the German law was already announced by posters nailed to trees all over the village. In defiance of these warnings, more Jews were taken in by Polish Catholic farmers: Tatiana, Estera, Jojne and Mendel Goldsztein and one known by the first name of Mosze. In retaliation, Germans took the offenders back to the Cegłow church and executed them there by the railroad tracks. Thus gave their lives: **Aleksandra Araszkiewicz, Marcin Dąbrowski, Franciszek Fiutkowski, Aleksander Gąsior, Henryk Geregra, Tadeusz Lipiński, Zygmunt Maluś, Sylweriusz Płatek, Tomasz Płatek, Stanisław Płatek, Stanisław Peżyk, Edward Rżysko, Władysław Saski, Eugeniusz Skwieciński, Marian Smater, Piotr Smater, Jan Szczęsny, Józefa Szyperska, Władysław Wójcicki, Jan Zagańczyk** and **Ludwik Zając.** With them died Estera, Jojne and Mendel Goldsztein. The village was burned down. One more step for the German "Drang nach Osten" (push to the East).

W.-Z. p. 361-3, 421. GKBZH WB VI A, 2, 10-11, 43, p. 68, 3. 866, Z 777.

112 Ciesie (2), Mińsk Mazowiecki county, voivodship of Warsaw. June 28, 1943. German military police, in a raid on Jewish escapees from a death train to Treblinka, punished by death **Rozalia Jaworska** and her two-year old **daughter** for the "crime" of giving them shelter.

Testimony of W. Romanowski in B.-L. p. 865-7. W.-Z. p. 363. GKBZH WB VI A 2

113. Ciesie (3), Mińsk Mazowiecki county, voivodship of Warsaw. June 28, 1943. In spite of German threats, **Jan Wąsowski** decided to hide Jews knocking at his door. Their hiding place was a loft over the stable. All of them were discovered, however, and shot. Together with them and their host, died **Aleksandra Wąsowska** and her son, **Mieczysław Wąsowski.** One of the Jews, though wounded, managed to escape with the aid of helpful Catholic peasants.

B.-L. p. 866. W.-Z. p. 421. GKBZH WB VI W.

114. Cudnów, Radom county, voivodship of Kielce. July 26, 1944. A Polish farmer named **Grosiak** and his wife, Julianna Grosiak, gave shelter to Judka Kania, Chil Kerstenberg, Mosze and Chaim Berneman, Rubinsztein (no first name) from Ćmielów, and Dutek (no first name); all Jews hiding from the German authorities. For this "transgression", their host was executed while his wife managed to escape.

GKBZH WB I 32.

Cumań see **Obórki.**

Czaplowizna see **Zarzetka.**

115. Czarna, Dębica county, voivodship of Rzeszów. November 1942. **J. Wiatr,** employed in a construction firm at Pustków, was executed for sharing his food rations with the Jewish inmates of Stalowa Wola steelworks.

T. Bi. p. 11.

116. Czarne (forest), Mińsk Mazowiecki county, voivodship of Warsaw. March 19, 1943. Germans have surrounded a forester's house which became a refuge for Mrs. Szpidler Malinowska and her mother, and for Teresa Powązek, her husband, and their friend, Abraham Słomka. In the ensuing fight, all the Jews were killed along with their host, **Stanisław Rokicki,** and two Russians, **Paweł Iwanow** and **Aleksander Popow.** Their bodies were consumed inside the house by the fire which was started with a hand grenade.

W.-Z. p. 417 (Ignaców) GKBZH WB VI 93 (Szpindler-Malinowska).

117. Czarny Dunajec, Nowy Targ county, voivodship of Kraków. May 20, 194 **Karol Chrąca,** 46, from Wróblówka was shot to death for bringing food to Joseph Lehrer and his daughter who were hiding from the Germans. All three were executed and buried in one common grave, in a Jewish cemetary.

B.-L. p. 832, 842. W.-Z. p. 405. GKBZH WB II Ch.

118. Czerlany, Gródek Jagielloński county, voivodship of Lwów. December 1942 or January 1943. An **entire Polish family,** name unknown, was executed by the Germans for giving shelter to Dr. Hammerschmidt and his wife from Gródek Jagielloński. The Jewish couple committed suicide.

Testimony of S. Gniazdowski in OKBZH of Opole, Kpp. 41/70.

119 Czermna, Jasło county, voivodship of Rzeszów. 1943. For hiding the Morgensztern family of four, **Andrzej Garboliński,** 55, his son, **Władysław Garboliński,** 21, and their neighbor, **Stanisław Owca,** 55, were shot to death by the Gestapo. The neighbor was punished for failing to inform the German authorities. Their farms were burned to the ground.

W.-Z. p. 431. GKBZH WB VI 4,5.

120. Czernie, Garwolin county, voivodship of Warsaw. June 1943. German Gestapo shot to death **Wiktoria Dąbek,** 40, together with ten Jews she was sheltering.

G.-L. p. 835, 839. S.D. p. 98 (Czernic) GKBZH WB VI 1396.

121. Częstochowa (1), voivodship of Katowice. April 2, 1943. By the decision of a special court (Sondergericht), two brothers, **Stanisław Kurdziel** and **Jan Kurdziel,** were executed for helping Jews.

J. Pi. p. 186.

122. Częstochowa (2), voivodship of Katowice. April 7, 1943. For the same offense of aiding Jews, **Bronisława Lang, Irena Bogucka** and **Marian Bogucki** were deported to KL Majdanek. Their fate remains unknown.

J.Pi. p. 186.

123. Częstochowa (3), voivodship of Katowice. April 15, 1943. **Wacław Żerkowski** perished in the KL Majdanek for helping Jews.

J.Pi. p. 186.

124. Częstochowa (4), voivodship of Katowice. June 9, 1943. Early in the morning German Schutzpolizei (security police), under the command of a Gestapo officer, Wilhelm Laubner, surrounded the rectory of St. Barbara's parish. Its leader, accompanied by two gunmen and a Jew who was previously caught with an identification card forged in that parish, entered the building and, with a burst of bullets, killed **Rev. Teodor Popczyk,** 33, who was pointed out by the Jewish informer as the person guilty of providing him with false papers.

J.P. p. 90-1. J.-W. v. 2, p. 156.

125. Częstochowa (5), voivodship of Katowice. June 18, 1943. **Tadeusz Bednarski** and his wife, **Czesława Bednarska,** suspected of sheltering Jews, were first doported to Auschwitz, then brought back to Częstochowa in order to find out the place where Jewish jewelry was hidden. One day Germans took them from the jail and no trace of them was ever found. In the meantime, the Jews managed to escape.

J.Pi. p. 186. Also the testimony of Zofia Majewska in the acts of the Częstochowa jail in the Archives of Częstochowa voivodship.

126. Częstochowa (6), voivodship of Katowice. August 2, 1943. Sixty-two years old **Antonina Sygizman,** accused of holping Jews, didn't survive cruel investigations and died in jail in the Zawodzie suburb of Częstochowa.

J.Pi. p. 187. Archives of Częstochowa voivodship, no. 3237.

127. Częstochowa (7), voivodship of Katowice. Summer 1943. Germans killed a Polish officer of the Home Army known as **Leutenant Langiewicz,** who was trying to save a wounded Jewish courier girl from Łódź. This was one of many lives given by the emissaries of the "Żegota" campaign to save the Jews. "Lieutenant Langiewicz" was commissioned to provide financial aid to the Jewish fighters of ŻOB (Jewish Fighters' Organization) who, with the aid of their Polish counterparts, left the Warsaw Ghetto in May 1943.

T.P. p. 231.

128. Częstochowa (8), voivodship of Katowice. August 17, 1943. The German police suddenly surrounded a little house owned by **Jakub Szmaciarski** and his wife, **Józefa Szmaciarska,** surprising there a group of Jews emploved in a nearby plant. The Jews were killed on the spot and the Polish couple sent to Auschwitz on August 22. Jakub was killed there on October 18, 1943, and this wife, Józefa, died on January 10, 1944, for the crime of befriending their Jewish neighbors.

J.Pi. p. 187. Testimony of Zofia Majewska in the Archives of Częstochowa voivodship.

129. Częstochowa (9), voivodship of Katowice. December 1943. **Bolesław Grzeliński,** an organist at the parish of St. Zygmunt, was engaged in the preparation of false identification papers for the Jews. It involved searching for an appropriate name of a deceased parishioner, marking the entry in the parochial books to prevent more than one id. for the same name and distributing the papers among the Jewish refugees. The organist was promptly arrested after several such documents were discovered in the ghetto. He was tortured to disclose the names of his beneficiaries. Shortly before Christmas, his wife was informed by the Gestapo that her husband died of a kidney ailment. His companion in prison cell, Eugeniusz Krawczyk, remembered seeing Grzeliński's back blackened from beatings over the kidneys during the interrogation which probably damaged his internal organs.

J.P. p. 105-6.

130. Częstochowa (10), voivodship of Katowice. January 19, 1944. On this day in Auschwitz Germans killed **Halina Polak** and the next day her mother, **Franciszka Polak,** both arrested together with their father and husband, Jan Polak, for giving shelter to a Jew who managed to escape. Jan somehow survived.

J.Pi. p. 187. Testimony of Jan Polak and Stanisław Sobczak in the Archives of Częstochowa voivodship.

131. Częstochowa (11), voivodship of Katowice. 1944. Since the formation of the ghetto on April 9, 1941, rector of the cathedral church, **Rev. Bolesław Wróblewski,** took care of more than 60 Jewish children by placing them in various Catholic institutions. Finally, sometime in 1944, the Germans became suspicious of his activities and of his entire household. After the intensive search disclosed no children present at the rectory, the 74-year old priest was pistol-whipped and his sister, **Miss Wróblewska,** was struck by the Gestapo officer Hintze with a rifle butt on head and died a few days later. Their maid who had a broken arm was pushed into a cellar and the bed-ridden aunt of the priest, Mrs. Wielowieyska, was severely beaten.

H.Pi. p. 180. C.T. p. 374.

132. Częstochowa (12), voivodship of Katowice. 1942-44. Among the personal acts of the jail in the Zawodzie suburb there are indications of **32 more cases** where Catholics paid with their lives for the aid given to Jews.

J.Pi. p. 186. Archives of Częstochowa voivodship, nos. 1602, 2348, 2349, 2354, 2359, 2361, 2365, 2366, 2371, 2372, 2406, 2477, 2478, 2573, 2574, 2575, 2803, 2951, 2990, 2991, 2992, 2995, 2996, 2997, 2998, 3055, 3059, 3233, 3242, 3303, 3358, 3736.

133. Czorsztyn, Nowy Sącz county, voivodship of Kraków. Summer 1942. **Anna Furca** was murdered by the Germans for permitting Jews to live in her house.

GKBZH WB II 104.

134. Czuszów, Miechów county, voivodship of Kraków. In a nearby estate Germans murdered a **Polish child** in retaliation for an attempt to shelter a fugitive Jewish child. A next door neighbor, guilty of the same "transgression" said: "I hope they will take my life first, if they catch me."

Testimony of F. Kohn in. B.-L. p. 556.

135. Czyżuny, Grodno county, voivodship of Wilno. A Catholic Pole named **Żukowski** and his wife, **Kazimiera Żukowska,** together with all members of their family, lost their lives for giving shelter to Jews.

GKBZH WB VII 115.

136. Daleszyce, near Chmielnik, voivodship of Kielce. Summer 1942. **Stanisław Furmanek** was arrested and later murdered in jail for transporting Jews in his carriage to the town of Chmielnik where they thought they had a better chance of survival. **Michał Malarecki,** also from Daleszyce, was arrested for the same reason. He died after being tortured in prison.

W.-Z. p. 407. GKBZH WB I 139,169.

137. Dąbrowa Górnicza, voivodship of Katowice. 1940 or 1941. For bringing ink supplies to a makeshift print shop which furnished fake food stamps to the starving Jews, Germans arrested and murdered **Tadeusz Torbus** (circumstances unknown).

Testimony of A. Koszowski in W.-Z. p. 368.

138. Dąbrowa Tarmowska (1), voivodship of Kraków. September 17, 1944. **Anna Gruchała** and her daughter-in-law, **Julia Gruchała,** paid with their lives for sheltering two Jewish families: Pinkas Cizer, along with his wife, Rozalia, and their son, as well as Mrs. Shifra, with her husband, two children and a sister. Four of the Jews were shot on the spot, others managed to escape. Julia's two children became orphans.

Testimony of J. Kozaczka in W.-Z. p. 344, also 437. GKBZH WB II 82-3. S. Datner in the "Biuletyn" of the Jewish Historical Institute, no. 75(1970) p. 27 (Jakub Derchowicz, Hirsch Lincenberg).

139. Dąbrowa Tarnowska (2), voivodship of Kraków. A Polish Catholic, **Franciszek Pula,** was arrested and taken to Brzesko. He was murdered there for sheltering a Jew.

W.-Z. p. 447. GKBZH WB II 1.

140. Dąbrówka, Kolbuszowa county, voivodship of Rzeszów. 1943 **Bronisław Wilk** was murdered in Auschwitz for giving shelter on his farm to Jankiel Szyja and Moszek Orgiel. Jankiel was killed on the spot and Moszek survived the German occupation.

W.-Z. p. 431. GKBZH WB II 1. T.Bi. p. 7.

Derewna see **Pińsk.**

Dębno see **Brzesko.**

141. Dobra, Limanowa county, voivodship of Kraków. April 7, 1941. Arrested for providing Jews with baptismal certificates, and tortured by a Gestapo officer named Hermann, **Rev. Adam Sekuła,** 27, assistant pastor of the local parish, was murdered in the jail of Nowy Sącz while refusing to betray the names of those he had helped.

J.-W. v. 4, p. 387.

142. Dobra, Łuck county, voivodship of Wołyń. Two Catholic Poles, **Stanisław Sawicki** and **Hilary Sawicki,** were murdered by the Germans for giving aid to Jews.

W.-Z. p. 439. GKBZH WB IV 344.

143. Dobra-Kolonia, Olkusz county, voivodship of Kraków. November 14, 1942. **Piotr Domagała** was shot to death together with Kajla June, her husband, their child and another Jewish woman he was sheltering. Their neighbor, **Stefan Ptak,** was arrested for not informing Germans about the offense. Mrs. Domagała managed to escape, returning only to bury her husband.

Testimony of Mrs. Domagała in W.-Z. p. 377-8. GKBZH WB II 15.

144. Dobroszyce, Radomsko county, voivodship of Łódź. December 20, 1943. **Zygmunt Kaczmarek** and **Jan Malczewski,** were shot for helping Jews; Kaczmarek in his home,

Malczewski in a field near Radomsko, along with Abram Zel-
kowicz and his 10-year son whom he was trying to save.

W.-Z. p. 429. GKBZH WB X 60, 63.

145. Doliniany, Rohatyn county, voivodship of Lwów.
Wawrzyniec Kolanko was arrested and executed by the Gestapo for keeping in his house two Jewish boys around the age
of 8 and 10, sons of Kunio Uszer, and two adult Jews. They all
died together.

GKBZH WB X 27.

146. Dornfeld, Lwów county, voivodship of Lwów. A
14-year old **Catolic boy** who refused to betray the hideout of
some Jewish friends was shot on the spot by the Germans.

R.P. p. 45.

147. Dulcza Mała, Mielec county, voivodship of Rzeszów. Winter 1943/44. For aiding Jews hiding in a forest, Germans rounded up **thirty six Poles** from Dulcza Mała and Ma-
lec. The Jews managed to escape with the aid of the Polish
Home Army. As a punishment, all the arrested were sent to
Auschwitz. Only eight persons returned alive.

Testimony of B. Bartyzel and Z. Kozaczka in W.-Z. p. 341.

148. Dulcza Wielka, Mielec county, voivodship of Rzeszów. 1944. German Gestapo shot to death **Zofia Gawęda** for
sheltering a Jewish family of eight in her house.

W.-Z. p. 441. GKBZH WB IV 348.

149. Dylągówka, near Hyżne, voivodship of Rzeszów.
December 30, 1943. **Jan Slemp** was arrested and executed by
the Germans on the next day, together with Meier Zalcman, a
Jew, whom he was sheltering.

GKBZH WB IV 13 (Dylęgówka) GKBZH V Ko 12/70.

150. Dzwonowice, Olkusz county, voivodship of Kraków. January 12, 1943. For keeping Jews in a forester's cotta-

ge, Germans burned down all the occupants together with the cottage. The forester, Bronisław Janus, who happened to be away at this time, upon his return, found in the ashes of his cottage remnants of the bodies of his wife, **Helena Janus**, 22, his son, **Krzysztof Janus**, 3, his mother, **Maria Janus**, 40, his sister, **Zofia Madej**, his brother-in-law, **Mieczysław Madej**, 23, and their daughter, **Krystyna Madej**, 2, along with six persons of two Jewish families of Berliński and Rusinek who shared the holocaust.

Court deposition of B. Janus in W.-Z. p. 377, also 413. GKBZH WB II 12, 176-8.

Eiszyszki see **Mirzance.**

151. Fabianówka, Bychawa county, voivodship of Lublin. September 1943. In a nearby forest Germans executed **Fabian Ciuraj** and his wife, **Jadwiga Ciuraj**, for giving shelter to Jews.

W.-Z. p. 425. GKBZH WB IV 120-1.

152. Faliszówka, Krosno county, voivodship of Rzeszów. Winter 1942/43. **Władysław Krzysztynik,**who for one year kept six Jews in his house, among them two women and one child, was shot to death and buried together with them.

Court deposition of L. Marszałek in W.-Z. p. 396-7. GKBZH WB IV 352.

153. Furmany, Tarnobrzeg county, voivodship of Rzeszów. 1943. **Józefa Stępień, Stanisław Osiecki** and **Walenty Rutyna** were executed for giving shelter to M. Barow, a Jew, who managed to escape.

W.-Z. p. 429.

154. Gamratka, Mińsk Mazowiecki, voivodship of Warsaw. July 27, 1943. For sheltering Jews, **Zofia Kur**, 43, and her son, **Aleksander Kur**, 17, were executed by the Germans.

Three persons they sheltered were also killed.

B.-L. p. 835, 840. S.D. p. 100, 113. W.-Z. p. 423. GKBZH WB I K.

155. Giebułtów, Miechów county, oivodship of Kraków. May 1944. **Mrs. Natalia Konieczna** and **her daughter** were executed for sheltering 17 Jews on their farm. Mr. Konieczny managed to escape.

Testimony of T. Seweryn in B.-L. p. 850. W.-Z. p. 435. GKBZH WB II 142-3 (Niekonieczna).

156. Glina, Węgrów county, voivodship of Warsaw. August 1943. Inhabitants of this village located near KL Treblinka were subjected to severe reprisals, including death, for giving aid to Jewish inmates who escaped from the camp. Local Home Army unit, headed by Stanislaw Siwek, helped the escaping Jews to cross the Bug river by boat, with **considerable losses in lives.**

F.Z. p. 124.

157. Glinik Nowy, Jasło county, voivodship of Rzeszów. For sheltering a Jew, **Anna Wietecha** was deported to KL Auschwitz and killed there.

W.-Z. p. 441. GKBZH WB IV 437.

158. Głęboka, Gorlice county, voivodship of Rzeszów. January 14, 1943. On the basis of a letter found on the person of a Jew named Schuman, Germans shot to death **Franciszek Belniak** for sheltering two Jews: Eizberg and Leon Gelcalder. T. Konik was sent to Auschwitz for a similar „offense".

T.Bi. p. 5. C.-G. p. 197. W.-Z. p. 413. GKBZH WZ IV 350.

159. Głogów Małopolski, county and voivodship of Rzeszów. March 1943. German policemen shot to death **Jan Samojedny,** 56, and his wife, **Maria Samojedna,** 52, for sheltering Jews.

B.-L. p. 834,838. S. D. p. 93 W.-Z. p. 417. GKBZH WB IV 134-5. GKBZH/B VI 11 (Dutkiewicz).

160. Gniazdowo, Wołomin county, voivodship of Warsaw. Autumn 1942. **Aleksander Dudkiewicz** was murdered by the Germans together with Mr. Frydman, a Jew he was sheltering.

B.-L. p. 843. S.D. p. 89, 112. W.-Z. p. 409. GKBZH WB VI 11 (Dutkiewicz).

161. Gniewoszów, Kozienice county, voivodship of Kielce. **Józef Suchecki** was executed by the Germans for giving refuge to a dozen Jews who had run away from a labor camp. All the Jews managed to escape.

GKBZH WB I 69.

162. Golcowa – Ropa, Krosno county, voivodship of Rzeszów. The German Gestapo from Nostrzec executed **Franciszek Tomoń** for hiding a Jew.

W.Z. p. 441. GKBZH WB IV 431.

163. Goniądz, Mońki county, voivodship of Białystok. May 1944. German military police shot to death **two Christians** and three Jews sheltered by them.

B.-L. p. 832. B.-R. p. 44. W.-Z. p. 435.

164. Grabanów, Biała Podlaska county, voivodship of Lublin. July 20, 1943. For giving aid to the Jewish population of the hamlet, **Jan Kuszneruk**, 52, and his son, **Józef Kuszneruk**, 21, were killed by a German policeman.

W.-Z. p. 423. GKBZH WB V 118.

165. Grabiny, Węgrów county, voivodship of Warsaw. March 4 and 5, 1943. Germans pursuing the Jewish escapees from KL Treblinka shot to death in the local school building **ten persons** suspeced of helping "the Jews and partisans". Several others were sent to various concentration camps.

T.Sz. p. 50.

166. Grabów Szlachecki, Ryki county, voivodship of

Warsaw. March or April 1943. German military police shot to death and burned in their house **Juliana Woźniak, Kazimierz Woźniak** and **Stanisław Woźniak,** for harboring Jews. Also, another couple of the same name, **Stanisław Woźniak** and **Genowefa Woźniak,** were shot to death for the same offense.

GKBZH ASG 42 p. 162. OKBZH in Warsaw Ds 4/69.

167. Grądy, Węgrow county, voivodship of Warsaw. August 1943. **Some inhabitants** were punished by death for giving aid to Jews escaping from KL Treblinka.

W.Z. in "Więź" monthly, 1972 p. 124.

168. Grodno, voivodship of Wilno. July 14, 1943. For secretly aiding persecuted Jews, the Guardian of the Conventual Franciscan monastery, **Rev. Michał Klimczak, O.F.M.Conv.,** 36, (Father Dionizy), was executed near the village of Neumowicze. For the same reason **Msgr. Albin Jaroszewicz,** 65, Dean and Pastor of the local parish lost his life.

Ph.F. p. 126. J.-W. v. 1, p. 209, 251.

169. Grodzisk Mazowiecki, voivodship of Warsaw. March 1943. **Jan Mielczarek** was executed by the Germans for bringing arms and munitions to the Warsaw Ghetto. He was caught with his cargo in Błonie, a suburban locality near Warsaw.

W.-Z. p. 417. GKBZH WB VI M.

170. Gródek Jagielloński, voivodship of Lwów. Winter 1942/43. **Michał Charchalis,** surprised by Germans breaking into his house, where he was harboring Jews, gave his life defending them. The Jews were also killed.

Testimony of S. Gniazdowski in GKBZH Kpp 58/70. GKBZH WB IV 353-4.

171. Gruszka Zaporska, Zamość county, voivodship of Lublin. March 22, 1943. For keeping a group of seven Jews in a special "bunker", the German military police from Szczebrzeszyn exterminated the entire Solowski family. **Mrs. Helena Solowska,** together with her two children, **Wanda Solowska,** 12, and **Marian Solowski,** 5, were taken behind the barn and shot to death with a hand gun. Their father, **Jan Solowski,** was fatally wounded and died shortly afterwards.

Testimony of Z. Klukowski in B.-L. p. 868. W.-Z. p. 417. GKBZH WB V 207-8.

172. Gruszów, Miechów county, voivodship of Kraków. November 1943. **Kacper Woda** was deported to KL Auschwitz for hiding Jews. He never returned.

Testimony of T. Seweryn in B.-L. p. 850. W.-Z. p. 429. GKBZH WB II 200 (Gruszowa).

173. Grzegorzówka, Przeworsk county, voivodship of Rzeszów. November 1942. During a raid on Jewish hiding places, German military police extorted from a Jewish woman the names of Christian Poles helping Jews. In consequence, Germans murdered **Henryk Gajda, Władysław Jasiński, Stanisław Pelc** and **Grzegorz Wojtulski.**

W.-Z. p. 360.

174. Gumniska, Dębica county, voivodship of Rzeszów. Autumn 1943. "Navy blue" police murdered **Rozalia Zielińska,** who was in a state of advanced pregnancy, as a punishment for sheltering a Jew, Winda, from Dębica. Mr. Zieliński was absent from his house at this time, thus escaped certain death.

W.-Z. p. 427. GKBZH WB IV 315.

175. Gwoździec, Brzesko county, voivodship of Kraków. January 20, 1944. German policemen, Wagner, from Zakliczyn shot to death **Maria Pirzyńska** for hiding two Jews: Benjamin Sukman and Roman Sukman. The execution took place behind the barn in an open field.

W.-Z. p. 431. GKBZH WB II 8.

176. Hadle Szklarskie, Przeworsk county, voivodship of Rzeszów. November 1942. Many Jews hiding in the local forests were provided with food by the villagers and, during bad wather, sought shelter in their houses. One of them, Małka Szinfeld, was caught away from her hiding place and – probably under stress – pointed out to the Germans those farmers who were giving food and shelter to them. As a result of this betrayal, all these people were executed; among them, **Bronisław Deć,** who was forced to watch from a locked room as his young sons were led out and killed, one by one, in his backyard: first, **Józef Deć,** then, **Stanisław Deć,** finally the youngest, **Tadeusz Deć,** who begged his executioners in vain to let him live. The father was killed last. Also, **Aleksander Dusza** was shot to death by the Germans on December 4, 1942 because of his aid to Jews.

W.-Z. p. 360. GKBZH WB IV 180, 203, 204. T.Bi. p. 4.

177. Hucisko, near Głogów Małopolski, voivodship of Rzeszów. June 10, 1943. Bloody reprisal for sheltering of the Jews took place when the Germans rounded up and massacred **21 Catholic Poles: Jadwiga Aczalik or Chezalik,** 41, **Adam Baran,** 29, Szczepan Baran, 36, **Franciszek Beskur,** 35, **Franciszek Drąg,** 31, **Anna Dworak,** 21, **Jan Dworak,** 29, **Anna Dworak,** 30, **Katarzyna Dworak,** 60, **Maria Dworak,** 62, **Michał Dworak,** 57, **Stefania Dworak,** 16, **Zofia Dworak,** 51, **Adam Gut,** 31, **Józef Gut,** 41, **Ludwika Gut,** 38, **Marcin Gut,** 46, **Marcin Kolanko,** 36, **Jakub Rumak,** 34, **Józef Rumak,** 31, **Józef Słuja,** 31 and **Adam Susich,** 53. During the massacre 17 houses and scores of farm buildings belonging to the victims were burned to the ground.

Testimony of M. Wrzosek in B.-L. p. 847. W.-Z. p. 421. GKBZH WB IV 306, 348, 349, 351, 359 a, 361-8, 383, 385, 386, 419, 430, 441, 580, 581.

178. Huta Pieniacka, near Sasów, Brody county, voivodship of Tarnopol. February 22-23, 1944. Three hundred eighty

Poles and Jews lived peacefully in the village before the war. When the Germans started persecution of the Jews, the entire Polish population engaged in giving aid to over one hundred Jews. Suddenly, the Germans surrounded the village. They poured gasoline on houses and farm buildings, burning all the inhabitants. Over one hundred households were consumed by fire together with their inhabitants, including horses, cattle, pigs and all other domestic animals. The fire raged the whole day, while the Germans guarded the burning houses, barns, pigsties, stables and sheds in order not to permit anybody to escape from the flames.

"Yad wa-Shem Bulletin", April 1957, p. 19-20. W.-Z. p. 433. GKBZH WB IV 343.

179. Huta Werchobuska, Złoczów county, voivodship of Tarnopol. March 23, 1944. As a punishment for helping Jews who hid in a forest, another raid was staged by the Germans on the village of Huta Werchobuska. The majority of inhabitants, however, due to an early warning, managed to run away. **All those who could not escape** were burned alive with their cattle and all the farm buildings. Only two farms were left out of one hundred and twenty. Afterwards, nobody dared to return to the smoldering ruins. It remained a wasteland for a long time. A scout of the Soviet Army, Matvey G. Perlin, eventually found about eighty Jews hidden in a forest where they survived in their two earthen underground shelters, supported by Christian inhabitants of the surrounding villages.

"Yad wa-Shem Bulletin", April 1957, p. 20. W.-Z. p. 433. GKBZH WB IV 336.

180. Ignaców, Lipsko county, voivodship of Kielce. December 14, 1942. **Franciszek Osojca,** his wife, **Aniela Osojca,** and their two-year old **child** were shot to death and their bodies burned together with the farm buildings for sheltering a Jewish woman.

Court deposition of P. Kotur in W.-Z. p. 374. E.F. p. 303-4. GKBZH WB I 176-8.

181. Ignaców (forest), Mińsk Mazowiecki county, voivodship of Warsaw. March 30, 1943. Two Polish rangers from the Czarne forest, **Jan Gawrych**, 50, and **Stanisław Skuza**, were killed by the Germans after excruciating torments. They were accused of giving shelter to David Rutkowski and other Jews.

B.-L. p. 844. S.D. p. 94, 114. W.-Z. p. 417. GKBZH WB VI 99, 844.

Iwkowa see **Brzesko.**

182. Jabłeczna, Biała Podlaska county, voivodship of Lublin. November 1939. **Korneliusz Rudzki** was shot to death by German guards while ferrying Jews across the Bug river to the Soviet-occupied area of Poland which was accorded to the Soviet Union in the infamous clause of the Ribbentrop-Molotov Agreement of August 23, 1939, and where a better treatment was expected by the Jews.

OKBZH in Lublin Egz. J.

183. Jadowniki, Dąbrowa Tarnowska county, voivodship of Kraków. 1942. For a long time **Wincenty Cebula** was suspected by the Germans of bringing food to the Jews confined in the Busko ghetto. Being unable to catch him, they killed his father, **Franciszek Cebula.** The long arm of German justice eventually reached the young Cebula also. He was killed while running from the ghetto area.

GKBZH WB I 189-90.

184. Jadowniki Mokre, Dąbrowa Tarnowska county, voivodship of Kraków. The commanding officer of the German military police by the name of Guzdek personally killed **Paweł Kostecki** and **Franciszek Kostecki** for giving aid to Jews. For the same reason, their neighbor, **Aleksander Grajdura,** was killed.

W.-Z. p. 448. W.-Z. 448. GKBZH WB I 139, 140.

Jakubowice see **Opatów.**

185. Jankowice, Jarosław county, voivodship of Rzeszów. May 25, 1944. German military police, with the aid of some "navy blue" policemen, executed **Szymon Fołta,** 65, along with five Jews he was sheltering: Jeremiasz Nadel, 33, a merchant, Necha Nadel, 35, a seamstress and her daughter, Mila; Regina Amada, 28, a seamstress, and Dora Ring, also a seamstress.

B.-L. p. 834. S.D. p. 107, 112. W.-Z. p. 435. GKBZH WB IV 296. T.Bi. p. 6.

186. Janowiec, Mielec county, voivodship of Rzeszów. The German Gestapo shot to death **Florian Szczurek** for sheltering Jews in a "bunker" built under his house.

W.-Z. p. 411. GKBZH WB IV 424.

187. Janów Poleski, Drohiczyn county, voivodship of Polesie. April 1944. A Polish teacher from Dolsk, Pińsk county, named **Siekierzyński,** his **wife** and their **two children,** 7 and 10 years old, were taken by the Germans to a wall of the watermill. First, the children were forced to lie face down on the ground to be shot and when the mother threw herself over them in order to protect them, all three were riddled with bullets. Their father who had to watch the massacre of his family, was killed at the end. Their "crime" was giving refuge and a friendly home to a little Jewish boy, son of a grain merchant named Czertak from Janów.

Court deposition of A. Boratowski in W.-Z. p. 400-1. GKBZH WB VIII 44, 47.

188. Januszkowice, Jasło county, voivodshsip of Rzeszów. For hiding a Jewish child named Korzennik, a Catholic farmer, **Stanisław Gacoń,** and his wife, **Apolonia Gacoń,** were shot to death. Also, **Józef Foryś** was executed and his farm burned to the ground for feeding Jews.

W.-Z. p. 441. GKBZH WB IV 438-9. T. Bi. p. 2. (Sonina)

189. Jasionów, Brody county, voivodship of Lwów. **Zbi-**

gniew **Wartanowicz** was murdered by the Germans for hiding Jews; among others, an attorney-at-law by the name of Grünseit.

GKBZH WB XI 33.

190. Jasło (1), voivodship of Rzeszów. During the deportation of Jews to a death camp, **Polish Catholic farmers** who had been giving them aid and shelter were tied with the Jews and marched at the front of the column. All were packed in railroad boxcars and taken to their common fate.

W.-Z. p. 439. GKBZH WB IV 343.

191. Jasło (2), voivodship of Rzeszów. **Roman Juryś,** accused of providing a Jewish woman with flour, paid for this with deportation to a concentration camp. He never returned.

S. Z. p. 190.

Jaworze Dolne see **Jaworzów Dolny.**

192. Jaworzno (1), voivodship of Kraków. July 1943. **Janina Posz** was arrested and deported with her baby daughter, **Bogusia Posz,** for giving shelter to a Jewish family. She died in KL Auschwitz and her baby perished in the Potulice concentration camp for Polish children.

Testimony of W. Kolka, dated August 26, 1979 in GKBZH Arch.

193. Jaworzno (2), voivodship of Kraków. 1943. Principal of a local elementary school, **Jan Prześlak,** and his wife, **Helena Prześlak,** a teacher, were arrested by the German authorities and sent to Auschwitz for allowing a large number of Jews to hide in the spacious cellars of the school building. Together with the Jews they were trying to save, they went directly to the gas chambers.

GKBZH WB VII 252-3.

194. Jaworzno (3), voivodship of Kraków. **Wiktoria Sto-**

żek who, together with her husband, Michał Stożek, was sheltering Mrs. Laufer and her two children, was arrested and died in KL Auschwitz for harboring Jews.

Testimony of W. Kolka, dated August 26, 1979 in GKBZH Arch.

195. Jaworzno (4), voivodship of Kraków. For hiding in the attic of her house the Jewish family of Nebenschal, **Helena Posz,** the grandmother of Bogusia (mentioned above), was sent to KL Auschwitz and was killed there.

Testimony of W. Kolka, dated August 26, 1979 in GKBZH Arch.

196. Jaworzów Dolny (1), Dębica county, voivodship of Rzeszów. February 4, 1943. Germans executed four Catholic farmers: **Józef Maduzia,** 68, **Maria Kałuża,** 28, **Jan Psioda,** 71, and his wife, **Wiktoria Psioda,** 71, along with their maid. Together with the Poles, six Jews were killed. For an act of Christian charity the price was death. Their house was put on fire.

S.D. p. 92. W.-Z. p. 415 (Jaworz Dolny) GKBZH WB IV 123 (Marianna K.) 122-3, 207 (Jaworze Dolne) 336. T.Bi. p. 5 (Jaworze Dolne, Psiad).

197. Jaworzów Dolny (2), Dębica county, voivodship of Rzeszów. February 4, 1944. Another detachment of German police surrounded the house of **Józef Ryba,** 24. A Jew staying there at that time was hidden in the chimney. Ryba was tortured in order to make him show other Polish houses where Jews were hiding. When he did not do that, he was shot to death while still unconscious from the beating he received.

T.Bi. p. 5.

198. Jazowa, Strzyżów county voivodship of Rzeszów. July 3, 1943. For giving aid to Jews, the German Gestapo arrested a Catholic farmer named **Walczak.** They took him to the town of Jasło and killed him there.

S.Z p. 200.

199. Jeziorko, Łowicz county, voivodship of Warsaw. **Two Polish families** which had taken care of persecuted Jews were denounced to German authorities by a Jew apprehended by the Germans. As a result of this betrayal, **thirteen Catholics** were killed, including children.

PZPR KC CA 202 (III) 7 p. 89. W. W. p. 128.

200. Kałusz, voivodship of Lwów. Summer 1943. **Maria Jajeśnica** and her adopted son, **Jan Jajeśnica,** were hiding the family of a Jewish photographer, Jeffe, in their small brick factory. Discovered by the Germans, they were forced into a brick-kiln together with Jews and were literally baked there over a slow fire.

GKBZH WB XII 4-5.

201. Kamienica, Limanowa county, voivodship of Kraków. November 1, 1942. **Franciszek Kuziel,** with his wife, **Katarzyna Kuziel,** and their 18-year old **daughter,** gave their lives for aiding Jews. The father of the family was probably executed in Nowy Sącz. The execution of the mother and her teen-age daughter was reserved as a spectacle for people leaving church on Sunday in order to discourage anybody from helping a Jew.

W.-Z. p. 407. GKBZH WB II 65-7.

Kamień see **Pińsk.**

202. Kamieniec, Siedlce county, voivodship of Warsaw. May 18, 1944. Germans raided a village in search for Jews and partisans sheltered by its inhabitants. The entire village was burned and the following farmers executed: **Leon Gajowniczek,** 23, **Stanisław Szczepanik,** 18, **Jan Kiełbasa,** 25, **Zygmunt Radosz,** 18, **Paulina Patolęta.** Many young people were deported from the village.

F.-R. p. 478.

203. Kamionka Strumiłowa, voivodship of Tarnopol. Winter 1943/44. A Catholic bricklayer named **Przywoda** was arrested and executed. While being led to the execution place, he was made to pull a sled through the streets of the town. On the seat of the sled sat a Jewish woman who was going to be executed with her protector. All along the way, the bricklayer was ordered to shout: "I was protecting a Jewess!" in order to warn anybody from following his example.

Court deposition of J. Tenerle in W.-Z. p. 393, also 433. GKBZH WB XI 1.

204. Kamyk, voivodship of Kraków. January 29, 1944. A Catholic farmer was condemned to death for "siding with Jews and helping them". His name, **Stanisław Kluba,** was printed in the official announcement of the sentence with this remark specifying the nature of his "crime".

A facsimile of the official poster in W.-Z. p. 431, also 444. GKBZH WB II 165.

205. Karczmiska, Ryki county, voivodship of Warsaw. **Stanisława Wiśniewska** was executed together with her younger sister, **Zofia Wiśniewska,** for helping Jews. Her farm was burned to the ground.

W.-Z. p. 443. GKBZTH WB VI W.

206. Karskie, Sokołów Podlaski county, voivodship of Lublin. April 1, 1943. German military police murdered **Stanisław Tonkiel** for sheltering Jews in his house. They were killed together with him.

GKBZH WB BI T.

207. Kawęczyn, Skierniewice county, voivodship of Łódź. Spring 1944. **Jakub Fedorowicz** and **Stanisław Trojanowski,** kept on their commonly-owned farm Abraham Rosenberg and his 18-year old son, along with a tailor from Rawa Mazowiecka and his Jewish girl friend. Arrested by two Gestapo men, all six were shot in the head and their bodies left in the fields.

Court deposition of S. Kowalczyk in W.-Z. p. 381, also 435. GKBZH WB X 5-6.

208. Kępa Kolczyńska, Puławy county, voivodship of Lublin. January 5, 1942. A **Catholic mother** and her **daughter,** names unknown, were shot to death for sheltering Jews.

B.-L. p. 833.

209. Kielce (1), 1942. Another Pole, **Jan Piszczyński,** was shot while bringing food to Jews starving in their ghetto.

Account of Piszczyński's brother-in-law, Bandrowski, in E.F. p. 433-4.

210. Kielce (2), 1942. **Krystyna Mojecka,** daughter of pharmacy owner Stefan Mojecki, was shot to death by a German policeman named Rumpel, for aiding the Jews in the ghetto of Kielce.

Account of K. Misiak, a salesman in Mojecki's pharmacy, in E.F. p. 435.

211. Kielce (3), 1942. **Stanisław Janusz,** a Catholic farmer from the village of Mąchocice, who went to the Kielce ghetto with a food delivery, never came back alive.

Deposition of his son in E.F. p. 434-5.

212. Kielce (4), During the deportation of Jews, a **Catholic Pole** was shot to death at the moment when he was trying to give a glass of water to the Jewish victims locked in a railroad car.

W.-Z. p. 439. GKBZH WB I 193.

213. Kielce (5). An inhabitant of the village of Bilcza, **Franciszek Nosek,** went to a sawmill in Kielce. There he was picked by the Germans and forced to drive into the ghetto to haul some Jewish posessions confiscated by the Germans. On his way back, he was taken to the wall of a synagogue and executed there. His offence was giving a piece of bread to a Jewish inmate who was begging for food. Nosek's body was buried

somewhere in a ravine close to Silnica creek, together with five
or six similar offenders who had shown mercy to Jews.

Account of J. Szuba in E.F. p. 435-6.

214. Kielnarowa, Rzeszów county, voivodship of Rzeszów. November 15, 1942. **Stefania Kamińska** was killed for
giving aid to Jews in the Tyczyn ghetto. She was buried in a
Jewish cemetery.

V.-L. p. 840. S.D. p. 010 (Kielmanowa). GKBZH WB IV 343. W.-Z.
p. 427.

215. Kiełrzec, Węgrów county, voivodship of Warsaw.
August and September 1943. Long after the desperate break-
out from the Treblinka death camp, German authorities kept
arresting and sending to Auschwitz **Catholic farmers** suspected of helping the Jewish escapees. Many of them perished
there.

F. Z. in "Więź" no. 4, 1972, p. 124.

216. Kietlin, Radomsko county, voivodship of Łódź. November 29, 1943. Two Germans in plain clothes and Tyrolian
hats entered the farm of **Władysław Librowski,** 35, and, after
a while, led him to the backyard where he was shot through
the head. In the same way, they shot his crippled mother,
Franciszka Librowska, 60. Also, **Gerwazy Bieńkowski,** 30,
who just happened to be there, was killed. It was the punishment for keeping two Jewish families of Chęcińskis and Bu-
gajskis from Radomsko. Men, women and children were shot
with pistols. Their bodies were thrown into the heap of manure behind the barn and buried there.

Court depositon of. S. Kowalczyk in W.-Z. p. 380-9, also 427. GKBZH
WB X 41-2.

217. Klamocha (forest) near Kunów, Starachowice county, voivodship of Kielce. December 6, 1942. Under the command of Stanisław Olczyk, ps. Garbaty, a forest "bunker" was

constructed for Jewish refugees from Radom, Ostrów and Starachowice. Catholic peasants from nearby villages provided
food. At 9:00 a.m. a Polish partisan unit, assigned to the protection of the camp, discovered a strong German force surrounding the area. A decisive partisan attack succeded in breaking through and leading out most of the Jews, but **twenty
partisans** gave their lives in the course of action. Two captured Jews preferred to die rather than to betray the names of
Polish game keepers involved in building the "bunker".

Testimony of A. Kantowicz in B.-L. p. 282-3. T.S. p. 40.

218. Klementowice, voivodship of Lublin. Autumn 1943.
A Catholic farmer named **Białkowski** was murdered by the
Germans for sheltering Jews.

R.G. in "Zeszyty Majdanka" v. X, p. 101.

219. Kleszczówka, Ryki county, voivodship of Warsav.
1943. German military police and the Gestapo murdered
Aleksandra Piątek together with six Jews and two Soviet prisoners who were hiding in her house.

GKBZH Egz. K 1.

220. Klikowa, Tarnów county, voivodship of Kraków.
April 8, 1943. **Anna Niepsuj,** 45, was put to death along with
two Jews who were hiding in her house.

B.-L. p. 831, 838, 847. S.D. p. 94, 114. W.-Z. p. 419. GKBZH WB II 59.

221. Kłobuczyn, Łuck county, voivodship of Wołyń.
Germans burned alive in a barn **twenty five Christian peasants** for giving aid to Jews and sheltering them.

W.-Z. p. 448.

222. Kobryń (1), Brześć on Bug county, voivodship of
Białystok. October 15, 1942. The Assistant Pastor of the Roman Catholic parish, **Rev. Władysław Grobelny,** 29, was killed for helping Jews. They were murdered together with him.

J.-W. v. 4, p. 284.

223. Kobryń (2), Brześć on Bug county, voivodship of Białystok. October 15, 1942. In the vicinity of the parish church, Germans shot to death **Msgr. Jan Wolski,** 56, for giving aid to some Jews from the Kobryń ghetto which was being liquidated on the same day.

J.-W. v. 4, p. 281.

224. Kobylanka, Gorlice county, voivodship of Kraków. November 27, 1943. German military police discovered in the household of **Helena Dyląg** the Jewish Morgensztern family, whose members were immediately put to death. Helena was arrested with her companion, **Anna Patla,** and deported to the concentration camp of Plaszów from which neither returned.

L.D. p. 198.

225. Kobyłka, voivodship of Warsaw. September 1, 1943. **Zofia Brzozowska** was shot to death by German Gestapo for hiding two Jews somewhere in her backyard. All three bodies were buried in the garden.

W.-Z p. 425. GKBZH WB VI 226.

226. Kock, Radzyń county, voivodship of Lublin. January 1940. German guards of the local Schutzpolizei killed a **Catholic Polish woman** who opened her door to some Jews trying to evade deportation to the ghetto.

GKBZH ASG Sygn. 16, p. 700.

227. Kolbuszowa Dolna, Kolbuszowa county, voivodship of Rzeszów. Autumn 1942. For aiding Jews, **Józef Wilk** was deported to a concentration camp in Pustków and later to Oranienburg from which he never returned.

W.-Z. p. 409. GKBZH WB IV 262.

228. Koluszki, Brzeziny county, voivodship of Łódź. December 24, 1942. **Szymon Bormański** and his daughter, **Danuta Opuchlik,** were murdered in Auschwitz. For helping

Jews, they were deported there together with **Mieczysław Bormański**, Szymon's brother. Their neighbor, **Mr. Boberek**, who failed to inform the German authorities, suffered the same fate.

W.-Z. p. 411. GKBZH WB X 11 (Barwański).

229. Kołomyja, voivodship of Stanisławów. 1944. Shortly before the German-Soviet front line approached the town, the local Gestapo executed in a Jewish cemetary **Emilia Dembska** together with her **maid** for hiding under her kitchen floor two dentist brothers by the name of Gotfryd, together with their wives and four other Jews. All eight Jews were killed on the spot.

Court deposition of S. Baraniuk in W.-Z. p. 387-8. GKBZH WB XI 83-4 (Dębska).

Kołdyczów see **Mir**.

230. Komarów, Zamość county, voivodship of Lublin. The bailiff of the village, named **Szyduczyński**, was executed by the German Gestapo for issuing "Aryan" identification cards to some Jews.

Testimony of L. Mont in the Catholic weekly "WTK", June 16, 1968.

231. Kombornia, Krosno county, voivodship of Rzeszów. The entire **Balawajda family** was exterminated for sheltering one Jew in their house.

W.-Z. p. 441. GKBZH WB IV 435.

232. Kopyczyńce, voivodship of Tarnopol. **Longin Gomułkiewicz** was killed by the Germans for hiding Jews in his barn.

Court depostion of W. Szepelowski in W.-Z. p. 380, also 447. GKBZH WB X 36.

233. Korchów, Biłgoraj county, voivodship of Lublin. 1943. **Michał Staroński** and his son, **Andrzej Staroński**, were shot to death for hiding two Jews, Herszek and Moszek, last names unknown today, from Tarnogród. While the Starońskis were being arrested by the German guard (*Schupo*), the two Jews managed to escape.

W.-Z.. p. 431. GKBZH WB V 25.

234. Korniaktów (forest), Łańcut county, voivodship of Rzeszów. Winter of 1942/43. A Jewish hideout was betrayed by snow prints leading to the bunker in the forest. German police, before executing its inmates, obtained from a Jewish woman the whereabouts of **a Polish gamekeeper** who was providing food for them. The whole family of the forester was executed. The Jewish hideout was blown up with hand grenade.

T. Bi. p. 4. W.J. p. 124.

235. Koszoły, Biała Podlaska county, voivodship of Lublin. Summer 1942. **Władysław Bednarek**, 30, was shot to death by the Germans in his honse with a Jewish woman seeking refuge there.

GKBZH Egz. V K. Ds 41/703 B.

236. Kotłówka, Siedlce county, voivodship of Lublin. March 12, 1944. A Catholic farmer **Jan Celeja** perished together with **Stefan Kapczyński** for sheltering a Jewish woman Terka Holtzhandler who was killed at the same time.

GKBZH WB V 1397.

237. Kowel (1), voivodship of Wołyń. 1943. For two years a Jewish woman hid in the house of a Catholic railroad man, **Marian Grabowski**. Both were shot to death on the spot when the German military police discovered her.

W.-Z. p. 447 GKBZH WB VI 62.

238. Kowel (2), voivodship of Wołyń. Winter 1942/43. **Kazimierz Piskorek**, a train conductor, permitted Józef Szpulman to travel by rail from Kowel to Chełm, contrary to

the German law, and was shot to death on the spot.
GKBZH WB VI 619.

239. Kowel (3), voivodship of Wołyń. A Catholic railroad
conductor named **Wąsowski** of Starokolejowa Street was sheltering a Jewish barber from across the street. Discovered by
the Germans, he was executed along with his **wife**, their **daughter** and their **daughter's playmate** who just happened to be
there.
W.-Z. p. 447. GKBZH WB VI W.

240. Kozłówek, Strzyżów county, voivodship of Rzeszów. June 1943. In the village of Markuszowa the German
military police from Wiśniowa executed **Władysław Śliwa**,
a non-commissioned officer of the Polish Army, for bringing
aid to Jews hiding in the forest. With him perished **Piotr Zagórski**, 45, **Józef Fąfara** from Markuszowa, **Aleksander Pirga**
and **Stanisław Oparowski**. Their bodies were buried on the
spot and moved later to the cemetery in Dobrzechów.
W.-Z. p. 421. GKBZH WB IV 54 (Wojciech Śliwa), 52, 307, 150, 53.
C.-G. p. 203.

241. Kraków (1). Spring 1943. **Stanisław Majchrzak**,
a Polish sculptor, was arrested for sheltering a Jewess. He was
shot to death in January 1944, along with a group of hostages,
on the corner of Ogrodowa and Lubicz streets.
W.-Z. p. 419. GKBZH WB II 131. T.W. p. 309.

242. Kraków (2). November 11, 1943. For his part in providing Jews with "Aryan" identification papers, **Michał Kliś**
pseud. Wojtek, was arrested and executed. He was a member
of the "navy blue" police and, at the same time, a soldier of the
Polish Home Army.
Testimony of T. Seweryn in B.-L. p. 847. W.-Z. p. 439. GKBZH WB II
164. T. W. p. 290.

243. Kraków (3). 1943. A German soldier caught **Józef
Adamski** throwing food packages, clothing and underground

papers to Jewish inmates of a forced labor camp he was passing on his way to work. He was beaten severely and died within few weeks.

Testimony of Dr. J. Aleksandrowicz in B.-L. p. 550. W.-Z. p. 447. GKBZH WB II 208.

244. Kraków (4). January 6, 1944. **Helena Jabłkowska** who, in cooperation with her sister Janina Kowalik of Warsaw, rendered assistance to many Jews and sheltered, among others, the Bardach family. was finally arrested and shot to death by the Germans.

Testimony of "Stefan" Sendłak in B.-L. p. 173. S.D. p. 103, 113. GKBZH WB II 196.

245. Kraków (5). January 29, 1944. Among 73 persons condemned to death by authority of the Head of SS and Military Police, the official public poster listed the following Catholic residents of the city as helping Jews: **Witold Sygiericz** – a municipal employee, **Tadeusz Paziuk** – a city marshall, and **Kazimierz Rachtan** – a furrier by profession.

Facsimile of the poster in W.-Z. p. 444, also 431, 445. GKBZH WB II 1966 (Sygiewicz). T.W. p. 321.

246. Kraków (6) March 14, 1944, **Tadeusz Kallo** was condemned to death by a Special Tribunal (Sondergericht) for giving aid to Jews and providing them with false identification cards.

GKBZH WB II 195.

247. Kraków (7). **Dr. Władysław Zapałowicz** was arrested with his wife and their son, **Zbigniew Zapałowicz**, for sheltering Jews. The whole family was deported to Auschwitz. None of them returned alive.

W.-Z. p. 439. GKBZH WB II 206.

248. Kraków (8). **Ada Próchnicka**, pseud. Irena from the Council for Aid to Jews know as "Żegota", the only organization of this kind in all of Europe, saved the lives of Róża Kfara (Janina Górnicka), Helena Szumańska, Dr. Zina Paduchowa, and Helena Ehrlich, by smuggling them from Lwów to Kraków, until a Jewish lady lost her nerve during a search on the railroad. Both were arrested and executed off the railroad tracks around the Stryj area.

B.-L. p. 190, 205. A.-P. p. 112. T.P. p. 311.

249. Krasnystaw (1), voivodship of Lublin. 1941. **Leon Pałaszewski** and his wife, **Helena Pałaszewska**, were executed in the Jewish cemetary and buried there for helping Jews.

GKBZH – OKBZH in Lublin, Egz. Kr.

250. Krasnystaw (2), voivodship of Lublin. 1941. **Bronisława Marszczycka**, 30, was executed in the forest called Borek for giving aid to Jews.

GKBZH – OKBZH in Lublin, Egz. Kr.

251. Krasnystaw (3), voivodship of Lublin. 1942. **Szymon Bielicki** was shot to death for giving assistance to Jews.

GKBZH – OKBZH in Lublin, Egz. Kr.

252. Krępa, Miechów county, voivodship of Kraków. April 23, 1944. to discourage the Polish Catholic population from sheltering Jews, the German authorities decided to give a frightful lesson by executing local farmer **Józef Wydmański** and burning all his farm buildings to the ground.

B.-L. p. 849. S.D. p. 111. F.R. p. 168. W.-Z. p. 439. GKBZH WB II 65. OKBZH in Kraków, S16/71.

253. Kronosz, Chełm county, voivodship of Lublin. May 26, 1942. The German Gestapo, with the aid of regular Army units (Wehrmacht), assembled at the village forge all the inhabitants, including women and children, and demanded extradition of those guilty of sheltering Jews and Soviet prisoners of war. When nobody volunteered, indiscriminate shots were fired into the crowd, killing fifteen persons: **Władysław Bana-**

szek, 18, **Feliks Brzoza**, 3, **Józef Buraczuk**, 37, **Maria Falkus**, 34, with her two daughters, **Irena Falkus**, 5, and **Janina Falkus**, 4, **Natalia Kozłowska**, with her two sons, **Ryszard Kozłowski**, 5, and **Zdzisław Kozłowski**, 3, **Stefania Lewczuk**, 36, **Tadeusz Piotrowski**, 25, **Ryszard Świechowski**, 2, **Katarzyna Tywoniuk**, 30, with her only son, **Jan Tywoniuk**, 8, and **Włodzimierz Wróblewski**, 36. Their bodies were buried in a common grave. Twenty six households were put to the torch.

Cz. M. p. 59. OKBZH in Lublin, Ds 193/67.

254. Kruszewo, Grójec county, voivodship of Warsaw. July 13, 1943. A Catholic farmer, **Teofil Pawlak**, was killed by the Germans for helping Jews.

W.-Z. p. 432. W.W. p. 127. GKBZH WB VI 167 (Kruszew, Teodor P.).

255. Kryg. Gorlice county, voivodship of Rzeszów. April 2, 1944. For sheltering a Jew from Libusza named Hilary Morgensztern, **Zygmunt Kmiecik**, 27, and his wife, **Maria Kmiecik**, 24, were shot to death by the Gestapo in the county jail of Jasło.

W.-Z. p. 435. GKBZH WB IV 338-339, 340. T.Bi. p. 10.

256. Krynica, Nowy Sącz county, voivodship of Kraków. **Antonina Kempa** was killed for sheltering a Jewish family of five persons.

Testimony of A. Korczak in W.-Z. p. 348. GKBZH WB II 175.

257. Książniczki, Miechów county, voivodship of Kraków. June 3, 1943. During a chase organized by the Germans, three Jews sought refuge in the farm of **Stefan Kaczmarski** and **Stanisław Sojka**. One of the Jews escaped, two were killed. For lack of cooperation in apprehending the fugitives, the owners of the farm were executed.

W.-Z. p. 421. GKBZH WB I 151, 168.

258. Kurzyna, Nisko county, voivodship of Rzeszów. In the local elementary school, Germans murdered **Bronisław Fedorek** for hiding Jews from the hand of the German law.

W.-Z. p. 445. GKBZH WB IV 343.

259. Latki, Stołpce county, voivodship of Nowogródek. Elementary school principal **Bednarczyk** was executed for helping Jews.

W.-Z. p. 445.

260. Lebiedniki, Lida county, voivodship of Wilno. Autumn 1943. **Jadwiga Bikiewicz**, who managed to hide some Jews from April till Fall of 1943, was killed for that "crime".

GKBZH WB VIII 114.

Leoncin see **Tarnawce**.

261. Librantowa, Nowy Sącz county, voivodship of Kraków. **Józef Ruchała** and his wife, **Weronika Ruchała**, perished in Auschwitz for giving shelter to a Jewish refugee by the name of Grybel.

B.-L. p. 848. W.-Z. p. 441. GKBZH WB II 187-8.

262. Libusza, Gorlice county, voivodship of Rzeszów, April 21, 1944. A Polish peasant, **Adam Czajka**, 30, who together with his sister, Mrs. Kmiecik of Kryg, helped the Jewish family of Morgensztern to hide, was executed in the Jasło jail.

T.Bi. p. 5.

263. Limanowa, voivodship of Kraków. September 7, 1939. In order to suppress Christian solidarity with persecuted Jews, the Nazis decided to have a drastic demonstration of the "new order". When a Catholic mailman, **Jan Semik**, was trying to intervene with the German authorities on behalf of a group of nine Jews slated for execution without any apparent reason, the German reply was swift and efficient: Semik himself was promptly arrested and executed with the Jews in a nearby forest.

B.-L. p. 179. S.D. p. 87, 114. W.-Z. p. 405. GKBZH WB II 192.

264. Lipiny, Dębica county, voivodship of Rzeszów. March 1943. German military police shot to death a Catholic farmer, **Jan Bobrowski**, 50, for sheltering Jews. He was later buried in the parish cemetery at Pilzno. His farm was burned to the ground. Bobrowski's wife and child managed to escape death.

B.-L. p. 838. S.D. p. 94, 112. W.-Z. p. 417. GKBZH WB IV 352 (Bobowski). T.Bi. p. 4.

265. Lipków, Pruszków county, voivodship of Warsaw. Spring 1944. **Marian Drożdż** perished in a concentration camp where he was sent with **Aleksander Sotomski** for attempting to give a decent burial to a Jewess murdered by the German military police and thrown into a ditch.

GKBZH WB VI 754.

266. Lipnie. Starachowice county, voivodship of Kielce. 1942. Germans burned to the ground the household of a Catholic peasant named **Moc** for feeding Ałtek, Moszek and Adam Grosman, three Jews hiding in a forest. His own fate remains unknown. The Grosmans fled to the household of Stanisława Dziuba in the vicinity of village of St. Catherine in the Holy Cross Mountains. All of them survived and emigrated to the West after the war. Their saviors remain in extreme poverty, but were fortunate enough not to be caught by the Germans.

Testimony of S. Dziuba in E.F. p. 445-52.

267. Lipno, Dębica county, voivodship of Rzeszów. A **Catholic farmer** was killed by the Germans for sheltering Jews.

I.C. p. 281.

268. Lipowiec Duży, Biłgoraj county, voivodship of Lublin. One of the Jews sheltered by Wojciech Kusiak fell into the hands of the Germans and betrayed, under pressure, the identity of his saviors. Their farm was immediately surrounded by the military police and all ists occupants shot to death. **Katarzyna Rybak**, 60, and another unidentified **visitor** died in this holocaust together with **Mrs. Kusiak** and her **two sons**, 28 and 5 or 6 years old. Their bodies were burned with the household. The father and one of his three sons escaped certain death by accidentally being absent during the raid. They returned only to find the charred remains of their beloved in the ashes.

Testimony of R.W. in B.-L. p. 867. W.-Z. p. 439. GKBZH WB V 146-8.

269. Lipownica, Przemyśl county, voivodship of Rzeszów. A Catholic gamekeeper, **Stanisław Kurpiel**, was shot to death by the Gestapo for sheltering twenty-four Jews. Only one Jew managed to escape.

B.-L. p. 843. S.D. p. 111, 113. W.-Z. p. 439. GKBZH WB IV 153-4.

270. Liszno, Przemyśl county, voivodship of Lublin. May 18, 1942. Under suspicion of "aiding Jews and partisans" the German Gestapo and SS murdered **sixty villagers**; among others, **Jan Błaszczyk**, 34, **Michał Błaszczyk**, 39, **Jan Garbula**, 39, **Józef Głogosz**, 21, **Stanisław Iwaniuk**, 19, **Stefan Jaroć**, 43, **Jan Kasjan**, 36, **Mieczysław Klin**, 31, **Edward Kosmowski**, 13, **Adam Łopaciak**, 30, **Adam Łusiak**, 33, **Aleksander Łusiak**, 21, **Władysław Parada**, 43, **Edward Serej**, 26, **Leon Serej**, 29, and **Jan Szachadyn**, 30. The names of the rest remain unknown. Their burial in a Catholic cemetery was forbidden.

Cz.M. p. 82. F.R. p. 57. OKBZH in Lublin, Quest. of 1968.

271. Lublin (1). April 30, 1941. The Vicar General of the Lublin diocese, **Msgr. Zygmunt Surdacki**, 36, after both its Bishops, Marian Fulman and Goral, were taken to their death in concentration camps, was deported to Auschwitz for aiding Jews. According to a notice sent to the Chancery by German authorities, he died there.

Testimony of Bishop Karol Niemira in B.-L. p. 241. S.D. p. 104, 117. J.-W. v. 3, p. 276.

272. Lublin (2). November 23, 1943. **Roman Włodarczyk** was condemned to death by the German *Sondergericht* (Special Court) according to the official poster in which, among 26 Catholic Poles, his name was listed with a specific "crime" of "giving aid and shelter to Jews".

Facsimile of the poster in W.-Z. p. 434, also 427. GKBZH WB V 427.

273. Lubomierz (1). Limanowa county, voivodship of Kraków. Spring 1943. **Stanisław Kowalczyk** was tortured to death by the German military police from Mszana for sheltering a Jew.

W.-Z. p. 419. GKBZH WB II 132 (Spring 1942).

274. Lubomierz (2). Limanowa county, voivodship of Kraków. A Volsdeutsch renegade, Władysław Gelb, tortured to death **Stanisław Adamczyk** in the Mszana Dolna jail for providing food to starving Jews, an offense punishable by death according to the decree of Governor Hans Frank, dated October 15, 1941.

B.-L. p. 848. S.D. p. 111. W.-Z. p. 441. GKBZH WB II 145 (Łącko).

275. Luszowice, Dabrowa Tarnowska county, voivodship of Kraków. During a raid on the rectory of the local Roman Catholic parish, Germans killed **two parish employees** while the Jew who had been sheltered by them escaped with the aid of some „navy blue" policemen.

Testimony of J. Kozaczka in W.-Z. p. 345.

Lutków see **Lutkówka**.

276. Lutkówka, Grodzisk Mazowiecki county, voivodship of Warsaw. March 1944. **Stanisław Siniarski**, 45, his wife, **Marianna Siniarska**, 43, and their three children: **Edward Siniarski**, 8, **Janina Siniarska**, 9, and **Marian Józef Siniarski**, 16, were shot to death along with two Jews sheltered by them. All were buried in the backyard of their farmhouse.

B.-L. p. 341-2. S.D. p. 106, 114. (Lutków) W.-Z. p. 435. GKBZH WB VI 1315-9 (3 Jews).

277. Lutowiska, Krosno county, voivodship of Kraków. **Eugeniusz Łukacz**, a Catholic pharmacist, and his wife, **Janina Łukacz**, were arrested for sheltering and feeding the Jewish families of Rotenman, Landau and Fisz. Eugeniusz was killed in Auschwitz and Janina died in the Tarnów jail.

W.-Z. p. 445. GKBZH WB VIII 29-30.

278. Lwów (1). February 21, 1942. Near the Rucker factory in Zamarstynów area **two Catholic priests** were shot to death by the Germans for attempting to bring two Jewish families into the safety of their monastery. Their bodies were buried in a cemetery at Hołosk. The Germans announced that as a punishment for helping Jews in the future, they would burn down the churches of the priests involved. The funeral rites were attended by throngs of Catholic Poles and Ukrainians.

J.W. p. 59.

279. Lwów (2). February 28, 1942. Germans shot to death a disguised **Catholic monk** for bringing food and money to the Jewish quarter. He was shot with an automatic weapon while running and the German police refused to surrender his body for a Catholic burial. They ordered Jews to bury it inside their ghetto.

J.W. p. 59.

280. Lwów (3). February 20, 1943. **Kazimierz Kolbuszewski**, a professor of literature at the University of Lwów, died in the Majdanek concentration camp, to which he was deported for giving shelter to one of his Jewish students.

B.-L. p. 67, 112. S.D. p. 93, 113. W.-Z. p. 415. I.O. p. 375. GKBZH WB V 146.

281. Lwów (4). December 14, 1943. Among the fifty-five Polish victims, executed by the order of the Commandant of the SS and Police District of Galicia dated of Dec. 14, 1943, eight Catholics were accused of helping Jews, seven of them from the city of Lwów: **Julia Irzek, Bronisława Józefek, Maria Józefek, Maria Kruszkowska, Natalia Susz, Michał Piastun, Wiktoria Malawska** born Wilczyńska, and **Halina Śladowska** born Krzymieniewska.

Facsimile of the poster in W.-Z. p. 438 (Josefek, Nastia Susch, obviously an Ukranian Catholic) also 439. B.-L. p. 973. Ph.F. p. 184. GKBZH WB IV 325, 338, 341, 345-6, 319, V 319.

282. Lwów (5). 1943. **Mrs. Biesiecka** was hung by the Germans for taking care of Jewish children.

Testimony of Zofia Tyszka in B.-L. p. 205.

283. Lwów (6). 1944. Among the eighty-four Poles executed by the order of the Commandant of the SS and the Police District of Galicia dated Jan. 28, 1944, four Catholics were accused of helping Jews, one of them Ukrainian: **Kazimierz Józefek, Anna Kufta, Bronisław Miga** and **Opanas Jewtusik**.

Facsimile of the poster in W.-Z. p. 442, also 1431. B.-R. p. 44. GKBZH WB IV 325, 338, 341, 347.

284. Lwów (7). **Stanisław Radomski**, 49, an electrician, was executed in the Brygidki prison for sheltering a Jewish woman.

B.-L. p. 845. S.D. p. 105, 114. W.-Z. p. 433.

285. Lwów (8). **Prof. Tadeusz Zadarecki**, a Catholic scholar who studied Judaism, spoke Hebrew and was familiar with the Jewish community which in Lwów amounted to 100,000, frequently slipped into the German-made ghetto and took notes containing details like dates, names and locations connected with the extermination of Jews, to be used later in the prosecution of German criminals. He perished on one of his trips, but the Polish underground saved his manuscript as a monument to this period of Polish-Jewish relations.

S.W. p. 275.

286. Lwów (9). **Stanisław Kaliniec**, a Catholic, was executed by the Germans for giving assistance to the persecuted Jews.

W.-Z. p. 447.

287. Lwów (10). The numerous Jewish population of the city, increased even more by the influx of thousands of refugees from other parts of Poland, while threatened with extermination by the advancing German forces, sought protection of their Catholic, Polish and Ukrainian neighbors. As a consequence of massive help given to the Jews, over **one thousand Catholics** were arrested and deported to the death camp of KL Bełżec as the only non-Jewish group there.

Testimony of P. Lisiewicz in B.-L. p. 204. I.O. p. 275. GKBZH IV 454.

288. Lwów (11). **Mrs. Zielińska** was arrested for giving shelter to a brother of her closest Jewish friend, Anna Feit. She perished in KL Majdanek for that.

GKBZH WB VIII 37.

289. Lwów (12). "A large number of Jews hid among the Poles and Ukrainians. No matter how the Germans endeavored to corrupt the hearts of people with the threat of death, actual executions, treachery and greed, there were nevertheless courageous and honest people capable of heroism. Educated Polish people saved many Jewish children from death, although for the most part they could take only girls for obvious reasons. Many Polish priests took in Jewish girls, hid them in the churches, and saved them from the death. **More than one**

of these noble people paid with their own lives for saving Jewish children."

Testimony of L. Hartz and N. Nacht in E.-G. p. 120.

290. Lwów (13). Two Jewish girls escaped from the ghetto. One of them by the name of Lily, suddenly remembered a **Catholic woman** she used to know. "Surely, she will help us", she said. After they knocked at her window, they were permitted to enter, served with a cup of coffee and hidden in a shed. Suddenly, some Germans came riding up on motorcycles. By accident only one girl was discovered. Her Catholic host did not escape the usual punishment by death.

E. G. p. 130.

291. Łagów, Zwoleń county, voivodship of Kielce. **Ignacy Dziurski** was arrested for bringing food to Jews and sheltering them in his house. He died in jail.

GKBZH WB I 48.

292. Łańcut, voivodship of Rzeszów. **Aniela Kozioł** was murdered by the Germans for giving shelter to the Wolkenfeld family of three persons. They met their death together with her.

GKBZH WB IV 88.

293. Łaskarzew, Siedlce county, voivodship of Lublin. December 22, 1943. **Stanisław Murawski** was shot to death by the Germans for sheltering ten Jews who, however, managed to escape.

GKBZH WB VI 1396.

294. Łąkoć, Puławy county, voivodship of Lublin. November 3, 1942. A team of Gestapo executioners was attacked on their way to the ghetto of Puławy. In order to discourage the Polish villagers from interfering with the extermination of Jews, the Germans forced all male inhabitants to assemble in the middle of the village which was surrounded by the troops. Ten of them selected for the execution were compelled to lie face down on the ground. Each of them separately was then shot though the back of his head. Thus perished: **Tadeusz Grzęda**, 33, **Edward Struski**, 22, **Julian Struski**, 32, **Jan Maruska**, 45, **Marian Mańka**, 9, **Eugeniusz Dąbrowski**, 28, **Mikołaj Dąbrowski**, 62 and **Władysław Bogusz** from Markuszów. They were joined by **Leokadia Kozioł** who was brought from the village Wielkie of Lubartów county to be executed together with the other offenders. One of selected men, Czesław Sturski survived with a wound in his head. In June, Germans came back in order to burn down the indomitable village and again, shot to death two persons during their flight from the burning houses.

Testimony of A. Struski in Z.M. p. 254.

295. Łęka Szczucińska, Dąbrowa Tarnowska county, voivodship of Kraków. **Wojciech Cieślak** was shot to death for hiding a Jewess from Pacanów in his house.

W.-Z. p. 343.

296. Łosice, Biała Podlaska county, voivdoship of Lublin. February 16 or 20, 1943. **Zbigniew Ilczuk** from the village of Czerpigórz was shot to death by the German military police for helping Jews.

GKBZH ASG Sygn. 17, p. 1013.

297. Łososin, Grodno county, voivodship of Wilno. **Mikołaj Umiński** smuggled out of Grodno ghetto his Jewish wife, Nina Buczyńska, his daughter, Anna, and his sister-in-law. While bringing food to their improvised hideout, he was severely wounded and jailed by the Germans. His family was killed together with other Jews. He never came out of jail alive.

Testimony of Jerzy Wiech in the Bulletin of Jewish Historical Institute, no. 71-2/1969/p. 23.

298. Łuck, voivodship of Wołyń. For sheltering a Jewish brewery owner named Sznajder, Germans executed **Mrs. Bobel** and her **mother**. Mr. Bobel managed to escape.

GKBZH WB IX 13-4.

299. Łukowica, Limanowa county, voivodship of Kraków. A housekeeper at the local parish, **Julia Żurawska**, was murdered for providing shelter to Jews. **Jan Wiśniewski**, a parish farm-hand implicated in this activity, gave his life with her.

GKBZH WB II 69, 80 (Łukowiecko).

300. Łuniniec, Pińsk county, voivodship of Polesie. July 4, 1944. the Dean and Pastor of the local Roman Catholic parish, **Rev. Fabian Poczobutt-Odlanicki**, 47, was killed in the village of Koźlakowice for organizing aid to Jews and partisans. His body was buried behind the cemetery chapel in Pińsk.

J.-W. v. 4, p. 258.

301. Łużna, Gorlice county, voivodship of Rzeszów. September 30, 1943. **Stanisław Radzik** and his wife, **Maria Radzik**, gave refuge in their household to Salomea, Rozalia and Anna Wynischer. Along with these three Jewish women, they also sheltered Jakub Hofman. Discovered by the German military police, Anna Wynischer was executed together with Stanislaw, in the Jewish cemetery. For refusal to disclose the whereabouts of other Jews, Maria was beaten so mercilessly that she died on January 26, 1944. Salomea and Rozalia Wynischer survived to the end of the war. The whereabouts of the whole group was given to Germans by Hofman.

W.-Z. p. 417. J.D. p. 115 (Wynishner). GKBZH WB IV 303. T.Bi. p. 6 (Wymisner, Hoffman).

302. Maciuńce, Lida county, voivodship of Nowogródek. **Józef Borowski**, along with his **family of eight** and **four vi-**

sitors, were shot to death for sheltering a group of Jews who
were killed together with them. All the farm buildings were
burned down.

W.-Z. p. 447. GKBZH WB VII 114.

303. Majdanek (1). Lublin county, voivodship of Lublin.
1943. A Polish Catholic lady, married to a Jew by the name of
Garfinkel, but using the name of **Garski** to conceal their Jewish identity from the Germans, voluntarily went to death
with her **two daughters** after the Germans discovered her
husband was a Jew.

A.S. p. 124.

304. Majdanek (2). Lublin county, voivodship of Lublin.
The Jewish chronicler and historian, Emanuel Ringelblum, in
his "Polish-Jewish Relations" related the story of an **entire
Polish family** condemned to Majdanek death camp for sheltering a Jewish surgeon.

W.-Z. p. 439.

Makoszka see **Ochoże**.

305. Maliszewo, Węgrów county, voivodship of Warsaw.
August 1943. For aiding Jews escaped from the Treblinka death camp **many villagers** were mistreated, arrested or murdered outright.

F.Z. in "Więź", 1972/4 p. 124.

306. Małec, Dąbrowa Tarnowska county, voivodship of
Kraków. Winter 1943/44. In retaliation for an unsuccessful
raid on Jewish refugees who were warned in advance by the
Polish Home Army and were able to escape on time, Germans
deported to Auschwitz **thirty-six persons** from the neighbo-
'ring villages of Dulcza Mała, Małec, etc. Only eight of them
returned alive.

Testimony of B. Bartyzel in W.-Z. p. 341.

307. Maniewicze, Kowel county, voivodship of Wołyń. November 2, 1942. As a reprisal for sheltering hundreds of Jewish refugees from local ghettos and execution sites, Germans murdered **one thousand twenty four Catholic farmers** from neighboring villages of Trojanówka, Poworsk, Mielnica and others.

Testimony of "Maks" Sobiesiak in W.-Z. p. 263.

308. Markowa, Łańcut county, voivodship of Rzeszów. March 24. 1943. A Catholic farmer, **Józef Ulma**, kept Jewish refugees in his household. Surprised by three carloads of German military police and cornered in the attic, all the Jews were shot to death there. Then, in reprisal, Ulma's **six children**: **Antoni Ulma, Barbara Ulma, Franciszek Ulma, Marian Ulma, Stanisław Ulma** and **Władysław Ulma**, aged from 1 to 8, were put to death. Their father and his pregnant wife, **Mrs. Ulma**, had to watch their children being killed one by one. Both parents were murdered last. All the Christians and Jews were buried in one common grave dug in the backyard. The youngest, a one-year old baby was smashed against a tree.

W.-Z. p. 429. J.S. p. 142. S.Z. p. 191-2. (Wiktoria Ulma) GKBZH WB IV 121. T.Bi. p. 7-8.

309. Markuszowa (1), Strzyżów county, voivodship of Rzeszów. June 1943. For bringing aid to Jews hidden in a forest, the German military police shot to death **Feliks Ciołkosz**, 58, his wife, **Mrs. Ciołkosz**, 50, and their son, **Jan Ciołkosz**, 6, together with other **two farmers** from Kozłówek.

B.-L. p. 839. S.D. p. 98, 112. W.-Z. p. 421. GKBZH WB IV 866.

310. Markuszowa (2), Strzyżów county, voivodship of Rzeszów. June 1943. **Wojciech Śliwa** was shot to death by the German military police from Wiśniowa for giving aid to Jews hiding in a forest shelter.

GKBZH WB IV 866. GKBZH/B v. X, p. 157.

311. Markuszowa (3), Strzyżów county, voivodship of Rzeszów. A **Catholic peasant** who was sheltering three Jewish families in his household, was sent to Szebnie, then to Plaszów, and finally, to Sachsenhausen concentration camp, from which he did not come out alive.

S.Z. p. 190.

Markuszowa see also **Kozłówek**.

Matysówka see **Tyczyn**.

312. Mauthausen (concentration camp) branch of Linz III. November 13, 1944. As a result of severe beating for sharing food with a Jewish inmate, **Czesław Luć**, 35, prisoner no. 92387, died as a victim of Christian charity.

W.-Z. p. 437. GKBZH WB II 444.

313. Medynia Kańczudzka, Przeworsk county, voivodship of Rzeszów. **Franciszek Lichtarski** was shot to death by the Germans for sheltering a Jew.

W.-Z. p. 439. GKBZH WB IV 345.

314. Mętów, Lublin county, voivodship of Lublin. November 1943. German military police from Lublin executed **Jan Joć**, 61, and his wife, **Jadwiga Joć**, for bringing food to Jews hidden in a nearby forest. The Germans killed twenty Jews there.

B.-L. p. 833, 841. S.D. p. 102, 113. W.-Z. p. 429. GKBZH WB V 124-5. GKBZH Egz. V M. (June 11, 1943).

315. Michniów, Kielce county, voivodship of Kielce. July 12-13 and August 17, 1943. The last bloody German reprisal, far surpassing Lidice and Oradeur-sur-Glane, didn't miss an element of punishment for those aiding Jews. One of the few survivors, Zofia Materek, mentioned her husband violently hushing her up at the mention of a strong Jewish partisan unit which was receiving aid from the villagers. A two-stage reprisal wiped the village out of existence. Nobody suspected anything when, after the Sunday Mass, a group of German officers came for a quiet visit, making notes and examining the whole lay-out of the village very closely. During the night, a strong German military force of various formations tightened a double ring around the village. Forest workers attempting to go to work in the morning were turned back by the police lying in ambush around the village. They were forced to lie down in roadside ditches. When the farmers started to get busy around their farms, the action began.

The first to die were the **brothers Gołębiowski** after they were driven out of their houses. Some minutes later, on the road leading to the school, seventeen men driven from their farms were likewise shot. Others, beaten and mistreated, were put on the waiting trucks and driven towards barns chosen the preceeding day. When the men driven to Gil's farm started to resist, they were pushed inside and a few hand grenades were tossed in. Other barns were quickly filled, doused with gasoline and turned instantly into gigantic torches, burning the people alive. The men who had been stopped on the fringe of the forest were brought from the ditches. They, too, had to die in the blaze.

While one German unit was murdering unarmed men, another was sent to the huosehold of the game keeper, Wikło, to bring to Materek's farm five of his children, shoot them, one by one, in front of their mother and toss their bodies into the flames.

At midday on July 12th, 1943, in the smoldering ruins of houses and barns lay the bodies of **103 persons,** mostly burned alive: **Szczepan Arendarski**, 30, **Józef Biela**, 31, **Jan Biskup**, 24, **Antoni Ciszek**, 55, **Julian Ciszek**, 18, **Piotr Dąbrowa**, 26, **Jerzy Duda**, 16, **Marian Duda**, 21, **Władysław Duda**, 31, **Jan Dulęba**, 37, **Stanisław Dulęba**, 20, **Bronisław Dupak**, 32, **Stanisław Gil**, 19, **Antoni Gołębiowski**, 38, **Jan Gołębiowski**, 40, **Roman Gołębiowski**, 17, **Gustaw Grabiński**, 19, **Walenty**

Gruba, 39, Jan Haba, 49, Franciszek Harabin, 30, Zygmunt Imiołek, 21, Franciszek Kaczmarek, 42, Eugeniusz Krogulec, 33, Julian Krogulec, 16, Julian Krogulec, 24, Stefan Krogulec, 20, Walerian Krogulec, 20, Stefan Krogulec, 19, Jan Kwaśniewski, 55, Władysław Lorenc, 21, Feliks Magdziarz, 17, Wacław Magdziarz, 38, Eugeniusz Malinowski, 21, Roman Malinowski, 57, Władysław Malinowski, 29, Dionizy Materek, 16, Florentyna Materek, 65, Henryk Materek, 32, Jadwiga Materek, 48, Jan Materek, 35, Józef Materek, 25, Kazimierz Materek, 37, Marian Materek, 20, Michał Materek, 31, Wacław Materek, 35, Wincenty Materek, 25, Witold Materek, 22, Witold Materek, 18, Władysław Materek, 59, Władysław Materek, 19, Zygmunt Materek, 20, Andrzej Matla, 49, Stanisław Michta, 31, Andrzej Miernik, 45, Eugeniusz Miernik, 19, Henryk Miernik, 24, Ignacy Miernik, 19, Julian Miernik, 55, Stanisław Miernik, 58, Stanisław Miernik, 16, Stefan Miernik, 23, Władysław Miernik, 23, Władysław Miernik, 38, Ryszard Morawski, 17, Antoni Obara, 35, Bronisław Obara, 40, Franciszek Obara, 63, Franciszek Obara, Jr., 39, Józef Obara, 37, Julian Obara, 18, Władysław Obara, 32, Józef Pająk, 38, Marian Rynkowski, 29, Stanisław Rynkowski, 55, Zdzisław Rynkowski, 17, Stanisław Salwa, 31, Witold Szampruch, 17, Marian Wąsik, 26, Jan Wątrobiński, 30, Henryk Więckowski, 20, Stanisław Więckowski, 23, Adolf Wikło, 24, Edmund Wikło, 18, Feliks Wikło, 19, Halina Wikło, 11, Ignacy Wikło, 40, Józef Wikło, 5, Julian Wikło, 22, Maria Wikło, 8, Michał Wikło, 59, Roman Wikło, 16, Stanisław Wikło, 30, Stanisława Wikło, 44, Stefan Wikło, 23, Witold Wikło, 24, Władysław Wikło, 48, Władysław Wikło, 33, Zdzisław Wikło, 16, Zofia Wikło, 14, Kazimimerz Zieliński, 31, and Tomasz Ziomek, 32.

On the morning of July 13th, 1943, a convoy of trucks appeared on the road from Kielce. Suspecting an oncoming raid, Michniow's remaining inhabitants began fleeing to the woods.

Just over one hundred people, mostly women and children, remained in the village. After entering the village, Germans continued their horrible work of extermination.

It was not a simple hunters' expedition: it was a thorough work of extermination. They shot everybody in sight – on streets, in backyards, in homes. To accomplish a wholesale effect, the groups of people were driven inside of houses and a torch was put to those wooden structures, burning everybody inside.

Only a dozen of people succeeded in escaping the holocaust, under exceptional cricumstances. Thus, for instance, sixteen citizens, who were guarding the plundered stock on the fringe of the forest, took advantage of a better chance to escape, although preparations were already made for their execution.

On the second day of the reprisal one hundred people died, among them 42 children between 9 days and 15 years of age. The youngest victim of the Michniów holocaust, the nine-day old **Stefan Dąbrowa**, had just been baptized in the church.

He was killed by a man whose tunic belt was marked with the words *"Gott mit uns"* – God with us – a Germanic god, a tribal deity of another "chosen nation", seeking their "promised land" in the East by exterminating its Slavic occupants like vermin.

Similar cases occurred on the previous Saturday in the neighboring village of Wzdoł when a German soldier yanked an 18-month old baby from its mother's arms and shot a bullet through its little body before killing its mother.

The bloody harvest took lives of: **Bogdan Biela**, 4, **Janina Biela**, 27, **Julian Biela**, 27, **Józefa Ciszek**, 45, **Elżbieta Dąbrowa**, 2, **Helena Dąbrowa**, 22, **Józef Duda**, 60, **Stanisław Duda**, 49, **Adam Duda**, 68, **Helena Dulęba**, 35, **Kazimierz Dulęba**, 7, **Wacław Dulęba**, 11, **Janina Dupak**, 13, **Maria Dupak**, 7, **Piotr Dupak**, 52, **Rozalia Dupak**, 50,

Stanisława Dupak, 21, Zofia Dupak, 16, Janina Dzierżyło, 16, Józefa Gołębiowska, 70, Felicja Grabińska, 43, Barbara Gruba, 7, Halina Gruba, 12, Witold Gruba, 16, Anna Haba, 48, Józef Haba, 14, Maria Haba, 19, Zofia Haba, 13, Katarzyna Harabin, 55, Antonina Imiołek, 48, Ignacy Imiołek, 46, Maria Imiołek, 19, Janina Kołomańska, Anna Krogulec, 5, Florentyna Krogulec, 49, Maria Krogulec, 25, Emilia Marcinkowska, 38, Andrzej Materek, 32, Karolina Materek, 56, Maria Materek, 60, Maria Materek, 20, Maria Materek, 10, Marian Materek, 10, Stefan Materek, 8, Stefania Materek, 60, Stefania Materek, 31, Tadeusz Materek, 2, Teresa Materek, 7, Witold Materek, 7, Witold Materek, 2, Władysław Materek, 13, Zofia Materek, 43. Franciszek Miazga, 49, Anna Miążek, 43, Halina Michta, 14, Jan Michta, 4, Rozalia Michta, 34, Antonina Miernik, 42, Janina Miernik, 10, Maria Miernik, 60, Maria Miernik, 38, Rozalia Miernik, 17, Zofia Miernik, 10, Florentyna Morawska, 65, Alfred Morawski, 10, Apolonia Obara, 13, Dionizy Obara, 16, Jan Obara, 7, Janina Obara, 7, Kazimierz Obara, 19, Lech Obara, 12, Maria Obara, 29, Marian Obara, 15, Stefania Obara, 35, Sylwester Obara, nine months, Zofia Obara, 32, Irena Majak, 28, Genowefa Przeworska, 24, Józefa Przeworska, 7, Wanda Przeworska, 7, Alojzy Przeworski, 10, Janusz Przeworski, six months, Marian Przeworski, 5, Wiesław Przeworski, 5, Władysław Przeworski, 32, Józefa Sanecka, 40, Katarzyna Wąsik, 24, Apolonia Więckowska, 72, Jadwiga Więckowska, 72, Kazimiera Więckowska, Antonina Wikło, 61, Stanisława Wikło, 30, and Zenon Wikło, 4.

Altogether, 250 farm buildings were burned to the ground, with all the human inhabitants consumed by fire. Only the livestock was spared. A special order of the German authorities, issued immediately after the reprisals, strictly forbade the reconstruction of the village and any assistance to the survivors of Michniów.

As late as Autumn 1943, several people who were picking

potatoes there were killed. The same happened to a girl who took a cow to pasture in this area.

Hundreds of Polish villages met a similar fate, especially in the area of Kielce and Zamość which were to be cleared for prospective Germanic (not only German!, but also of Danish, Dutch and Norwegian descent). How many victims of these events were additionally charged with aid to Jews, nobody knows.

Out of a handful of Michniów inhabitants who managed to get away alive, nine were caught and dispatched to Auschwitz. **Piotr Charasymowicz**, 7, **Władysława Daniłowska**, 40 – a teacher, **Feliks Daniłowski**, 50 – also a teacher, **Antoni Materek**, 49, **Jan Roman Materek**, 51, **Teofil Materek**, 34, never returned. Only three survived to tell their gruesome story unknown to the young German generation and unrepented.

F.-R. p. 136-9. L.K. p. 175-80.

316. Miechów (1), voivodship of Kraków. February to April 1943. German *Jagdkommando* (formation calling itself a "hunting party"), disguised as Polish peasants, killed 176 Polish peasants, among them **three Catholic families** "guilty" of helping Jews.

Testimony of Z. Bieszczanin in. W.-Z. p. 274.

317. Miechów (2), voivodship of Kraków. A court clerk, **Bronisław Falencki**, was a member of the Polish Home Army charged with the distribution among persecuted Jews of fake identification cards produced by Marian Urbański on the basis of false baptismal certificates furnished by the local organist, **Franciszek Grzebieluch**. When the applicants for these "Aryan" papers looked too "Jewish" to risk a public appearance, he directed them to selected peasant families, among others to the Catholic Baranek family in Siedliska (see case no. 452). One of his Jewish clients, Maria Bochnar, who was arrested in Przemyśl on March 12, 1943, and questioned about the source of her false documents, pointed out Falencki. He was promptly arrested and sent to Auschwitz. There his genitals were crushed with pliers in order to extract from him the names of his accomplices. He was killed when the desired information couldn't be extorted from him even in this cruel way.

Testimony of Zofia Olas in W.S. p. 222.

318. Miechów (3), voivodship of Kraków. **Two Catholic Poles**, father and son, were executed by the Germans for aiding Jews.

Cz.M. v. 2, p. 330.

319. Milanówek, Pruszków county, voivodship of Warsaw. May 17, 1943. German military police, with the aid of an informer, apprehended and shot to death **Hanna Brühl** along with four Jews sheltered by her. All five were buried at the place of execution.

B.-L. 835. S.D. p. 97, 112. W.-Z. p. 419. GKBZH WB VI 1311.

320. Mińsk Mazowiecki (1), voivodship of Warsaw. May 17, 1943. Germans killed **seven Polish Catholics** for giving shelter to Jews.

W.W. p. 128. PZPR KC CA 202/III/7 p. 78.

321. Mińsk Mazowiecki (2), voivodship of Warsaw. May 1944. **Marian Woźniak** was executed for giving shelter to Jews and otherwise helping them.

GKBZH WB VI 897.

322. Mir (1), Stołpce county, voivodship of Nowogródek. November 14, 1942. **Rev. Antoni Mackiewicz**, pastor of the local parish, was executed in Kołdyczów, together with other Poles, for helping Jews.

W.-Z. p. 445. GKBZH WB IX 41.

. 323. Mir (2), Stołpce county, voivodship of Nowogródek. A Catholic gardener on a nearby estate by the name of **En-**

glert was punished with death by the Germans for giving shelter to Jews.

W.-Z. p. 445. GKBZH WB IX 40.

324. Mierzańce, Lida county, voivodship of Nowo-gródek. March 1942. **Leokadia Daglis**, a Lithuanian Catholic, was shot to death by the Germans for sheltering a Jewish child. The execution took place under the command of an officer Kleitner.

W.-Z. p. 405. GKBZH WB IX 20 (Ejszyszki, Daglys).

325. Mława, voivodship of Warsaw. April 1942. For the purpose of racial education, the entire population of the town was summoned by the German Gestapo to witness an execution of fifty Jews. The moral indignation of the crowd was expressed by **one of the witnesses** who shouted: "Innocent blood is being spilled". For this he was seized by the Germans and shot before the crowd.

W.-Z. p. 405.

326. Mociesze, Brasław county, voivodship of Wilno. An unidentified **Polish family of twelve persons** was burned alive by the Germans who found out they were sheltering Jews. The Jews shared the fate of the entire family.

W.-Z. p. 405.

327. Modryń, Hrubieszów county, voivodship of Lublin. December 1942. **Rozalia Baran** was cruelly beaten and later executed for giving her identity card to a Jewish lady who thus was able to leave for Germany. There she was recognized and her identity card traced back to Rozalia.

W.-Z. p. 270, 411. GKBZH WB V 139.

328. Mokre (1), Biała Podlaska county, voivodshiop of Lublin. July 1943. Germans murdered the entire **Makarewicz family**, including two children and **several other persons**, altogether eleven, accused of helping Jews.

GKBZH – OKBZH in Lublin, Ank. M.

329. Mokre (2), Biała Podlaska county, voivodship of Lublin. August 1943. German military police from Wiszniewice shot to death **Władysław Szuk** and his mother-in-law, **Marianna Dżyg**, 65, for giving aid to Jews. The ececution took place in front of their house.

GKBZH – OKBZH in Lublin, Ank. M.

330. Mołczadź, Słonim county, voivodship of Polesie. Winter 1942/43. **Halina Sienkiewicz**, 20, was arrested and executed by the Germans because her family served food to twenty Jewish partisans. Their farm was burned to the ground. The rest of the family, however, was able to escape.

GKBZH WB VI 222 (Mołczady).

331. Motycz – Józefin (1), voivodship of Lublin. March 15, 1942. German military police executed **Agnieszka Paprotna**, 60, and **Bronisława Paprotna**, along with her three chldren: **Maria Paprotna**, 3. **Stanisław Paprotny**, 2, and **Zofia Paprotna**, 6, as punishment for giving aid to Jews.

GKBZH, Egz. V, p. 22/71/Lp.

332. Motycz – Józefin (2), voivodship of Lublin. February 12, 1944. **Tadeusz Bukowski**, 21, was murdered by the German military police for giving shelter to a Jewish lady, Mrs. Maziarczyk. She was killed at the same time.

GKBZH, Egz. V M.-J.

333. Mszana Stara, Kozienice county, voivodship of Kielce. Winter 1943. German military police from Zwoleń arrested and shot to death **Stanisław Pawelec** and his son-in-law, **Bronisław Błazik**, both accused of hiding a Jewish refugee named Glassman who was caught by the Germans and forced to show his hiding place.

W.-Z. p. 41. GKBZH WB I 16, 188.

334. Mszanka, Włodawa county, voivodship of Lublin. June 29, 1943. During a series of raids on villages where persecuted Jews were being sheltered, German military police arrested and executed a Catholic farmer, **Józef Wójtowicz**.

J.D. p. 198.

335. Mykanów, Częstochowa county, voivodship of Katowice. October 16, 1944. German military police from Chorzenice shot to death a **Catholic Pole** along with three Jews he was sheltering.

B.-L. p. 832.

336. Mystków, Nowy Sącz county, voivodship of Kraków. Two brothers, Chaim and Szmul Neigreschel, were caught by the Germans and betrayed their hiding places. As a result, **Ludwik Borek**, as well as **another man** from Ptaszków, lost his life.

W.-Z. p. 349.

337. Nadole (1), Krosno county, voivodship of Rzeszów. 1943. In the yard of Dukla prison the Germans executed **Bronisława Krzywda**, together with six Jews, for sheltering a Jew in her house. The local trash collector, Jan Frysik, when ordered to load all seven bodies together with refuse, broke down and was beaten severely. Two bystanders were forced to perform this gruesome task.

Testimony of J. Frysik in GKBZH Ds 61/68. GKBZH WB I B 10.

338. Nadole (2), Krosno county, voivodship of Rzeszów. 1944. **Katarzyna Zajdel** was shot to death in the yard of Dukla prison for hiding a Jew in her house, who was killed while trying to escape.

T.K. p. 102. C.-G. p. 89.

Naliboki see **Pińsk**.

339. Natalin, voivodship of Lublin. August 1943. Two Jewish brothers, one bearing the name of Janiszewski, the other known only by his first Jewish name, Herszek, were sheltered successively by various families of the village. The last of Herszek's host was **Stanisław Kosior** who was shot to death by the German policeman König from Jastków immediately after Herszek was discovered and murdered behind the barn. Kosior was killed in a forest and buried there. After the war his remains were transferred to the cemetery.

Court deposition of J. Szymański in W.-Z. p. 378, also 423. GKBZH WB I 33, 38.

340. Niepla, Jasło county, voivodship of Rzeszów. For hiding the Jewish Szlem family from Przykówka, which included four children, **Michał Owczarski** was killed by the Germans.

GKBZH WB IV 122.

341. Norta, Miechów county, voivodship of Kraków. **Jan Gądek** and his pregnant wife **Władysława Gądek**, were killed by the Germans for sheltering the Jewish Wandelsman family.

GKBZH WB II 105-6.

342. Nowa Wieś, Kolbuszowa county, voivodship of Rzeszów. 1943. The German Gestapo shot to death in the Rzeszów prison **Józef Posłuszny** for sheltering five Jews.

W.-Z. p. 431. T.Bi. p. 6.

343. Nowy Sącz (1), voivodship of Kraków. August 21, 1941. **Rev. Tadeusz Kaczmarczyk**, 33, an Assistant Pastor in a Roman Catholic parish, had his fingers crushed between doors by a German Gestapo man, Heinrich Hamann. He was distributing baptismal certificates to Jews and refused to betray their names to the Gestapo. While being carried to his execution, he blessed his companions with a cross made out of crust of the prison bread.

J.-W. v. 4, p. 380, 387.

344. Nowy Sącz (2), voivodship of Kraków. August 21, 1941. An American citizen born in Pittsfield, Mass. the **Rev.**

Władysław Deszcz, was arrested, along with another Polish priest, for providing Jews with birth certificates which could save their lives. Twice he went through underground passages to the local ghetto bringing Holy Sacraments to those converted to the Catholic faith. He was executed with 25 others in Biegonice, diocese of Tarnów.

J.-W. v. 4, p. 378.

345. Nowy Sącz (3), voivodship of Kraków. March 1942. **Eugeniusz Stępniowski**, a postal employee, was arrested for destroying evidence against the Jews and was so badly tortured by the German henchman, Heinrich Hamann, that he died in the Tarnów jail.

B.-L. p. 949. S.D. p. 110, 114. W.-Z. p. 405. GKBZH WB II 169.

346. Nowy Sącz (4), voivodship of Kraków. 1942. A Catholic boy, **Stefan Kiełbasa**, 18, was shot to death together with his **companion** for providing their Jewish schoolmates with "Aryan" Iidentification papers.

B.-L. p. 844. S.D. p. 91. W.-Z. p. 411. GKBZH WB II 162-3. Bulletin of Jewish Hist. Institute 71-72, p. 231.

347. Nowy Sącz (5), voivodship of Kraków. A retired Polish judge, **Jan Wołyniak**, 70, who took in a homeless Jewish child for just one night, was sent to Auschwitz and later, to KL Buchenwald. He died there in 1945, just moments before the liberation by the advancing British troops.

Testimony of Dr. A. Korsak in W.-Z. p. 348. GKBZH WB II 189.

348. Nowy Sącz (6), voivodship of Kraków. In this area alone, the action of "Żegota", the organization sponsored by the Polish government to aid Jews, unique in all of Europe, took **two hundred and ten lives** of Catholic Poles; among others, **Anna Sokołowska**, who died in Ravensbrück, **Stanisław Wąsowicz**, mundered in Auschwitz, **Klemens Gucwa**, executed in Koszyce, etc.

Testimony of Dr. A. Korsak in W.-Z. p. 348.

349. Nowy Targ, voivodship of Kraków. December 4, 1941. Germans executed a bank director form Łódź, **Mieczysław Jarowski**, for refusing to part with his Jewish wife. Along with them, died **their son,** who followed his father's example.

Testimony of T. Seweryn in B.-L. p. 180 . S.D. p. 87, 113. W.-Z. p. 405. GKBZH WZ II 159.

350. Obórki, Łuck county, voivodship of Wołyń. November 8, 1942. The Gestapo and the German military police surrounded the village, inhabited by **22 Polish Catholic familes**, mostly named Trusiewicz and Domalewski, who were giving shelter and feeding Jews from Zofiówka. All males were beaten and taken for execution to Cumań. After several days, the village was surrounded again and the rest of its inhabitants, mostly women and children, but also the elderly – altogether **over seventy persons** – were massacred, their households plundered, burned to the ground and their site plowed down, without any trace left.

Testimony of I. Zielińska in W.-Z. p. 361. GKBZH WB II 86.

351. Ochoże, Siedlce county, voivodship of Warsaw. 1942. **All inhabitants** of the hamlet were killed and their households burned, for giving shelter to persecuted Jews.

S.L. p. 252.

352. Ojrzanów (1), Grodzisk Mazowiecki county, voivodship of Warsaw. 1943. In the woods of Kostowiec, a massive execution took place in which Germans exterminated Jews and **Catholic Poles** attempting to save their fellow citizens. Exact numbers are unknown.

T.F. p. 411.

353. Ojrzanów (2), Grodzisk Mazowiecki county, voivodship of Warsaw. The entire **family of Jan Jacek** was exterminated for hiding two Jews from Tarczyn.

W.-Z. p. 443. GKBZH WB VI J.

Okocim see **Brzesko**.

354. Oleśniki, voivodship of Lublin. 1943. A Polish Catholic, **Stanisław Małysz**, was shot to death by the German military police for aiding Jews crowded in the ghetto of Trawniki.
GKBZH WB V 95.

355. Opatów, voivodship of Kielce. Autumn 1942. During the entire existence of the local ghetto, from June 1 to October 1942, there was close cooperation between the Jews and the Catholic peasants of the area who provided food and, sometimes, facilitated escape from the confines of the ghetto. One of the local youth, **Stanisław Zajcew**, accused of aiding the Jewish escapees, was caught by the Germans in the railroad station of Jakubowice and shot to death when trying to board the train.
E.F. p. 55.

Orla see **Antopol**.

356. Orzełek, Węgrów county, voivodship of Warsaw. 1944. Germans killed **two Catholic Poles** for aiding Jews who escaped from a concentration camp.
T.Sz. p. 51.

357. Osobnica, Jasło county, voivodship of Rzeszów. January 1943. For sheltering three Jews, **Józef Lazar** was shot to death and his wife, Maria Lazar, was deported to Auschwitz. Together with Lazar, Germans also killed **two other Poles** for the same offense.
W.-Z. p. 415. GKBZH WB IV 355. C.-G. p. 209.

358. Oświęcim (1), voivodship of Kraków. **Anna Szalbut** was executed by the Germans for smuggling into the camp food, medicine and underground papers for the Jewish inmates. **Jan Mosdorf** was killed for sharing with the Jews contents of his food packages. Before the war he was accused of being a leading anti-Semite in Poland.

Testimony of J. Nowak in B.-L. p. 276. W.-Z. p. 439. GKBZH WB II 194.

359. Oświęcim (2), voivodship of Kraków. **Kazimierz Jędrzejowski**, known as "Kazik" in the Polish Home Army of Silesia, was sent to Auschwitz and executed there for providing Jews with "Aryan" identification cards and with arms.

Testimony of J. Nowak in B.-L. p. 276. W.-Z. p. 439. GKBZH WB II 210.

360. Pagorzyn, Gorlice county, voivodship of Rzeszów. 1943. **Piotr Oleszkowicz**, his wife, **Katarzyna Oleszkowicz**, and **Adela Kokoczka** were shot to death by the Germans for sheltering Jews.

W.-Z. p. 431. T.Bi. p. 10 (Oleśkiewicz).

Panewnik see **Borszczów**.

361. Pantalowice (1), Przeworsk county, voivodship of Rzeszów. November 1942. **Władysław Deć** was murdered by the German military police for bringing food to Jews hiding in the forest of Hadle Szklarskie. His name was extracted from a Jewess, Małka Szinfeld, who also betrayed other members of his family.

W.-Z. p. 360. GKBZH WB IV 205.

362. Pantalowice (2), Przeworsk county, voivodship of Rzeszów. December 4, 1942. To prevent the villagers from taking Jews who were leaving the forests on account of winter, Germans executed **Wincenty Lewandowski** and his wife, **Emilia Lewandowska**, suspected of sheltering them; also, **Emilia Hałyś, Jakub Kuszek** and his wife, **Zofia Kuszek**, as well as **Zofia Kubicka** and **Justyna Kubicka** who were known to them from the previous denunciation of Małka Szinfeld.

W.-Z. p. 409. F.R. p. 282. OKBZH in Rzeszów IS 86/70. GKBZH WB IV 176-7, 178, 180, 206.

363. Paprotnia, Garwolin county, voivodship of Warsaw. 1944. **Wacław Kurek** was shot to death by the German military police from Sobolewo for giving aid to six Jews hidden in the forest. For the same reason Germans killed **Jan Rzeszotek** from the village of Strych and two inhabitants of Piotrowice, **Kabot** and **Zygan**, all Catholics.

W.-Z. p. 437. GKBZH WB VI 68, K, S.

364. Parypse, Chełm county, voivodship of Lublin. May 22, 1942. On this day all the villagers were assembled in the market place, where an officer of the *Wehrmacht* (German armed forces) challenged those present to denounce the persos engaged in helping Jews and Soviet prisoners of war. Then, he proceeded to select eight men: **Jan Gałan**, 45, **Jan Karpiuk**, 40, **Józef Litwin**, 22, **Wasyl Piecuch**, 22, **Jan Rudnik**, 26, **Józef Rudnik**, 19, **Marian Smolina**, 18 and **Andrzej Wereniczuk**, 30, to be executed in case of non-compliance with his orders. When nobody volunteered to betray their neighbors and those hiding under their protection, all eight were shot to death in front of the crowd and one household was burned down as an example of what may happen to all.

GKBZH V Ds 192/67.

Pastewnik see **Borszczów**.

365. Patków, Kozienice county, voivodship of Kielce. A Catholic peasant named **Kopeć** was murdered for sheltering Jews from German persecution.

P.A.G.B. p. 70.

366. Paulinów, Sokołów Podlaski county, voivodship of Warsaw. February 24, 1943. A German agent, disguised as a Jew, received aid from Polish workers. Three weeks later, the German SS executed on this ground: **Franciszek Augustyniak**, 30, **Zygmunt Dryga**, 54, **Ewa Kotowska**, 54, **Józef Kotowski**, 56, **Stanisław Piwko**, 31, **Jan Śliwiński**, 48, **Aleksandra Wiktorzak**, 63, and the night watchman, **Franciszek Ki-**

rylski, 56. In addition, **Stanisław Kusiak** and **Stanisław Mazurek** were deported to Treblinka and died there. **Czesław Borowy, Jan Brzozowski**, 16, and **Stanisław Hendoszko** were ordered to dig ditches for their graves and were shot afterwards.

GKBZH Zh III/50/68, court deposition from Sokołow Podlaski of May 8, 1970. F.-R. p. 344-5.

367. Pawłoszów, Jarosław county, voivodship of Rzeszów. July 7, 1943. **Franciszek Czerwonka**, 56, his wife, **Julia Czerwonka**, 56, and their son, **Stanisław Czerwonka**, were murdered by the Germans for sheltering Jews.

B.-L. p. 834. S.D. p. 101, 112. W.-Z. p. 423. F.-R. p. 286 (Pawłosiów) OKBZH in Rzeszów, I Ds 53/69. GKBZH WB IV 218-20. (December 7, 1943).

368. Pawłów, Dąbrowa Tarnowska county, voivodship of Rzeszów. **Franciszek Woźniak** and **Michał Wójcik** were murdered by the Germans for sheltering Jews and ferrying them across the river.

GKBZH WB II 68, 897.

369. Pełczyn, Lublin county, voivodship of Lublin. December 7, 1942. German military police from Cyców, arrested on a highway three Polish farmers, **Jan Pięta, Stanisław Suryś**, 26, and **Wacław Wawszczak**, 29, all suspected of keeping contacts with Jews. Upon refusal to disclose the whereabouts of the Jews, all three were executed.

W.-Z. p. 411. GKBZH WB V 151, 157, 159.

370. Piaseczno, Mińsk Mazowiecki county, voivodship of Warsaw. A Jew escorted by members of the Polish underground from Lublin to a safer place in Warsaw, panicked at the sight of Germans around the station of Dęblin, but was calmed down. However, some time later, his frightened behavior gave him and his **Catholic companions** away, with fatal results for all of them.

J.M. p. 159.

371. Piastów, Przasnysz county, voivodship of Warsaw. April 26, 1944. **Irena Grabowska** was arrested and executed for giving shelter to Jews; among others, to the family of a well known publisher, Mortkowicz.

GKBZH WB VI 1383.

372. Pilica, Olkusz county, voivodship of Kraków. January 15, 1943. For sheltering three Jewish women, German military police shot to death **Maria Rogozińska**, 35, from the village of Wierbka, along with **Piotr Podgórski** who failed to inform German authorities that his neighbor was hiding Jews.

B.-L. p. 833, 837. S.D. p. 92. W.-Z. p. 413. GKBZH WB II 18-9.

373. Pilzno, Dębica county, voivodship of Rzeszów. **All persons** from this willage who had been involved in helping Jews in the construction of their hideout in a nearby forest were executed by the Germans.

S.Z. p. 192.

374. Pińczów (1), voivodship of Kielce. May 3, 1943. **Emil Niechciał** and his wife **Genowefa Niechciał** were arrested for sheltering the Haberman family of four and brought to Busko jail on May 1, 1943. For this offense, they were shot to death.

GKBZH WB IV 194-5.

375. Pińczów (2), voivodship of Kielce. Two Catholics, **Roman Jabłoński** and **Stanisław Jabłoński**, shared the fate of the Niechciał family for previously keeping also in their house the Haberman family. They were executed in the Busko jail.

GKBZH WB IV 191-2.

376. Pińsk, voivodship of Polesie. January 22, 1943. The Vicar General of the Roman Catholic diocese, **Msgr. Witold Iwicki**, was executed in Janów Poleski for organizing aid to persecuted Jews of this region. Included in a group of forty Catholics brought to Janów for execution, he was offered freedom by the commanding officer who had orders to execute only thirty eight persons and wanted to release the priest. Following the example of St. Maximilian Kolbe, Msgr. Iwicki gave his privilege to a married man, head of the railroad station. He was the last to descend into the ditch, already filled with corpses, to be shot there.

B.-L. p. 241. S.D. p. 104, 113. W.-Z. p. 431. I.O. p. 152, 185. J.-W. v. 4, p. 268, 275.

377. Pińsk (diocese), voivodship of Polesie (1), **Derewna**. August 8, 1943. The Pastor of the Roman Catholic parish, **Rev. Paweł Dołżyk**, 72, was shot to death in the forest of Jankowice by the German–controlled Vlassov bands for aiding Jews and partisans.

J.-W. v. 4, p. 268, 271, 274.

378. Pińsk (diocese), voivodship of Polesie (2), **Naliboki**, August 1943. The Pastor of the Roman Catholic parish, **Msgr. Józef Bajko**, 53, and his assistant, **Rev. Józef Baradyn**, 32, were locked in a barn and burned alive by the Germans for aiding "Jews and partisans".

J.-W. v. 4, p. 268, 271.

379. Pińsk (diocese), voivodship of Polesie (3) **Kamień**. August 1943. The Dean and Pastor of the Roman Catholic parish, **Rev. Leopold Aulich**, 49, and his assistant, **Rev. Kazimierz Rybałtowski**, 34, were killed by the Germans under suspicion of aiding "Jews and partisans".

J.-W. v. 4, 268, 271, 279.

380. Piotrków Trybunalski, voivodship of Łódź. **Two Polish guards** were arrested and sent to KL Auschwitz for giving financial aid to Jews. They never came back alive. Two Jewish families involved were executed on the spot.

A.-B. p. 113.

Piotrowice see **Paprotnia**.

381. Podborek (1), Radom county, voivodship of Kielce. January 1943. The Ruciński family fell under suspicion of aiding Jews. One morning, their little daughter, **Janina Rucińska** 10, was killed by the German military police. The police then entered their house and murdered father, **Antoni Ruciński** and mother, **Aleksandra Rucińska** who was then in the last month of her pregnancy.

GKBZH WB I 179-81.

382. Podborek (2) Radom county, voivodship of Kielce. July 11, 1943. Under suspicion of having sheltered Jews, German military police from Górki murdered **Jan Kowalczyk**, 43, and his wife, **Stefania Kowalczyk**, along with their little son, **Jan Kowalczyk**, 2, also **Marianna Ambroży**, 75, **Katarzyna Szepietowska**, 40, and her son, **Józef Szepietowski**, 7, who just happened to be there. Among the murderers were: Gottfried Omer, Josef Pasek, Adolf Kloderl, Anton Fischer and Otto Hober, who were never prosecuted in their country for their crimes against humanity which were considered to be their patriotic duty.

F.-R. p. 311. OKBZH in Kielce, Ds 56/69.

383. Podborze, Mielec county, voivodship of Rzeszów. April 23, 1943. A German police force came from Mielec in search of Jewish families known to be hiding in the village and, although not one Jew was caught there, six buildings were set on fire and 21 farmsteads were burnt down. **The number of losses among the inhabitants** remain unknown.

T.Bi. p. 8.

384. Podiwanówka, Kowel county, voivodship of Wołyń. For giving massive help to persecuted Jews, Germans murdered about **two hundred inhabitants** of Berecz and Podiwanówka.

Testimony of "Maks" Sobiesiak in W.-Z. p. 263, also 445.

385. Poizdów colony, Radzyń Podlaski county, voivodship of Lublin. June 29, 1943. German military police from Kock shot to death **Feliks Brygoła**, 50, his two children, **Janina Brygoła**, 13, and **Stanisław Brygoła** 18, in addition to **Florentyna Zdunek**, 18, and her little sister, **Alfreda Zdunek**, 1, all in retaliation for sheltering an undisclosed number of Jews.

L.S. in "Zeszyty Majdanka" v. 2, p. 182. W.-Z. p. 421. GKBZH WB V 152-6. GKBZH ASG, p. 660.

386. Polanówka, Zamość county, voivodship of Lublin. August 1942. German military police shot to death **two Catholic Poles** arrested in the Żabia Wola forest for bringing food to Jews hiding there.

B.-L. p. 833. GKBZH ASG, p. 652.

387. Połom Mały, Brzesko county, voivodship of Kraków. December 26, 1944. **Michał Wójcik**, 48, was shot to death and burned inside of his house for hiding a Jew, Henryk Goldfinger. His wife managed to run away.

G.-L. p. 832, 842, 852. S.D. p. 108, 114. GKBZH WB II 6.

388. Połomyja (1), Dębica county, voivodship of Rzeszów. September 7, 1943. For sheltering Jews, members of a Catholic peasant family, **Anna Rębis**, 57, **Józef Rębis**, 61, **Zofia Rębis**, 27, **Karol Rębis**, 19, and **Wiktoria Rębis**, 24, were shot to death along with their **maid** and their guest, **Piotr Gawryć**, 20. Their house and all the farm buildings were burned to the ground.

B.-L. p. 397. S.D. p. 100, 114. F.-R. p. 425 (Sept. 9) W.-Z. p. 421.

389. Połomyja (2), Dębica county, voivodship of Rzeszów. September 1943. An elderly Catholic lady, **Zofia Miela**, was killed by the Germans for sheltering ten Jews in her household. The Jews managed to escape.

S.Z. p. 191. GKBZH IV 330.

390. Połomyja (3), Dębica county, voivodship of Rzeszów. 1943. German military forces (Wehrmacht) and the Gestapo executed twenty Catholics and Jews. **Eight Catholics** among eleven executed were specifically charged with sheltering Jews.

B.-L. p. 834. W.-Z. p. 425.

391. Poniatowa, Puławy county, voivodship of Lublin. 1943. The German *Wehrmacht* executed **Jan Gil**, a photographer named **Zdaniewicz**, and another worker, **Jarosiński**, all three Catholics, for attempting to bring aid to Jews in the labor camp.

R.G. p. 101.

392. Popradowa, Nowy Sącz county, voivodship of Kraków. For sheltering five Jews of the Kaufer family, Germans executed **Maria Rumin** and her son, **Jan Rumin**. The Jews were shot to death in the backyard of the house, while the Rumins were taken to a Jewish cemetery for execution.

Testimony of A. Korsak in W.-Z. p. 349, also 448. GKBZH WB II 190-1.

393. Posada Górna, Sanok county, voivodship of Rzeszów. **Maria Bolanowska** and her son, **Piotr Bolanowski**, were executed by the Germans for sheltering Jews.

W.-Z. p. 411. GKBZH WB IV 433-4.

394. Posądza, Proszowice county, voivodship of Kraków. June 22, 1943. For shelterig Jews. Germans shot to death **seven Catholics**, including **two infants: Stanisław Wierzbanowski**, 60, **Maria Wierzbanowska**, 60, **Katarzyna Żmuda**, 40, **Teresa Żmuda**, 18, **Zdzisław Żmuda**, 1, **Mr. Nowak, Teofil Nowak**, 2, and **Mr. Zębala**.

GKBZH WB II 181-2, 207, 213-4, 215-7.

395. Potok Górny, Tomaszów Lubelski county, voivodship of Lublin. December 19, 1943. The Pastor of a Roman Catholic parish, **Rev. Błażej Nowosad**, 40, suspected by the Ukrainians of sheltering Jews, was assaulted in the attic of his church. After having been beaten with a rifle butt in order to extract from him the location of Jews remaining in his care, he was shot to death.

Testimony of Bishop Edmund Ilcewicz in "Tygodnik Powszechny" weekly of April 15, 1980. J.-W. v. 3, p. 268.

Powórsk see **Maniewicze**.

396. Poznań. A Catholic surgeon, **Dr. Parczewski**, perished in a concentration camp. He was deported there with **Mrs. Parczewska** for accepting food packages mailed from Hamburg for a Jew who was brought from there to Poland. The Jew was hanged after a package, addressed to Dr. Parczewski, was found in his possession.

GKBZH WB XVI 45.

397. Promna-Kolonia, Radom county, voivodship of Kielce. 1943. Michalina Milas permitted a Jewish couple, Mr. Libertman and his wife, to hide in their house. She already sheltered there two other Jews, Millensztajn and Szóstak, the last one so-called because he had six fingers. One day, while returning from the field, she saw the dead bodies of all four Jews scattered about her backyard. **Mr. Milas** was taken away and was never seen again. His wife was arrested and deported, first to the Pawiak prison in Warsaw, then to Auschwitz, and finally to Ravensbrück. She was beaten so cruelly that her entire body formed an open wound, and she could rest only on her elbows and knees. After the war, when she returned to her native village, she found the personal documents of her husband and a statement that he died on August 10, 1945 in Loewens near Holzmünden.

Deposition of M. Milas in E.F. p. 452.

398. Przemyśl (1), voivodship of Rzeszów. 1942. Due to the extensive help of Polish local population, 500 Jews were saved at the evacuation of the ghetto. **Three Polish women**

paid for this with their lives. They were executed at the main cemetery with a Jewish mother and child they were trying to save.

T.Bi p. 2.

399. Przemyśl (2), voivodship of Rzeszów. September 6, 1943. A Pole, **M. Kruk** was hanged for sheltering Jewish escapees from the local ghetto.

T. Bi. p. 3.

400. Przemyśl (3), voivodship of Rzeszów. Maksymilian Diament (Józef Burzmański) testified at the Eichmann trial in Jerusalem that he had witnessed the Germans killing **eight members of a Catholic family for giving aid and shelter to a Jewish child.**

W. Bartoszewski: Operation "Żegota" (typescript).

401. Przemysławice, voivodship of Kielce. August 27, 1943. **Józef Grzywnowicz**, 23, and **Franciszek Grzywnowicz**, 22, were executed by the Germans for sheltering and feeding a Jewish family of five persons for eight months.

GKBZH WB I 166-7 (Przesław).

402. Przewłoka, Biała Podlaska county, voivodship of Lublin. June 5, 1943. For sheltering Jews, the German authorities executed the Haciak family: **Mr. Haciak, his wife** and **their son**.

GKBZH WB I 166-7. Egz. V.P.

403. Przewrotne (1), Rzeszów county, voivodship of Rzeszów. March 13, 1943. In reprisal for sheltering Jews and partisans, German military police gathered all the villagers near the fire station, selecting **thirty six persons** for public execution. They shot to death: **Marcin Borkowski**, 42, **Wojciech Brudz**, 34, **Walenty Brudz**, 57, **Antoni Brudz**, 22, **Andrzej Drąg**, 50, **Łukasz Drąg**, 47, **Wojciech Drąg**, 43, **Michał Ga-**

weł, 38, **Adam Klecha**, 19, **Zofia Klecha**, 31, along with **Emilia Klecha**, 2, and 8-months old **Józef Klecha**, **Jan Kopeć**, 34, **Adam Organiściak**, 66, **Franciszek Organiściak**, 31, **Józef Organiściak**, 62, **Józef Organiściak**, 23, **Aniela Organiściak**, 34, **Tekla Organiściak**, 45, **Wojciech Organiściak**, 50, **Piotr Ożga**, 30, **Łukasz Pomykała**, 58, **Katarzyna Pomykała**, 42, **Wojciech Pomykała**, 30, **Weronika Pomykała**, 10, **Antoni Rusin**, 40, **Michał Sondej**, 34, **Jan Walc**, 43, **Szymon Warzocha**, 53, **Józef Warzocha**, 20, **Szymon Warzocha**, 25, **Franciszek Warzocha**, 48, **Paweł Warzocha**, 17, **Franciszek Warzocha**, 43, **Jan Wilk**, 24, and **Józef Wilk**, 28. All were buried in a common grave.

Testimony of Dr. M. Wrzosek in B.-L. p. 846. W.-Z. p. 41. F.-R. p. 321-2 (March 14). GKBZH WB IV 301, 350-4, 371, 421, 467-8. OKBZH in Rzeszów II Ds 77/68.

404. Przewrotne (2), Rzeszów county, voivodship of Rzeszów. May 9, 1943. In the second bloody reprisal for sheltering Jews and partisans, Germans killed **twenty-four persons** outright. They were picked according to a prepared list and brought near the fire station. From there, in small groups, they were conducted to the edge of a dried-out pond belonging to Marysia Pokrywka and liquidated there by means of individual shots through the head. Their names were: **Stefania Chrząstek**, 16, **Marcin Chuchro**, 35, **Michał Chuchro**, 50, **Franciszek Fila**, 40, **Andrzej Gola**, 40, **Antoni Granat**, 29, **Ludwik Gut**, 29, **Kacper Jarochowicz**, 74, **Jakub Jarosz**, 37, **Jakub Klus**, 37, **Józef Klus**, 27, **Józef Kuś**, 40, **Paweł Laska**, 58, **Paweł Laskorzec**, 47, **Katarzyna Magdziak**, 45, **Jan Marszał**, 41, **Anna Pawłowska**, 23, **Franciszek Rusin**, 60, **Piotr Suszek**, 35, **Józef Tyburski**, 30, **Franciszek Wilk**, 42, **Jan Wyka**, 22, **Stanisław Żak**, 60, and **Fanciszek Żmuda**, 41. The clothing of dead victims was collected and taken to Rzeszów. Their naked bodies were pushed into the pond and covered with dirt. A little chapel was later erected over this common grave. Another group of **forty-nine persons** was taken to the camp in Pustków, where most of them were killed in another execution, witnessed by Emil Gębala who counted about **twenty-four bodies**. They were also undressed and put in a huge pyre made of wood and pieces of tar paper which was ignited. Very few came back to their native village.

W.-Z. p. 419. F.-R. p. 322. S.Z. p. 178-9. OKBZH in Rzeszów II S 99/70. GKBZH WB IV 357, 354-5 (Chubro), 377-8.

405. Ptaszkowa, Nowy Sącz county, voivodship of Kraków. May 3, 1944. According to an official poster, signed by the Commandant of the Security Police and SS for Kraków, among eighteen men condemned to death there is the name of **Jakub Tokarz**, accused of "aiding Jews".

Facsimile of the poster in W.-Z. p. 446, also 349, 447. GKBZH WB II 141.

406. Pustelnik, near Marki, voivodship of Warsaw. October 1943. A pious Catholic widow, **Marianna Banaszek**, mother of three children, took into her little house a Jewish family of three persons. Warned by a friendly bailiff named Feler, she managed to pass the warning of an impending German raid to her guests who promptly got away. When the Germans arrived, they found only two children of Marianna, **Stanisława Banaszek**, 17, and **Władysław Banaszek**, 20, in the house. Enraged by the disappearance of the Jews, they took them to a nearby pond and shot them both there. The desolate mother did not even even try to run away. Appalled by the disaster she brought upon her own children by taking strangers into her house, she went to church for an examination of conscience to discover whether what she did was right. In these circumstances, she didn't see the reason why her own life should be spared. She went home and prepared herself for the inevitable. The Germans surprised her in prayer and shot her on the spot when she came out to open the door. The wall of the hall had to be painted several times to cover the blood which sprinkled from her body when she was shot. She was buried right there in front of the entrance, and only after the war had ended, her body was exhumed and moved to the cemetery, together with the remains of her two sons. Her third and the oldest child, **Wiktoria Banaszek**, was traced by the Germans in Warsaw where she was working as a maid. She was punished there for the "sin" of her mother, but her burial place remains unknown. After the war, the Jews saved by these tremendous sacrifices, arrived in a limousine of the Israeli Embassy; one of them found a briefcase in the attic, probably containing some valuables; they exhumed the body of their little daughter who had died from a disease and had been buried under a cherry tree in the garden. They departed without leaving any sign of their gratitude to the Banaszek family for having saved their lives at the expense of their own, not even a plaque on their grave. There is also no mention of them in the "Alley of the Just among the Nations" at Yad Vashem in Jerusalem which is supposed to be a token of Jewish gratitude to their Christian saviors.

Testimony of H. Szewczyk, dated Nov. 1979, in GKBZH. GKBZH WB VI B. Also the personal inquiry of the author on the spot.

407. Radgoszcz (1), Dąbrowa Tarnowska county, voivodship of Kraków. August 25, 1942. German military police shot to death **Zofia Wójcik** and her **two children**, 2 and 3 years of age, along with a Jew who had been sheltered by her. All four were buried on the site of the murder.

B.-L. p. 836. S.D. p. 88, 115. W.-Z. p. 407. GKBZH WB II 202-4 (October 25, 1942).

408. Radgoszcz (2), Dąbrowa Tarnowska county, voivodship of Kraków. September 13, 1942. Catholic peasants, **Bronisław Kmieć**, 17, with his mother, **Anna Kmieć** and **two children**, 2 and 3 years of age, were shot to death for sheltering Jews; Szyja Grinstman, a farmer, and, also, a son of a Jewish baker. Together with them, were killed **Maria Sołtys** and

Maria Wójcik. All the Catholics and Jews were buried in the same grave.

B.-L. p. 832. S.D. p. 88, 113, 115. W.-Z. p. 407. GKBZH WB II 91-2, 201.

409. Ragdoszcz (3), Dąbrowa Tarnowska county, voivodship of Kraków. **Tomasz Jużba** and his wife, **Bronisława Jużba**, in the eighth month of her pregnancy, were killed by the Germans for giving shelter to two Jews in their house.

GKBZH WB II 89-90.

410. Ragdoszcz (4), Dąbrowa Tarnowska county, voivodship of Kraków. **Stanisław Lach** was murdered by the Germans for sheltering Jews.

GKBZH WB II 93.

411. Radgoszcz (5), Dąbrowa Tarnowska county, voivodship of Kraków. Spring 1943. **Stanisław Stopa** gave his life for helping Jews. Also, some **other Poles** were killed for giving aid to Jews.

GKBZH WB II 94.

412. Radgoszcz (6), Dąbrowa Tarnowska county, voivodship od Kraków. **Jan Nadolski**, together with his wife, were killed by the Germans for aiding Jews in the Dąbrowa Tarnowska area.

GKBZH WB II 95-95a.

413. Radom (1), voivodship of Kielce. 1942. **Jan Rogala**, who aided a Jewish couple, Mr. and Mrs. Korngold, and introduced them to Leszek Ziółkowski who was to provide them with "Aryan" documents, was apprehended and executed by the Germans.

E.F. p. 208.

414. Radom (2), voivodship of Kielce. April 3, 1943. Two Jewish women, Sala Rubinowicz and Elka Szwarcman, were condemned to death by the German Special Court (*Sonderge-richt*) of Radom for leaving the ghetto area. Also condemned to death were five Poles who helped them: **Wincenty Buzo-wicz**, with his wife **Anna Buzowicz**, **Maria Różańska**, **Jan Pinkus** and **Zenon Poloński**. The same German decree which forbade leaving the ghetto area under the penalty of death, imposed the same punishment on the Catholic Poles who dared to help the Jews break this law.

Facsimile of death sentences in W.-Z. p. 432, also 419. GKBZH WB I 155-6, 157 (Szwarcblat), 159 (Gubinowicz).

415. Radzików – Stopki, Siedlce county, voivodship of Warsaw. April 10, 1943. For hiding Jews, the German military police executed **Antoni Domański**, 35, **Franciszek Domański**, 30, and their father, **Piotr Domański**, 70.

B.-L. p. 838. S.D. p. 95, 112. W.-Z. p. 423, 419.

416. Radzyń Podlaski, voivodship of Lublin. Summer 1941. German military police shot to death **eighteen Polish citizens** of Polish and Jewish descent, among them two women. The execution took place in the Jewish cemetary.

GKBZH V Ds 131/67 p. 271.

417. Raków, Częstochowa county, voivodship of Katowice. 1944. During a routine search by a German guard (Werkschütz) in the Jewish labor camp at Hasag Eisenhütte, some letters were intercepted in the possession of **Jan Brust**, a Polish foreman and a secret functionary of the Polish Aid to Jews "Żegota", in addition to some money he was bringing to the Jewish inmates. In order to protect confidential letters he was carrying for the Jews inside, Jan started to run while chewing the incriminatory letters, which could endanger many lives if they were seized by the Germans. He was shot to death.

Testimony of I. Jakobson in B.-L. p. 387-92, also 391-2. S.D. p. 106 (Brus), 112, B.-R. p. 97. W.-Z. p. 312, 434. GKBZH WB VII 251.

418. Rekówka, Lipsko county, voivodship of Kielce. December 6, 1942. The German SS, under the command of officer Bierner, burned alive **ten Catholic farmers** accused of sheltering Jews. Those who died were: **Piotr Skoczylas**, 58, his baby daughter, **Leokadia Skoczylas**, 8, his son-in-law, **Stanisław Kosior**, 40, his grandchildren, **Jan Kosior**, 8, **Mieczysław Kosior**, 5, **Marian Kosior**, 4, and **Teresa Kosior**, 3, with their mother **Marianna Kosior**, 27. Also murdered was **Marianna Kościńska**, 60, and **Henryka Kordula**, 13, a babysitter who just happened to be there at this time. All were locked in a barn which was set on fire. None was allowed to escape from flames. Among the Germans executioners were: Arno Fichtner, Martin Froede, Rudolf Neubauer, Gustav Eichler, Jakob Hofmann, Karl Biagi and Paul Vogel.

B.-L. p. 863, 865. F.-R. p. 305. S.D. p. 90, 103 B.-R. p. 48. W.-Z. p. 409. OKBZH in Kielce, Ds 85/69. E.F. p. 397-400. GKBZH WB I 88 (Kiścińska) 79, etc.

419. Roguziec, Siedlce county, voivodship of Warsaw. March 1943. **Alfons Skolimowski** was shot to death by the Germans under the suspicion of sheltering Jews.

B.-L. p. 838. S.D. p. 93, 114. W.-Z. p. 417. GKBZH WB VI 1398.

420. Romaszki, Biała Podlaska county, voivodship of Lublin. June 5, 1942. A Polish underground unit of 50 men challenged a German military force guarding a Jewish work camp and set free 180 inmates, also burning the buildings. German military police succeeded in recapturing around 100 Jewish inmates while the rest went free. There were **losses in lives** in the Polish unit.

S.L. p. 249.

421. Ropa (1), Gorlice county, voivodship of Rzeszów. Autumn 1943. In Michał Dec's barn German police found and shot to death the Jewish Schwimer family of six. Subsequently, **Katarzyna Dec** was arrested and taken away. She never came back.

L.D. p. 198.

422. Ropa (2), Gorlice county, voivodship of Rzeszów. **Franciszek Rowiński** and **Bruno Szupina** were killed by the Germans for giving shelter to Jews.

L.D. p. 116-7. T.Bi. p. 10.

423. Rozdziele (1), Gorlice county, voivodship of Rzeszów. 1944. For hiding Josek Lejba, a Jew, Germans shot to death **Anastazja Tylawska**.

W.-Z. p. 437. GKBZH WB IV 341.

424. Rozdziele (2), Gorlice county, voivodship of Rzeszów. 1944. A Catholic farmer, **Piotr Dragon**, was executed by the Germans for giving assistance to and sheltering a group of Jews. They were killed on the spot.

W.-Z. p. 437. GKBZH WB IV 342. T. Bi. p. 10 (Dragan, Rozdziel).

Rożny see **Zarzetka**.

425. Równe (1), Krosno county, voivodship of Rzeszów. November 14, 1943. For sheltering in their barn a Jewish famiily composed of seven persons, the **entire Daszkiewicz family** was exterminated by the Germans, except Anna Daszkiewicz who somehow escaped. On May 7, 1981 she was awarded Yad Vashem decoration, without mention being made in press of the rest of her family or having them counted with the "Just among the Nations".

Information, found in the list of decorations distributed in ZBOWiD (Polish Veterans' Association) in Warsaw, routinely transmitted to the Jewish Historical Institute in Warsaw.

426. Równe (2), Krosno county, voivodship of Rzeszów. 1943. In the yard of Dukla prison, Germans have executed **Władysław Braja**, a Catholic peasant, accused of sheltering three Jews in his household.

Court deposition of M. Braja in W.-Z. p. 397. GKBZH WB IV 9.

427. Różan, Maków Mazowiecki county, voivodship of Warsaw. March 11, 1943. A Jew from a labor camp was caught by the Germans and promised forgiveness if he revealed the addresses of Polish families which had given him assistance. After complying with this request, he was murdered together with **all the families** concerned.

S.L. p. 253.

428. Rudańce, Lwów county, voivodship of Lwów. November 14, 1943. Among the fifty five executions decreed by the German Commandant of the SS and Police in Galicia and announced in an official poster, "Nastia Susch condemned to death for sheltering Jews" seems to be identical with **Anastazja Susz**, an Ukrainian born Diachenko who committed this "crime" in her native town.

Facsimile of the poster in W.-Z. p. 438, also 429. GKBZH WB IV 325.

429. Rudka, Lubartów county, voivodship of Lublin. Among the Catholic population of the area, the most active in rescuing Jews and warning them about the oncoming German raids was the **Sidor family**, including Bolesław and Kazimierz, with their sisters, Maria and Józefa. **Bolesław Sidor** paid for this with his life when caught by the Germans on his errand of mercy.

Testimony of G. Alef-Bolkowiak in W.-Z. p. 269.

430. Rudka, Piotrków county, voivodship of Łódź. **Stefania Furmańczyk** was executed in Auschwitz where she was deported for giving her own identification card to Pola Watyńska, a Jewess, in order to save her from the Germans.

GKBZH WB X 66.

431. Ryczów, Zawiercie county, voivodship of Katowice. **Adam Rysiewicz**, known for opening channels for smuggling Jews over the Tatra Mountains to Hungary and Slovakia where the persecution was less violent, lost his life on one of those expeditions which took fifty Jews to safety.

Testimony of T. Seweryn in W.-Z. p. 293.

432. Rypin (1), Włocławek county, voivodship of Bydgoszcz. 1940. **Stanisław Paprocki** was arrested for helping Jews named Mendel, Blumencwajg and Anyż (with his wife and daughter) to pass illegally over the border. He perished in Auschwitz.

GKBZH WB XV 36.

433. Rypin (2), Włocławek county, voivodship of Bydgoszcz. 1940. A **Catholic guide** was shot to death by the German Wehrmacht for trying to smuggle Jews into relative safety across the border.

GKBZH WB XV 35.

434. Rytwiany, Staszów county, voivodship of Kielce. November 1943. **Jan Kalina** was killed while passing the house of his daughter, Genowefa Szelest, where six Jews were discovered hiding. Genowefa managed to ecape with her family.

W.-Z. p. 42. GKBZH WB I 134. (Szeleś).

435. Rzepędź, Sanok county, voivodship of Rzeszów. 1943. Nine Gypsies and **one Catholic Pole** were executed by the Gestapo, the Pole for hiding Jews.

B.-L. p. 834. GKBZH/B v. X. p. 185.

436. Rzeszów (1). 1943. **Anastazja Dobrowolska** fell into the German hands when some of the "Aryan" identification cards which she was distributing among the Jewish refugees from ghetto were traced back to her.

S.Z. p. 247.

437. Rzeszów (2). March 1944. The father of one of Polish guards, **Marian S.**, lost his life for giving shelter to the Jewish family called Throms. His wife and son, arrested with him, were saved by a Polish "navy blue" policeman who testified that both were in disagreement with the Throms and, for this reason, were denounced by them to the German authorities.

There were many cases of blackmailing Catholic families by Jews who refused to leave their hideouts at the request of their hosts when the Germans became suspicious and there was a danger of a raid and execution for everybody concerned, Poles and Jews alike.

S.Z. p. 52.

438. Rzędowice, Miechów county, voivodship of Kraków. March 1943. Two Catholic farmers, **Franciszek Chybowski**, 60, and his wife, **Julia Chybowska**, 54, were executed by the Germans for sheltering Jews.

Testimony of T. Seweryn in B.-L. p. 850. W.-Z. p. 417. GKBZH WB II 153-4.

439. Sadkowa Góra, Mielec county, voivodship of Kraków. December 1943. A Polish farmer named **Russakow** was shot to death by the Germans for hiding the Jewish Landers family and refusing to betray their hiding place. The Jewish family was saved.

GKBZH WB IV 122 (Landners).

440. Sadowne, Węgrów county, voivodship of Warsaw. January 13, 1943. **Leon Lubkiewicz**, 59, a baker who gave a loaf of bread to two Jewish girls, Czapkiewicz and Enzel, was executed with his wife, **Marianna Lubkiewicz**, 44, and his son, **Stefan Lubkiewicz**, 25, when the girls were caught with the bread in their hands and indicated the place where they got it. The girls were also shot on the spot. Among their murderers was a German by the name of Schulz.

W.-Z. p. 448. W.W. p. 128. PZPR KC CA DR 202/III/37, p. 78. GKBZH WB VI 194-6.

441. Sambodzie, Otwock county, voivodship of Warsaw. June 1, 1943. Germans arrested **Władysław Jedynak**, 54, for sheltering in his home the Jewish Ajzyk family. The Jews were executed on the spot, but their host was tortured for several days. He was forced to run over one mile, tied to a galloping horse and was shot to death in the village Wilga on the river of the same name.

GKBZH WB VI 1397. Also a letter from Stanisław Jedynak, addressed to the author, based on the information from his nephew, Wacław Jedynak from Antopol near Nałęczów.

442. Samoklęski (1), Lubartów county, voivodship of Lublin. 1944. **Bolesław Dąbrowski**, 38, from Starościn, was shot to death by the Germans for sheltering thirty eight Jews who were executed together with him.

B.-L. p. 837. S.D. p. 92, 112. W.-Z. p. 413. GKBZH WB VI 140 (27 Jews) DSW 8/242/69 W. 727.

443. Samoklęski (2), Lubartów county, voivodship of Lublin. 1944. Catholic farmers, **Antoni Mastelarz** and his wife, **Aniela Mastelarz**, were murdered by the Germans for saving the Jewish Buksbaum family from death.

W.-Z. p. 437. GKBZH WB IV 70-1.

444. Sanok (1), voivodship of Rzeszów. April 19, 1944. German judge Pooth, assisted by Dr. Aldenhof, Dr. Naumann and Hagelstein, presiding with him on the Special Court (Sondergericht), issued a death sentence to **Stanisława Kornecka**, 25, accused of giving shelter to Jews. After the war, hundreds of such judges went back to their country without a threat of prosecution, to occupy honorable positions in German courts.

Facsimile of Sondergericht sentence in S.Z. p. 192. GKBZH WB IV 223.

445. Sanok (2), voivodship of Rzeszów. April 19, 1944. **Stanisław Stojowski** and his wife, **Zofia Stojowska**, were shot to death for sheltering three Jews in their house.

Court deposition of W. Stojowski in W.-Z. p. 398, also 419. GKBZH WB IV 304-5.

446. Sędziszów, Ropczyce county, voivodship of Rzeszów. Catholic farmer, **J. Szafirowicz**, supplied food to Jews hiding in a forest. One day the German police surrounded his house. First wounded, he was killed while trying to escape.

T.Bi. p. 3.

447. Siedlce (1), voivodship of Warsaw. June 1941. One of local teachers, **Władysław Makarczuk**, who worked closely with the Jews, especially with Chaim Majer, was arrested and perished before the end of this year in KL Auschwitz.

S.L. p. 132, 248.

448. Siedlce (2), voivodship of Warsaw. November 27, 1943. By order of the Commandant of the SS and Police District of Warsaw, **ten Catholic Poles** were executed for the crime of *"Judenherbergung"*, sheltering of Jews. They were: **Kazimierz Księżopolski**, 27, **Jerzy Lorkiewicz**, 23, **Jan Ston**, 29, **Bolesław Ston**, 31, **Ludwik Zacharczuk**, 31, **Franciszek Zakrzewski**, 46, **Stanisław Cabaj**, 29, **Bronisław Kondraciuk**, 35, **Piotr Zakrzewski**, 48, and **Jan Włodarczyk**, 55. This list was printed on posters in German and in Polish, for the purpose of deterrence. If all the death sentences on Poles were to be printed on posters "there would be not enough lumber in the Polish forests", said German Governor of Poland, Dr. Hans Frank.

Facsimile of the poster in W.-Z. p. 436. L.S. p. 252.

449. Siedlce (3), voivodship of Warsaw. December 17, 1943. To frighten the Catholic population even more, another order of the Commandant of the SS and Police District of Warsaw announced the execution of ten more Poles with the crime of *"Judenherbergung"*, (sheltering of Jews), prominently displayed among other "crimes". Thus executed were: **Jan Perycz**, 20, **Zbigniew Perycz**, 19, **Tadeusz Perycz**, 61, **Zenon Szmurło**, 20, **Zdzisław Kalinowski**, 19, **Wiesław Kniaziński**,

17, **Eliasz Bartniczuk**, 27, **Jan Bartniczuk**, 27, **Franciszek Sojka**, 43, and **Jerzy Papliński**, 20. To avoid further such executions, the civilian population was warned to denounce to the German authorities any further occurrence of such "crimes".

Facsimile of the poster in W.-Z. p. 440. L.S. p. 252.

450. Siedlce county (1), voivodship of Warsaw. A **Catholic farmer** was executed simply because a Jew was apprehended by the Germans in the vicinity of his farm, carrying food supplies.

L.S. p. 386. A case described by Stanisław Łukasiewicz in Okupacja, 1956.

451. Siedlce county (2), voivodship of Warsaw. A similar case occured in the same area when a Jewish child, caught with his parents outside of their usual hideout, while seeing his parents tortured, volunteered the information asked of them and pointed out the Catholic family which was taking care of them. The **whole family** was executed together with the Jews.

L.S. p. 253.

452. Siedliska, Miechów county, voivodship of Kraków. March 15, 1943. Two little boys of the Baranek family were frequently seen carrying heavy bags of food, not responding to the overtures of other children, always taciturn and a little frightened. Their mother sometimes was seen crying her eyes out, as in expectation of something disastrous. This "terrible secret" was best known to the father, who – in performance of his duties as a bailiff – had to warn everybody about grim reprisals for sheltering Jews. When the fatal day arrived, Germans first shot the Jews, all four of them from the Koplewicz family who had been sheltered by the Baraneks. The Germans tied their legs to horses and dragged them behind a barn to be buried there. Next came the Baraneks: **Wincenty Baranek**, 44, and his wife, **Łucja Baranek**, 35, were locked in the barn and their children, **Henryk Baranek**, 12, and **Tadeusz Baranek**, 9, visibly trembled holding each other's hands. The boys were shot first and then their parents, who were forced to witness their execution. People who later went into the barn to see their bodies, noticed in Łucja's hands lots of her own hair which she had pulled out in a moment of terrifying realization that her decision to keep the Jews meant a disaster for her good and obedient children. This was not a ficticious "Sophie's choice", but a historical "Łucja's choice" which will not appear in novels and films. It didn't even place Baraneks in the Yad Vashem's "Just among the Nations" alley. Conveniently forgotten, also, was **Grandma Kopeć** who was killed quietly and permitted to be buried in her own grave for her part in saving the Jews.

B.-L. p. 832, 838, 850, 855-9. S.D. p. 93, 112. S.M. p. 218-21. W.-Z. p. 375, 417. GKBZH WB II 146-9.

453. Siedliszczowice, Lipsko county, voivodship of Kielce. March 11, 1942. **Wacław Sochacki** was killed by the Germans in his own backyard for giving shelter to a Jewish boy, Antoś Adamus.

GKBZH WB I 122.

454. Sielice, Lipsko county, voivodship of Kielce. December 14, 1942. **Józef Owczarek**, arrested under suspicion of aiding Jews from the village of Chotcza, was shot to death by the Germans in the forest of Wólka Ciepielowska.

GKBZH WB I 122.

455. Siemianówka, Lwów county, voivodship of Lwów. February 1943. A Catholic farmer, **Stanisław Balicki**, was murdered by the Germans for hiding two Jews.

W.-Z. p. 415. GKBZH WB IV 442.

456. Sieniawa, Jarosław county, voivodship of Rzeszów. **Bronisław Stawarski** was killed together with the Jews he was sheltering, while his wife, **Mrs. Stawarska**, was deported to a death camp from which she never returned.

W.-Z. p. 441. GKBZH WB IV 429-30.

457. Skarżysko (1), voivodship of Kielce. Spring 1944. In the German ammunition factory Hasag, the German authorities publicly hanged a young Polish Catholic named **Nowak**, 25, for bringing food to Jewish inmates in the forced labor camp.

W.-Z. p. 441. GKBZH WB I 164.

458. Skarżysko (2), voivodship of Kielce. 1943. In a forest around the village of Michałowiec Germans executed a Polish woman employed at Starachowice by the name of **Wróblewska**, along with **her mother**, for hiding a Jewish child, son of Dr. Kramer in their apartment at 91 Robotnicza Street. At the same time, two **other Poles** of German descent (Volksdeutsch) were killed for aiding Jews, one of them named Bielański.

L.K.H. p. 96-97.

459. Skórnice, Piotrków county, voivodship of Kielce. April 13, 1943. The German military police found a Jewish family hiding on one of Polish farms. Together with the Jews, all the Poles were executed on the spot. In this massacre **13 persons** were killed, including three men, four women and six children. **Eight Catholics** gave their lives in attempt to save Jews. In the same reign of terror more than a dozen villages of the area were totally or partially wiped out, some of them for no obvious reason, possibly also for harboring Jewish refugees.

A. J. p. 5. OKBZH in Kielce, testimonies and witnesses, 1968 questionaire of GKBZH.

460. Skrzynice, Bychawa county, voivodship of Lublin. October 1943. During a raid by the German military police, **Bolesław Kwiatosz**, 28, was discovered sheltering a 15-year old Jewish boy, Chaim. Both were murdered on the spot and buried in a common grave.

B.-L. p. 844. S.D. p. 101, 113. W.-Z. p. 427. GKBZH WB V 105.

461. Skrzynka, Dąbrowa Tarnowska county, voivodship of Kraków. A Volksdeutsch renegade named Wendland from Mądrzechów, with the aid of dreaded German henchmman, Guzdek, discovered that the Polish Piekielniak family was sheltering a Jewish family. The Jews were shot on the spot and both Piekielniaks beaten so cruelly that **Mrs. Piekielniak** died soon afterwards. Her husband, Józef Piekielniak, somehow survived the ordeal.

Testimony of J. Kozaczka in W.-Z. p. 342.

462. Słomniki, Miechów county, voivodship of Kraków. March 1943. For aiding Jews, a Catholic farmer, **Władysław Michalski,** was executed in Miechów together with his son.

W.-Z. p. 417. S.D. p. 94, 114. GKBZH WB II 179-80.

463. Słonim, voivodship of Nowogródek. December 19, 1942. The Gestapo broke into the convent of the Sisters of the Immaculate Conception where many Jewish children were hiding. They arrested Mother Superior **Kazimiera Wołowska** (Sister Marta) and **Bogumiła Noiszewska,** M.D. (Sister Ewa). Most Jewish orphans were brought to the convent by Jesuit Pastor of the Żyrowice parish, **Rev. Adam Sztark,** S.J., who also paid with his life for hiꞏ heroic errands of charity.

J.-W. v. 5, p. 596. GKBZH WB 755 (Marta Wołowska), 462 (Ewa Noyszewska).

464. Słupia, Skierniewice county, voivodship of Łódź. May 25, 1944. **Walenty Nowak** and his son, **Tadeusz Nowak,** for two years sheltered a Jew with a pseudonym "Tomczak", committed to their care by the Polish Home Army. For this offence, the father was executed in KL Mauthausen and his son was ctuelly beaten at the Gestapo quarters in Tomaszów

Mazowiecki. His massacred body was thrown into a heap of manure and ordered to be carted away by a trash collector.

GKBZH WB X 98-9. OKBZH in Łódź, Okt/Kpp 18/79, testimony of J. Paczkowska.

465. Słuszczyn, Lipno county, voivodship of Kielce. February 1943. During a raid on the Borek family house, a group of Germans named Mesel, Himmel, Werner and a local Volksdeutch renegade, Fosch, discovered there was a shelter for Jews. While looting the house, they kept the Boreks tied with a clothline in a barn, with the exception of their daughter, Honorata, who was holding a crying baby in her arms. After everything of value was removed, they brought together **Stanisław Borek**, 68, his wife, **Stanisława Borek**, 60, their son, **Czesław Borek**, 20, and their son-in-law, **Jan Wójtowicz**, 30. They ordered everybody, including **Honorata Wójtowicz**, 30, to take a sheaf of straw from the barn and carry it to the house in order to be burned alive there, together with the **baby Wójtowicz**, ten months of age. In the last moment, Stanisław was taken out and driven to Lipna to be tortured there in order to find the whereabouts of the Jews. A few shots into the house ignited the straw, and the house, with all its occupants, was burned to the ground. Stanisław died in the dungeons of Lipno, without giving any information.

Court deposition of J. Wyroda in W.-Z. p. 373-4, also 415,. F.-R. p. 306. GKBZH WB I 147-9, 48-50. K.-M. p. 8 (Starzyno).

466. Sobianowice, Lublin county, voivodship of Lublin. Autumn 1942. **Władysław Piątek** was shot to death, together with a Jewish father and his daughter who sought refuge in his home. Their executioners were the German military policemen from Rybnik.

GKBZH Osn 8/219/69/W-1089.

467. Sobujew, Sierpc county, voivodship of Warsaw. May

8, 1942. **Jan Machulski** was shot to death for hiding Jews who, in the meantime, managed to escape.

W.-Z. p. 405. GKBZH WB IV 23.

468. Sokal, voivodship of Lwów. February 1942. A woman named **Wysoczańska** was murdered by the Germans together with three Jewish children she was trying to save from death by bringing them to her house.

GKBZH WB XI 71.

469. Sokołów Małopolski, voivodship of Rzeszów. Summer 1943. **Agnieszka Gałgan** was drenched with gasoline together with **two farmers** from Trebuska and set on fire for hiding three Jewish men and one woman who, under duress, betrayed to the Germans their hiding place. One of German executioners pushed Agnieszka, still alive, into a ditch and finished her off with a pistol.

Court deposition of K. Kozak in W.-Z. p. 395-6, also 425. GKBZH WB IV 261.

470. Solinki, Biała Podlaska county, voivodship of Lublin. In reprisal for helping Jews, Germans murdered **Józef Rosa** on the spot and deported **twenty-eight persons** to the dreaded prison in the castle of Lublin and to KL Majdanek. Some of them returned alive; those who died included, among others: **Edward Celiński**, b. 1917, **Wacław Celiński**, b. 1915, **Wacław Dębowski**, b. 1909, **Józef Fijoł**, b. 1907, **Wacław Krasuski**, b. 1917, **Aleksander Szczygielski**, b. 1902, **Władysław Rosa**, b. 1917, and **Franciszek Nożyński**, b. 1917.

W.-Z. p. 443. GKBZH WB V 158, 176-7, 179, 180, 182-3.

471. Sosnowice, Chełm Lubelski county, voivodship of Lublin. May 1942. **Hipolit Kamiński**, his wife, and their daughter, **Halina Kamińska**, were shot to death for sheltering a Jewish family. They were cruelly beaten before being killed.

W.-Z. p. 445. GKBZH Egz. S.

GENERALGOUVERNEMENT
DISTRIKT RADOM
Der Stadt-Kommissar der Stadt Ostrowiec
(Kreishauptmannschaft Opatow)

BEKANNTMACHUNG

Es ist wiederholt festgestellt, dass geflüchtete Juden von Polen aufgenommen sind. Ich mache auf die 3. Verordnung über Aufenthaltsbeschränkung im Generalgouvernement vom 15. 10. 1941. VO. Bl. GG S. 595 aufmerksam. Danach werden diejenigen Polen, die den geflüchteten Juden Unterschlupf oder Beköstigung gewähren oder ihnen Nahrungsmittel verkaufen, mit dem Tode bestraft. Ich weise hierauf letztmalig hin.

Ostrowiec, den 28. September 1942.

Der Stadtkommissar

(gez.) Motschall

OGÓLNE GUBERNATORSTWO
DYSTRYKT RADOM
Komisarz Miasta w Ostrowcu
Starostwo Powiatowe w Opatowie

OGŁOSZENIE

Stwierdzono powtarzające się wypadki ukrywania się żydów uchodźców u polaków. Zwracają uwagę na 3 rozporządzenie z dnia 15. 10. 1941 r (VO. Bl. GG. str. 595) w sprawie ograniczenia pobytu na terenie Generalnego Gubernatorstwa, pouczam, że kto udziela żydom uchodźcom pomieszczenia i żywności lub sprzedaje żydom środki żywnościowe, będzie karany śmiercią. Pouczenie jest ostateczne.

Ostrowiec, dnia 28 września 1942 r.

Komisarz Miasta

(—) Motschall

BEKANNTMACHUNG

Betrifft:
Beherbergung von geflüchteten Juden.

Es besteht Anlass zu folgendem Hinweis: Gemäss der 3. Verordnung über Aufenthaltsbeschränkungen im Generalgouvernement vom 15. 10. 1941 (VO. Bl. GG. S. 595) unterliegen Juden, die den jüdischen Wohnbezirk unbefugt verlassen, der Todesstrafe.

Gemäss der gleichen Vorschrift unterliegen Personen, die solchen Juden wissentlich Unterschlupf gewähren, Beköstigung verabfolgen oder Nahrungsmittel verkaufen, ebenfalls der Todesstrafe.

Die nichtjüdische Bevölkerung wird daher dringend gewarnt

1) Juden Unterschlupf zu gewähren,

2) Juden Beköstigung zu verabfolgen,

3) Juden Nahrungsmittel zu verkaufen.

Tschenstochau, den 24. 9. 42.

OGŁOSZENIE

Dotyczy:
przetrzymywania ukrywających się żydów.

Zachodzi potrzeba przypomnienia, że stosownie do § 3 Rozporządzenia o ograniczeniach pobytu w Gen. Gub. z dnia 15. X. 1941 roku (Dz. Rozp. dla GG. str. 595) żydzi, opuszczający dzielnicę żydowską bez zezwolenia, podlegają karze śmierci.

Według tego rozporządzenia, osobom, które takim żydom świadomie udzielają przytułku, dostarczają im żywności lub sprzedają artykuły żywnościowe, grozi również kara śmierci.

Niniejszym ostrzega się stanowczo ludność nieżydowską przed:

1) udzielaniem żydom przytułku,

2) dostarczaniem im jedzenia,

3) sprzedawaniem im artykułów żywnościowych.

Częstochowa, dnia 24. 9. 42

Der Stadthauptmann
Dr. Franke

472. Sosnowiec, voivodship of Katowice. Summer 1943.
Roman Kołodziej undertook the mission of saving Dr. Liberman, a Jewish surgeon, from the local ghetto which, at this time, was in process of being liquidated. He was shot to death by a German military policeman.

Testimony of J. Goldkorn in B.-L. p. 442. W.-Z. p. 425. GKBZH WB VII 250.

473. Sośninka, Garwolin county, voivodship of Warsaw. November 19, 1943. Germans shot to death **five Catholic farmers** together with the two Jews they were sheltering.

GKBZH WB VI 60.

474. Spytkowice, Jordanów county, voivodship of Kraków. May 28, 1944. **Franciszek Długopolski**, 44, was arrested under suspicion of sheltering Jews. He was executed as one of the hostages in a camp located in the area of two Jewish cemeteries in Płaszów near Kraków. In this camp, at a special order of the Commandant, some Catholic victims were hanged by the Jewish inmates.

GKBZH WB II 60. ZG 31/46, court deposition taken at Jordanów.

475. Stara Łomża, Łomża county, voivodship of Białystok. Autumn 1943. **Czesław Kowalewski** was hanged over one of the gates leading to the ghetto area for bringing aid to Jews incarcerated there.

GKBZH WB II 12. Ko 39/70, court deposition taken in Łomża.

476. Stare Bystre, Nowy Targ county, voivodship of Kraków. July 1943. Józef Synaj, a Jew who came to **Franciszek Ligas**, asking for help, was caught by the Germans. For not denouncing his guest to German authorities, the Catholic farmer was arrested and sent to the dreadful Montelupi prison in Kraków where he was tortured to death. Synaj was shot on the spot.

W.-Z. p. 423. GKBZH WB II 96.

477. Starzyna, Hajnówka county, voivodship of Biały-stok. German military police shot to death **Gierasim Kozak**, a Byelorussian, who died together with four Jews he was trying to save.

W.-Z. p. 429. GKBZH WB III 133.

478. Staw, Chełm county, voivodship of Lublin. May 26, 1942. German military police, with the aid of Ukrainian rene-gades, gathered over two hundred Polish Catholic villagers in a public square and demanded extradition of those guilty of ai-ding "Jews and partisans". When nobody volunteered this kind of information, eight hostages were selected and murde-red in front of the crowd which didn't budge. Those killed were: **Jan Bień**, 33, **Adam Dużyc**, 35, **Władysław Jaszczuk**, 30, **Tadeusz Natalski**, 32, **Jan Nowosad**, 45, **Wasyl Szady**, 18, **Józef Wasyńczuk**, 28, and **Stanisław Nowosad**, 18. Their bo-dies were buried in an open field, not in a cemetery.

F.-R. p. 59. OKBZH in Lublin Ds 152/67.

479. Sterdyń, Sokołów county, voivodship of Warsaw. March 25 to April 23, 1943. The German SS performed a sum-mary execution of **forty-seven Christian farmers** for the of-fence of sheltering Jews, and **forty** for helping them otherwise. In addition, **one hundred forty persons** were arrested and ta-ken away. The entire village was put to torch and burned to the ground.

PZPR KC CA 202/III/33 p. 354. S.L. p. 252.

480. Stoczek, Węgrów county, voivodship of Warsaw. 1943. For helping Jews, **thirteen farmers** were put to death by the Germans. Together with the Sadowne and Łochów area, more than **one hundred Christian farmers** were assassinated for this reason by the Germans.

B.-L. p. 835. W.-Z. p. 429. S.L. p. 86. GKBZH WB VI S.

481. Stróże, Gorlice county, voivodship of Rzeszów. **Michał Dywan** was shot to death for hididng Hamek Kant, a Jew.

W.-Z. p. 443. GKBZH WB II 209.

Strych see **Paprotnia**.

482. Stryj (1), voivodship of Stanisławów. 1943. In the middle of a square, next to the city hall, Germans erected gallows for a **Catholic teacher**, 40, and **his wife** to be hanged publicly for the "crime" of sheltering a Jewish family. The event was announced through louds peakers installed in the city streets and all the inhabitants were forced to come out of their houses to witness the execution.

W.-Z. p. 431. GKBZH WB IV 333-4.

483. Stryj (2), voivodship of Stanisławów. January 28, 1944. According to the order signed by the German Commandant of SS and Police for the district of Galicia, **Bronisław Jaroszyński** was condemned to death as one of eighty–four victims, five of them sentenced specifically for sheltering and otherwise helping Jews. The purpose of printing this poster was to frighten the population. Normally, similar killings were executed on the spot, without any such formalities.

Facsimile of the poster in W.-Z. p. 442, also 431. B.-L. 873. S.D. p. 104, 113. B.-R. (Jaroziński). GKBZH WB IV 387.

484. Studzieniec, Rzeszów county, voivodship of Rzeszów. December 1, 1942. German military police, with the aid of especially trained dogs, discovered a Jewish family of five in a forest dug-out near the village of Przewrotne. A hand grenade was tossed inside and took the lives of Lejb, Gitla, Srul and Gnedla Zeler, while the oldest among them, Metla Zeler, somehow survived. Questioned about the names of Catholic farmers who were supplying Jews with food and other necessities, she pointed out **Franciszek Dziubek**, 30, who made the door to their shelter, **Franciszek Drąg**, 31, who brought hinges, **Józef Drąg**, 32, **Jan Pomykała**, 52, and **Jan Żak**, 32, who performed other services. Captured by her spirit of cooperation, Germans made her undress and dance for them in the snow while they were taking pictures. Finally, the old woman was brutally pushed into a ditch where all the condemned Catholics had already been shoved. They were photographed, before being killed, and their bodies covered with dirt. On this day Germans killeds **even Christian farmers** for aiding Jews.

S.Z. p. 144-5. F.-R. p. 321. OKBZH in Rzeszów, Ds Ii 4/71.

485. Swaryszów, Jędrzejów county, voivodship of Kielce. April 27, 1943. Germans executed a **Catholic woman** from Wodzisław for helping Jews.

B.-L. p. 832.

486. Swoszowa Wola, Jasło county, voivodship of Rzeszów. 1944. For hiding eighteen Jews in a dug-out under his house, **Władysław Kozak** was shot to death by the Germans while some Jews managed to escape. Seven members of the Feigenbaum family, whom he had saved, emigrated to Israel.

Testimony of T. Seweryn in W.-Z. p. 292, also 441 (17 Jews) B.-L. p. 180. GKBZH WB IV 171, also II 35/70.

487. Szarwark (1), Dąbrowa Tarnowska county, voivodship of Kraków. July 5, 1943. The Gestapo, aided by the "navy blue" police, surrounded the farm of the Mendala family, suspected of helping Jews. They found there one hundred hard boiled eggs, obviously intended for the Jews hiding in the forest. For this, the Germans killed **Franciszek Mendala**, 48, his wife, **Teresa Mendala**, 40, their **two children**, 10 and 12 years of age, and their mother-in-law, **Wiktoria Wężowicz**, 67. The slaughter took place inside their house which was later set on fire. According to some accounts, children were killed in a barn and their bodies were tossed into the raging flames.

Mendala's farm was never rebuilt. Whatever remained of their bodies was collected in a box and buried in the local cemetery under an inscription on a wooden cross which simply says that they "died a tragic death". Even the local pastor does not know why and how they died. There were too many such deaths for the Poles to remember and Yad Vashem, as a rule, does not commemorate Catholic Poles who died trying to save the Jews, especially when their heroic efforts were not crowned with success.

B.-L. p. 68, 839, 847. S.D. p. 99, 113. W.-Z. p. 341-2, 375, 423. GKBZH WB II 97-100.

488. Szarwark (2), Dąbrowa Tarnowska county, voivodship of Kraków. July 5, 1943. German Gestapo surprised a Catholic farmer **Władysław Starzec** who was sheltering a Jew in the attic of his stable. The Jew managed to escape, but his presence was betrayed by his bed dug out in the hay. The captured delinquent was cruelly beaten and tossed alive into the burning house of Mendala.

B.-L. p. 68, 839, 847. S.D. p. 99, 113. W.-Z. p. 341-2. GKBZH II 102.

Szczepanów see **Brzesko**.

Szczurowa see **Brzesko**.

489. Szerzyny (1), Jasło county, voivodship of Rzeszów. February 5, 1944. Catholic peasants, **Józef Augustyn** and his wife, **Józefa Augustyn**, were executed by the German military police for sheltering two Jewish families of Eliasz and Hersz Heskel. The farmers were shot to death together with the Jews.

W.-Z. p. 433. GKBZH WB IV 6-7.

490. Szerzyny (2), Jasło county, voivodship of Rzeszów. For sheltering Jews, two Polish peasants, **Franciszek Figura** and **Jędryś**, were sent to Auschwitz. They never returned.

W.-Z. p. 441. GKBZH WB IV 436. T.Bi. p. 6 (B. Figura).

491. Szerzyny (3), Jasło county, voivodship of Rzeszów. **Bronisław Mitoraj**, betrayed by the very Jews he was sheltering in his house, fell into German hands. He was arrested and never came back.

GKBZH WB IV 8. T.Bi. p. 6 (Mikołaj).

492. Szklary, Rzeszów county, voivodship of Rzeszów. 1942. The Gestapo shot to death **Wojciech Patroński** in front of his own house along with three Jews he was sheltering. The Jews were buried in a common grave in the Buczyna forest and their benefactor's body was transferred to the local cemetary after the Germans were gone.

B.-L. p. 834, 837. S.D. p. 92, 114. W.-Z. p. 413. GKBZH WB IV 416. T.Bi. p. 4.

493. Sztuki, Wysokie Mazowieckie county, voivodship of Białystok. A Catholic named **Andrzejczyk** was executed by the Germans in his own backyard for giving shelter to twenty Jews.

W.-Z. p. 443. GKBZH WB III 1361. K.-M. p. 8 (Czyżewo Sutki, J. Andrzejczak).

Szumin see **Zarzetka**.

494. Szwejki, Sokołów Podlaski county, voivodship of Warsaw. For her aid to some hidden Jews, **Marianna Kur** was arrested and disappeared without trace.

Testimony of. K. Witt in J. K. p. 220.

Szymbarzyna see **Zarzetka**.

495. Szynwałd, Tarnów county, voivodship of Kraków. August 1944. **Stanisław Kopacz** was murdered by the Germans for sheltering Jews.

Testimony of T. Seweryn in B.-L. p. 848. S.D. p. 107, 113. W.-Z. p. 437. GKBZH WB II 211.

Szyszczyce see **Chmielnik**.

496. Świesielice (1), Lipsko county, voivodship of Kielce. November 8, 1942. **Maria Skwira**, 40, was shot to death by the Germans for sheltering Jews. The rest of her family managed to escape.

F.-R. p. 306 (Dec. 7, Marianna S.) W.-Z. p. 407. OKBZH in Kielce, Ds. 58/69.

497. Świesielice (2), Lipsko county, voivodship of Kielce. November, 1942. A few days after Mrs. Skwira was executed, her neighbor, **Stanisław Czapka**, 30, was punished by death for looking after Maria's farm, thus making a common cause with her concern for Jews.

W.-Z. p. 407. F.-R. p. 306 (Nov. 7, Czapla). GKBZH WB I 194.

498. Świesielice (3), Lipsko county, voivodship of Kielce. December 7, 1942. **Benedykt Wdowiak**, 58, his daughter, **Aleksandra Wdowiak**, 16, and his mother, **Marianna Wdowiak**, 90, were murdered by the German military police from Ciepielów for harboring Jews and taking care of them.

W.-Z. p. 371. F.-R. p 300 (Aleksander W.) GKBZH WB I 115-7. OKBZH in Kielce Ds 58/69.

499. Świesielice (4), Lipsko county, voivodship of Kielce. December 7, 1942. To deter Catholic Poles from giving support to the Jews, German military police committed a wholesale slaughter of the Wojewódka family, killing **Ignacy Wojewódka**, 50, his wife, **Maria Wojewódka**, 45, and all their children: **Jan Wojewódka**, 18, **Stanisława Wojewódka**, 12, **Józef Wojewódka**, 7, and **Wacław Wojewódka**, 21.

W.-Z. p. 371. F.-R. p. 306 (Marianna W.) GKBZH WZ I 145, 146.

500. Tarnawce, Przemyśl county, voivodship fo Rzeszów. A Catholic forester, **Stanisław Kurpiel**, and his wife, **Franciszka Kurpiel**, both from Leoncin, were shot to death by the Germans for sheltering three Jewish families in a "bunker" built next to their house. Together with them perished the families of Rubinfeld, Golinger and Spiegel.

B.-L. p. 718. W.-Z. p. 439. GKBZH WB IV 153-4.

501. Tarnawka, Łańcut county, voivodship of Rzeszów. **Stanisław Piechuta** was executed for bringing food to Jews hiding in the Hadelski forest.

T.Bi. p. 4. OKBZH in Rzeszów.

502. Tarnów, Chełm county, voivodship of Lublin. May 1942. German military police units murdered **fifteen Catholic peasant** accused of sheltering "Jews and partisans": **Paweł Bażan, Genowefa Ciepłowska, Katarzyna Hajdaczuk, Natalia Kalinowska, Stefan Kolańczuk, Jan Kudeniec, Józef Lec, Jan Świętowicz, Maria Misztalska, Mieczysław Misztalski, Maria Paszczuk, Jan Świętowicz, Katarzyna Świętowicz, Zofia Szarun** and **Anastazja Szczepaniuk**. Together with them died five Jewish families: Esta, Josek, Lajza, Mendel, Nysek and Felka from the Hajbor family; Dawid, Chaim, Esta, Herszek, Manaszek, Lata, Majka, Idka and Pejsa of the Karp family; Aron, Esta, Hanka, Szmul and Humka of the Lajzeron family; Józek Lejzorek; and Berko, Manach, Sura of the Machenbaum family. Many houses were looted by the German military police, two of them burned to the ground.

F.-R. p. 60.

503. Tarnów (1), voivodship of Kraków. August 22, 1942. On Krakowiecka Street, the Gestapo killed **two Polish boys** for bringing food to Jews. For the same reason, they murdered three Catholic women: **Mierzejewska**, 70, **Sabina Orlik** and **one**, unknown by name.

A Pietrzyk in the Calendar of events, "Zeszyty Tarnowskie", 1972, p. 88.

504. Tarnów (2), voivodship of Kraków. February 1943. For hiding Rozalia, a seven-year old Jewish girl from Rumania, **Maria Wcisło**, mother of a thirteen – year old Kazimierz

Wcisło, was shot to death.

GKBZH WB II 117. GKBZH Ko 93/98, a court deposition made in Brzeg July 25, 1978.

505. Tarnów (3), voivodship of Kraków. **Julian Maciejko**, who entered the ghetto area to supply aid to Jews inside, never came back. He was killed there.

W.-Z. p. 445. GKBZH WB II 174.

506. Tomaszowice (1), Lublin county, voivodship of Lublin. Summer 1943. **Stanisław Zawada** was murdered by the German military police for the aid given to Jews.

GKBZH V Egz. T.

507. Tomaszowice (2), Lublin county, voivodship of Lublin. February 28, 1944. German military police, under the command of officer König, used hand grenades to kill **Leonard Pietrak**, his wife, **Maria Pietrak**, their son, **Stanisław Pietrak**, his companion, **Franciszek Chęć**, 15, and also their neighbor, **Stanisław Wierzbicki**. The Pietrak family was executed for sheltering Jews, the others for failing to inform the German authorities, which also was punishable by death, according to the German law.

Court deposition of I. Woźniak in W.-Z. p. 379, also 433. GKBZH WB V 126-7, 130.

508. Treblinka (1), Węgrów county, voivodship of Warsaw. Summer 1942. Prospective victims of the dreadful death camp were not aware of its real nature. A foreign-born Jew, when lost in transport, even bought his own ticket there in order to join his group which allegedly was being shipped to a rural settlement. He was warned by a Polish conductor and ran away. On another occasion, however, a similar warning from a **Catholic worker** resulted in his immediate execution when the Jew complained to a German guard, mistrusting the "anti-Semitic" Pole.

F.Z. p. 44-5.

509. Treblinka (2), Węgrów county, voivodship of Warsaw. Summer 1942. A Catholic railroad employee, **Jan Maletko**, was shot to death by a German guard while bringing water to Jews locked in a box car. His companion, Remigiusz Pawłowicz, who also went to the aid of Jews, was saved by falling into a ditch. Maletko's body was loaded into a railroad car to be burned with Jewish corpses in the death camp, but was released for a burial in the cemetery of the Prostynia parish at the request of his foreman.

F.Z. p. 46. Also author's interview with R. Pawłowicz in Małkinia on August 3, 1983,

510. Treblinka (3), Węgrów county, voivodship of Warsaw. May 1943. In connection with the Polish Home Army desigh to attack the death camp and free the Jewish inmates prepared by Franciszek Ząbecki, plans of the camp were made, some weapons smuggled in and contacts made. Due to a mishap, **Grzegorz Ząbecki**, pseud. Zbroja, was arrested, taken to Pawiak prison, sent to Auschwitz and later to Mauthausen, in which he gave his life as prisoner no. 45330 (tatooed on his arm).

F.Z.W. p. 123, 124. S.L. p. 250. J.G. p. 17, 18-19 L. S. p. 250-1. W. Razmowski: Akcja Treblinka in "Dzieje Najnowsze" periodical, 1964, nr. 1.

During the premature outbreak of revolt in Treblinka, one unit of the Polish Home Army, under the command of Stanisław Siwek, assisted the escapees in crossing the Bug river and taking a correct direction in flight through the woods. Among those sheltered by the Polish farmers and nursed back to health was one of the Jewish leaders, Henryk Paswolski, who was invited often from Rio de Janeiro to testify in many Treblinka processes – a living denial of the defamatory book by J. F. Steiner on the subject.

511. Treblinka (4), Węgrów county, voivodship of Warsaw. Near the electric fence surrounding the death camp known as Treblinka 2, German guards apprehended a **Catholic girl** about 20-years old who was trying to pass some food to the starving inmates through the fence. Brought inside, she was executed in front of the prisoners.

W.-Z. p. 439. GKBZH WB V 136.

512. Treblinka (5), Węgrów county, voivodship of Warsaw. A Catholic farmer, **Jan Samsel**, residing close to Treblinka 2, was commissioned by the Polish Home Army to deliver
arms to the Jewish inmates through the intermediary of a
friendly Ukrainian guard. Germans, however, probably through a Jewish informer known as "Ignac", found out about the
imminent action and arrested the **entire Samsel family** in the
village of Grędy. All of them perished in the death camp.

S.L. p. 251. Also, author's interviews with Eugenia Samuel and Józef Wu-
jek, both living in the neighborhood of Treblinka at this time, themselves inmates of Treblinka 2.

Their visas were cancelled by the American Consulate in Warsaw in order
to prevent them from testifying at the Cleveland Treblinka trial. Only Jewish
"survivors" were allowed to testify.

513. Trębaczew (1), Rawa Mazowiecka county, voivodship of Łódź. November 11, 1943. **Stanisław Szczepaniak**,
who was sheltering a Jewish family in his attic, died at the
hands of the German military police. He was shot to death together with **Antoni Szczepaniak** and **Władysław Szczepaniak**. After the Germans were gone, they were buried in the
Catholic cemetery of Lubanie.

GKBZH WB X 2-3, 4. A court deposition in GKBZH Ko 23/68.

514. Trębaczew (2), Rawa Mazowiecka county, voivodship of łódź. November 11, 1943. A Polish Catholic, **Jan Do-
maradzki**, was executed by the Germans for helping the Jews.

GKBZH WB X 1. A court deposition in GKBZH Ko 23/68.

515. Trębaczew (3), Rawa Mazowiecka county, voivodship of Łódź. Spring 1944. German military police shot to death **five Catholic peasants** for sheltering Jews.

W.-Z. p. 435.

516. Trzebuska (1), Kolbuszowa County, voivodship of Rzeszów. July 20, 1942. Four Jewish refugees, three men and one woman, were hiding on the farm of **J. Gołojuch**. Discovered by the Germans, all Jews and the entire Catholic Gołojuch family were murdered.

T.Bi. p. 6

517. Trzebuska, (2), Kolbuszowa county, voivodship of Rzeszów. Summer 1943. Together with four Jews from Sokołów, **Bartłomiej Gielarowski** and his wife, **Mrs. Gielarowska**, as well as **Karolina Marciniec** and another **Catholic woman** from Sokołów Podlaski, unknown by name, were shot, drenched with gasoline, pushed into a ditch and cremated. Their offense was giving a helping hand to Jews...

Court deposition of K. Kozak in W.-Z. p. 395-6. GKBZH WB IV 272-3 (five Jews). T.Bi. p. 7. (Gielarowski).

518. Tworki, Siedlce county, voivodship of Lublin. January 1944. **Zofia Krasuska**, 38, and her little son, **Stanisław Krasuski**, 5, were put to death by the Germans together with seven Jews sheltered by them.

B.-L. p. 833. W.-Z. p. 433. GKBZH WB VI 1392.

519. Tyczyn, Rzeszów county, voivodship of Rzeszów. October 15, 1943. For giving aid to Jewish refugees from the Tyczyn ghetto, German Gestapo executed **Józef Jędrzejewski**, 27, **Józef Głowiak**, 21, his father, **Walenty Głowiak**, 50, from Biała, and **Jan Pająk**, 21, from Matysówka; they were buried in a common grave in a Jewish cemetery.

B.-L. p. 834, 840. S.D. p. 101. GKBZH WB IV 342-3. W.-Z. p. 427.

520. Tymienica (1), Lipsko county, voivodship of Kielce. January 1943. For giving aid to Jews, **Szczepan Lasek**, 12, and **Zdzisława Lasek**, 14, were murdered by the Germans.

Court deposition of J. Mirowski in W.-Z. p. 372. GKBZH WB I 173.

521. Tymienica (2), Lipsko county, voivodship of Kielce. Winter 1942/43. **Józef Rutkowski** was murdered with **six other Poles** for giving aid to the Jews. He was burned alive.
GKBZH WB I 173.

522. Uszew, Brzesko county, voivodship of Kraków. May 1944. German military police shot to death a Catholic peasant, **Wojciech Koftis**, 70, who was supplying food to five Jews–Pinkas Federgrün, Mrs. Goldberg, and her three children under 5 years of age, hiding in a nearby forest. All the Jews were killed with him.
S.D. p. 107, 112. W.-Z. p. 435.

523. Użowa, near Rożyszcze, voivodship of Wołyń. 1942. **Józef Juchniewicz** was killed by the Germans and burned with his farm building for sheltering some Jews for one year in his house.
GKBZH WB XI 24.

524. Waniewo, Łapy county, voivodship of Białystok. September 8, 1943. German military police from Tykocin shot to death on the spot **Stanisław Krysiewicz**, and his wife, **Władysława Krysiewicz**, was murdered in Tykocin. Their five little children were saved by their neighbor, Marianna Wołosik. Eight Jews sheltered by them were burned alive with Krysiewicz's house in which they were hiding. They were: Lejzor Różanowicz with his wife, S. Jaskóła with his wife Lsza, B. Różanowicz with his wife, and two girls, one of them being from Warsaw.
Testimony of M. Wołosik in W.-Z. p. 366-7, also 425. B.-L. p. 868. GKBZH WB III 16-7 (Waplewo). K.-M. p. 8.

525. Wapowice, Przemyśl county, voivodship of Rzeszów. Mrs. **Maria Kawa** was shot to death by the Germans for sheltering a Jewish family.
W.-Z. p. 443. GKBZH WB IV 443.

526. Warsaw (1). January 1940. With the aid of his Polish friends, a Pole of Jewish descent, Andrzej Kott, managed to escape from jail. Among those who helped him and were killed by the Germans was **Szymon Lubelski**, a teacher of the German language. In the apartment of **Maria Brodacka**, where his chains were filed off and his hair tinted to a different hue, the remains of the chains were found and Maria was executed on June 14, 1940 as the first Catholic Pole in Warsaw to be so punished for aiding a Jew. Many other Poles connected with this rescue were killed in the Palmiry forest.

S.D.T. p. 138-40. W.S. p. 147. Also Author's interview with Mrs. Brodacka's son in Warsaw, on March 4, 1984.

527. Warsaw (2). November 19, 1940. An unidentified **Polish boy** was killed by the Germans for tossing a bag of bread over the wall of the ghetto to starving Jews. Many similar cases were noted by the Jewish chronicler of the Warsaw Ghetto, Emmanuel Ringelblum, in his book entitled "Polish–Jewish relations".

W.-Z. p. 405. GKBZH WB VI'87.

528. Warsaw (3). Winter 1940. The Board of Directors of the Polish Bar Association rejected the German demand that Jewish lawyers be disbarred. Even the lawyers who, before the war, were critical of the excessive number of Jews in their profession, like **Jan Nowodworski**, President of the Association, **Jerzy Czarkowski**, **Bolesław Bielawski**, **Jerzy Czerwiński**, **Ludwik Domański**, **Jan Gadomski**, **Władysław Młodzianowski**, **Leon Nowodworski**, **Stanisław Perzyński**, **Jan Podkomorski**, **Mieczysław Rudziński**, **Michał Skoczyński**, **Bogdan Suligowski**, **Feliks Zadrowski** and **Leopold Żaryn**, refused to disbar their Jewish colleagues at their meetings in February 1940, and in the Spring of 1941 supported their decision. Many of them were sent to the dreadful Pawiak prison between July 10 and 12, 1940, and subsequently deported to Auschwitz from which hardly anybody returned.

Testimony of W. Szyszkowski in B.-L. p. 114-7. W.-Z. p. 38.

529. Warsaw (4). June 12, 1941. **Jerzy Szurig**, 48, a journalist by profession, was caught in the ghetto while bringing aid to its Jewish inmates. He was executed, with thousands like him, in the Palmiry forest where Christian crosses are intermixed with the Stars of David over the symbolic graves of the cemetery.

B.-L. p. 1024.

530. Warsaw (5). Spring 1941. German police shot to death **Stanisława Iwańska**, 68, mother of Major Henryk Iwański whom the Polish Underground authorities had put in charge of aiding the Jews. She refused to disclose the whereabouts of these activities. Her husband, one of her sons, her daughter-in-law and two grandsons, died for the same noble cause, each in his own line of duty.

S.D. in the ”Biuletyn” of the Jewish Historical Institute, nr. 76 (1970 p. 81).

531. Warsaw (6). September 3, 1941. **Rev. Wojciech Kopliński, O.F.M.Cap.,** known as Father Anicet from the Capuchin monastery at Miodowa Street, was caught helping Jews. Deported to Auschwitz, he gave his life in a gas chamber on October 16, 1941 as prisoner no. 203676, in the first gassing of inmates. He died only two months after St. Maximilian Kolbe. There are two German biographies of this saintly man, but none in Polish.

Testimony of Bp. K. Niemira in B.-L. p. 421. S.D. p. 91. I.O. p. 152. W.-Z. p. 419. J.-W. v. 5, p. 233. GKBZH WB VI 1372 (Kapliński).

532. Warsaw (7). September 27, 1941. **Stefan Dworznik** died from the wounds he received while smuggling weapons into the Warsaw Ghetto in the course of ”action AK-J”.

GKBZH WB VI 569.

533. Warsaw (8). June 10, 1942. A Catholic gardener from Bukowińska St., Aleksander Smolarek, and his son **Kazimierz**

Smolarek, supplied food for the Warsaw ghetto; they also had a cache of arms and provided shelter for Jewish escapees; among others, the Biegunek family – with four children, as well as Rita Ryczywół. Discovered by the Germans, Kazimierz was shot with Rita in the ruins of the ghetto.

T.B. p. 100.

534. Warsaw (9). August 1942. Several **Catholic Poles**, unknown by name, were killed by the Germans while smuggling food to the starving Jerws of the Warsaw Ghetto.

Testimony of Dr. E. Ringelblum in W.-Z. p. 407. GKBZH VI P.

535. Warsaw (10). October 15, 1942. In a hall of the Warsaw courthouse on Oct. 3, 1942 Germans arrested **Tadeusz Koral** and **Ferdynand Grzesik** who used to meet there regularly with those rare volunteers, among others M. Klepfisz, from the Warsaw Ghetto who were willing to fight the Germans. They were being trained for the preparation of explosives for sabotage and self-defense. Grzesik was hanged on Leszno Street along with 50 persons from Pawiak prison and Koral passed through several concentration camps before he succumbed.

W.-Z. p. 405. B.L. p. 266-7. GKBZH WB VI G.

536. Warsaw (11). Autumn 1942. The father of Henryk Iwański, **Władysław Iwański**, 68, was murdered by the Germans together with fourteen Jews, hidden by his son in his workshop on their way out of the ghetto. One of his helpers, who told the Germans about the Jews hiding there, was condemned and executed as a traitor by Polish Underground authorities. Poland was the only country in Europe to pass such sentences for betraying Jews, even when committed by the Jews.

S.D. in "Biuletyn" of the Jewish Historical Institute, no. 76 (1970) p. 81.

537. Warsaw (12). December 19, 1942. A city employee,

Mr. Malicki, with the help of his wife, **Maria Malicka**, his brother, **Marian Malicki**, an artist, and a **Catholic priest**, provided Jews with baptismal certificates and "Aryan" identification cards. Betrayed, probably under duress, by one of their Jewish clients who was caught with one of those false documents, the priest was shot to death on the spot and the Malickis were deported to the death camp of Treblinka. Since their arms and legs were already broken by beating, they had to be carried to the death train, ready for a gas chamber. Among the persons they helped was Maria Reibenbach and her sister who survived.

Testimony of M. Reibenbach in B.-L. 552 (Janina Kapcińska) I.O. p. 274. GKBZH WZ VI 1385-6.

538. Warsaw (13). December 1942. "While taking Greenberg over the ghetto wall, Henik Tuchman and **his Christian landlord** were arrested. The Germans searched the apartment, found the hidden Jews and discovered a store of arms in the basement... Both were taken to the Befehlstelle at Żelazna St. no. 103. There they were fatally beaten and finally shot".

B.G. p. 172.

539. Warsaw (14). 1942. From a burning house in the ghetto a Jewish mother was saved along with four little children, two of them blinded by the fire. They were placed in the residence of a **Catholic teacher** who lived there with her **elderly mother**. At the sight of German military police approaching, the Jews were hidden in a nearby ditch and the Germans, in order to extort information about their hiding place, stood the elderly mother in a hole, dug in the ground and gradually were filling the hole with dirt, adding one shovel each time the old lady refused to answer their question. Finally, only her head remained above the ground and she died from suffocation. Suddenly, one of the blind children inadvertently walked out of the ditch, thus betraying the hiding place. The

Jews were killed outright and the teacher was sent to Auschwitz where she died during the winter of 1943.

W.Sm. p. 281.

540. Warsaw (15). Winter 1942. In a house at Słoneczna St. no. 50, apt. 40, Germans surprised **Mrs. Kuzyk** and another **Catholic person**, along with the Jews who were sheltered by them. Before killing them, they ordered all five to stretch out on the floor, their heads together and legs pointing in five different directions. In this position they shot them through their heads with hand guns. After the murderes left, neighbors found their bodies forming a star, all together, Catholics and Jews.

W.-Z. p. 411. GKBZH WB VI K.

541. Warsaw (16). 1942. At Barska St. **Zdzisław Gręcki** from the Gray Ranks was publicly executed for bringing aid to Jews in the Ghetto.

Testimony of S. Kowalski in W.-Z. p. 166, also 411. GKBZH WB VI 166 (Grędzki).

542. Warsaw (17). 1942. Another member of the Gray Ranks, **Mr. Podwysocki**, was caught in the Warsaw Ghetto supplying arms for the Jewish resistance movement which was already initiated in 1940 by H. Iwański and was not approved by the official leader of Jewish community. Podwysocki was taken to the Pawiak prison and shot to death.

Testimony of S. Kowalski in W.-Z. p. 166, also 413. GKBZH WB VI P.

543. Warsaw (18). 1942. Two elderly ladies, **Jadwiga Ponikowska**, a cousin of an interwar minister of Poland, and **Regina Prokulska**, were murdered in the headquarters of the Gestapo for hiding a Jewish intellectual and a girl of 5 or 6 years of age in their boarding house.

Testimony of J. Lasowski in B.-L. p. 624. W.-Z. p. 413. GKBZH WB VI 87.

544. Warsaw (19). **Loda Komarnicka,** who in 1942 gave shelter to dozens of Jews and provided them with "Aryan" papers, hid two Jewesses in her loft. She fell into the German hands while on trip to Łowicz to make some arrangements for a Jewish woman. She was killed there.

Testimony of M. Jiruska in B.-L. p. 454-5, also 291. W.-Z. p. 447.

545. Warsaw (20). Since 1942, a group of five headed by **Kazik,** his last name unknown, was engaged in smuggling Jews out of the Ghetto to the "Aryan" side. One day, while jumping over the wall, Kazik was shot to death by the guards.

GKBZH WB VI 707.

546. Warsaw (21). 1942. A troop of twenty-six young Polish boy-scouts undertook the task of smuggling into the Warsaw Ghetto sorely needed anti-typhoid shots to fight the dreadful epidemic which was killing thousands of Jews. In the course of this dangerous operation, **seven Catholic scouts** were shot to death. A few others, severely wounded, had to be transferred to another post. Among those who remained was 16-year old **Staszek,** his family name today unknown, who was caught by the Germans with one of those precious ampuls in hand. To prevent the Germans from learning the purpose of his mission, he quickly placed the glass container in his mouth, crushed it with his teeth and swallowed. Soon blood started to spurt from his mouth and he died in torsions before a medical aid could be provided.

W.Sm. p. 63-5.

547. Warsaw (22). January 17, 1943. The Rector of the Archidiocesan Seminary of Warsaw, **Msgr. Roman Archutowski,** a prominent church historian, was arrested and sent to KL Majdanek. He died there for helping Jewish escapees from the Warsaw Ghetto.

B.-L. p. 95. Ph.F. p. 116. I.O. p. 275. W.-Z. p. 353. GKBZH VI A3.

548. Warsaw (23). January 21, 1943. **Edward Bonisław-**

ski, who, as a member of the Polish Home Army, helped the Jewish freedom fighters within the walls of the Ghetto, was killed in the area of Żoliborz by the German military police.

B.L. p. 24. Caption on his photograph in the CAF archives on Foksal St. in Warsaw.

549. Warsaw (24). April 19, 1943. In support of the Ghetto revolt, an action was undertaken by the Polish Home Army with the purpose of making a breach in the wall at Bonifraterska Street. It took the lives of **Eugeniusz Morawski** and **Józef Wilk**. Their bodies were blown to pieces by a landmine; however, in the resulting confusion, a few dozen Jews managed, to get away through the Jewish cemetery where they were aided by the subordinates of Major Iwański.

Report of W. Bartoszewski in B.-L. p. 354. T.B. p. 140. I.O. p. 159-60. W.-Z. p. 190. GKBZH WB VI 95, 1358 (April 13, 1943).

550. Warsaw (25). April 20, 1943. A five-man Polish group led by Józef Lejewski brought a supply of arms for the Jewish Military Association (a Rightis organization, ignored by most Communist and also Jewish historians). It remained inside the Ghetto walls and fought the following two days of the Ghetto Uprising around Miła Street. When the order was issued for their withdrawal, **four members** of the team were dead and Lejewski himself wounded.

Ch.L. p. 279. T.B. p. 140 (two dead, two seriously wounded).

551. Warsaw (26). April 22, 1943. Report of the German commander, Gen. Stroop, mentions the capture of "thirty-five Polish bandits" who supported the Jewish revolt and were promptly executed.

Facsimile of the report in W.-Z. p. 193.

552. Warsaw (27). April 23, 1943. The Polish action on Leszmo St. in support of the Jewish revolt inside the Ghetto took the life of **Jerzy Lerski** or **Lerner** ps. Mietek, who blew himself up with a hand grenade to avoid falling into German hands.

Report of W. Bartoszewski in B.-L. p. 357. W.-Z. p. 192, 419. T.B. p. 141. GKBZH WB VI 1359 (Lernel).

553. Warsaw (28). April 25, 1943. Another report of General Stroop, dated this day, mentions a group of "**seventeen Poles**", among them two members of the "navy blue" police, apprehended and executed by the Germans for their part in aiding the Jewish revolt.

Facsimile of the report in W.-Z. p. 188.

554. Warsaw (29). April 27, 1943. A task force of eighteen men from the Security Corps of the Polish Home Army entered the ghetto area, with arms, hand grenades and ammunition under the command of Henryk Iwański and Władysław Żarski, or Zajdler, in cooperation with the Jewish Military Association, Among them was Tadeusz Bednarczyk still living in Warsaw. They entered through a tunnel on Muranowska St. and took active part in heavy fighting, shoulder to shoulder, with their Jewish comrades. The son of the commanding officer, **Roman Iwański**, 16, and the officer's brother, **Wacław Iwański**, died during the combat. This demonstration of solidarity also took the lives of **Wincenty Jędrychowski**, 30, and "Czapa" **Pilichowski**, 35. Almost all the participants of the action were wounded. After having used all the ammunition, the task force retreated through the sewers, taking with them 34 wounded Jewish fighters The well-known author of the "Uprising in the Warsaw Ghetto" (Shocken Books), Ber Mark, was among those rescued.

Testimony of B. Mark in B.-L. p. 239. S.D. p. 96. I.O. p. 152. T.B. p. 142. W.-Z. p. 192.

555. Warsaw (30). April 1943. Among the stories of "Polish Easter Fireworks of 1943", peddled abroad by the leftist authors like Adolf Rudnicki, Aleksander Donat (recte: Michał Berg), Jerzy Andrzejewski and Stefan Otwinowski, one significant element is missing: spontaneous help to the Jewish victims. Far from enjoying the Jewish misfortune, great majority of Catholics sympathized with the Jewish victims and even risked their own lives in their rescue attempts. Maria Kann, the author of the first eye-witness account "In the Full View of the Whole World", relates the instances where the Polish firemen defied German orders to limit themselves to the firebrands on the "Aryan" side. One **Catholic fireman** was machine-gunned by the Germans for trying to extinguish the flames which engulfed a Jewish child. There were dozens of similar sacrifices among the Catholic firemen who also secretly admitted Jews into their ranks. If discovered by the Germans, all those involved would be executed.

M.K. p. 121. T.B. p. 125-34.

556. Warsaw (31). April 1943. **Jerzy Vogel** took advantage of his German name and excellent knowledge of the German language to smuggle out of the Ghetto area around three hundred Jews and, even at the moment of his arrest, managed to save a Jewish girl, Dorota Gelbert who was sheltered in his house. On April 9, 1943 he was arrested for refusing to sign a German Volksliste. He and the majority of his family perished in various concentration camps.

T.B. p. 118.

557. Warsaw (32). May 3, 1943. The youngest participant of the Polish support action on Bonifraterska St., **Feliks Sobczyński**, 16, was apprehended and executed by the Germans ten days after the action.

Report of W. Bartoszewski in B.-L. p. 534. W.-Z. p. 190, 419.

558. Warsaw (33). May 1943. Another task force of fifteen men from the Security Corps of the Polish Home Army was led by Henryk Iwański through the city sewers, bringing food supplies, drugs and munition, also rescuing the wounded Jews on their way back. While being lowered into the manhole in a street of the Ghetto, another son of the commanding officer, **Zbigniew Iwański**, 18, was severely wounded and died while being carried in a bag through the sewers. Two of his companions, **Stanisław Gładkowski** and **Jan Cieplikowski**, died from their wounds after they were brought to a clandestine hospital. The story of these dramatic events was told by Major Iwański himself: "We entered through the sewers, loaded with drugs, food and bandages and, on our way back, we took the wounded. Each of us was moving through the sewers dragging the wounded in a specially made bag with openings for legs and a grip at the head. Some-times we had to bend in two and, in such posture, crawl in the stinking fluid to the exit. My wife "Janka" was waiting there to take care of our precious cargo. One day she fainted when the head emerging from the filthy sack was the head of her teen-age son, Zbigniew". He was the second son of Iwański's to die helping the Jews.

Testimony of B. Mark in B.L. p. 239. S.D. p. 98. I.O p. 152. W.Z. 419 GKBZH WB VI t. 5, 5, 9. Testimony of H. Iwannski in "How the Poles Helped the Jews", Warsaw, 1968, p. 10-12.

559. Warsaw (34). May 8, 1943. As one of the last defenders of the Ghetto revolt headquarters of Mordechai Anielewicz at Miła St. no. 18, a Polish girl, **Halina Rotblatt**, unknown by her maiden name, was shot by her husband in a Massada-like suicide, only moments before an underground passage was discovered which provided an escape for four survivors: Tosia Altman, Michał Rojzenfeld, Yehuda Węgrower and Menachem Bejgelman. Halina, while being of non-Jewish descent, decided to share the fate of the embattled Ghetto fighters to the bitter end.

R.E. p. 637.

560. Warsaw (35). May 10, 1943. **Jerzy Zołotow**, one of Polish rescures, died together with Ryszard Moselman while leading the Ghetto survivors through the city sewers to the forest of Kampinos.

B.-L. p. 379.

561. Warsaw (36). May 15, 1943. In the course of Polish rescue activities, while trying to aid Jews still escaping from the ruins of Ghetto, **Franciszek Bartoszek** was killed by the Germans.

B.-L. p. 52, 349, 361.

562. Warsaw (37). May 28, 1943. **Stanisław Skrypij**, 29, who was in charge of the action on Bonifraterska St., fell into German hands on May 18th and was executed ten days later.

B.-L. p. 360.

563. Warsaw (38). May 29, 1943. A police lieutenant, **Ryszard Stołkiewicz**, who, together with Capt. Tadeusz Żmudziński, provided Jews with "Aryan" identification cards, kept Jewish refugees in his apartment on Pasteur St. no. 4/6. Discovered by the Germans, he was executed. Many of his collegues in the "navy blue" police acted likewise, as members of the underground Home Army.

T.B. p. 108. GKBZH WB VI 1269.

564. Warsaw (39). June 1943. On Czerniakowska Street, a Jewish family of 7 prepared a hideout for themselves and stayed there under the care of a **Polish janitor**. Denounced to the Germans by his own wife in a moment of anger, he was executed together with the other Jews, among them a 5-year old girl.

L.Sch. p. 243.

565. Warsaw (40). July 1943. The Gestapo arrested and executed in the ruins of the Ghetto **Jeremi Niewęgłowski**, who, as a city official, took advantage of this position and removed from the files addresses of army officers, some of them

Jewish, thus saving them from being deported to a concentration camp.

Testimony of E. Chądzyński in the "Biuletyn" of the Jewish Historical Institute, no. 75 (1975) p. 130. Bogdan Nowak in the Jewish "Folks-Sztyme", May 22, 1982.

566. Warsaw (41). November 3, 1943. Manager of an underground office which provided Jews with thousands of false identification cards, **Aleksander Weiss**, was caught at Pius XI St. 3 by the Gestapo. Brought to the infamous Al. Szucha place, he disappeared without a trace. He was probably tortured to death or committed suicide in order not to disclose any damaging information.

T.P. p. 156. S.T. p. 288.

567. Warsaw (42). 1943. A crippled **Catholic shoemaker** from Prądzyńska St. was murdered by the Germans together with his **wife** as a result of denunciation by a Jew, previously sheltered by him. All three were executed at the spot.

GKBZH WB VI 167-8.

568. Warsaw (43). 1943. Two Catholic ladies in their seventies, **Janina Pławczyńska** and **Rena Laterner**, were in charge of passing letters between the Warsaw Ghetto and the Polish Underground. After the Ghetto revolt, they sheltered ten Jewish escapees in an underground "bunker" near their house. Discovered by the Germans, all were executed together.

B.-L. p. 307. W.-Z. p. 441. GKBZH WB VI P.

569. Warsaw (44). November 24, 1943. **Ewa Rybicka**, a scout leader and a prominent psychologist, arrested with her Jewish husband and her ther-in-law, died in the Pawiak prison. Her father, **Kazimierz Rybicki**, was shot to death also in November.

Testimony of M. Wasserman in B.-L. p. 523. W.-Z. p. 447. GKBZH WB VI 136.

570. Warsaw (45). 1943. A Polish scout and a member of the Gray Ranks, known only by his first name of **Bolek**, was killed for bringing arms to Jews and leading the escapees through the city sewers to freedom.

GKBZH WB VI 137.

571. Warsaw (46). 1943. **Stefan Siewierski**, ps. Sawicki, caught by the Germans while escorting a group of Jewish ghetto fighters to the Kampinos forest, was tortured by the Gestapo at the dreaded Szucha Alley and shot to death for refusing to indicate the location at Chłodna St. where his sister, Anna Wąchalska, worked with David Klin and Stanisław Choromański in aiding Jews.

B.-L. p. 90, 262-5. W.-Z. p. 441. GKBZH WB VI 137.

572. Warsaw (47). 1943. A lieutenant of the Polish Home Army (OW.-KB), **Aleksander Zielonkiewicz**, was killed by the Germans for giving shelter to the Jewish Szapiro family in his villa at Ossów. His wife escaped through the back door the moment she saw her husband approaching the front door in the company of German police. A Jew informing Germans on his own family constituted an additional risk to Christians trying to save Jews.

T.B. p. 56.

573. Warsaw (48). December 13, 1943. On November 25, 1943. German military police arrested **Ludomir Marczak**, 36, a musician, and **Jadwiga Sałek** on Świętojańska St., not far from the ruins of the Ghetto. They found 13 Jews sheltered there. In spite of tortures, Marczak did not betray the location of a second shelter that he, together with Marianna Bartułd, ran on Pańska St. He and Jadwiga were executed. Of the Jews involved, only one, by the name of Świnarski, was saved.

Testimony of M. Bartułd in B.-L. p. 513-5. (Dec. 31) W.B. p. 66-7. I.O. p. 278. W.-Z. 429. GKBZH WB VI 1364.

574. Warsaw, (49). December 20, 1943. In the office at St. Augustin's rectory **Rev. Franciszek Garncarek**, 61, was murdered by the Germans for helping Jews. He had previously spent some time at the Pawiak prison.

Testimony of Bishop K. Niemira in B.-L. p. 241. I.O. p. 274. W.-Z. p. 429. GKBZH WB VI 1372.

575. Warsaw (50). 1941-1943. Polish streetcar conductors, at first driving through the Ghetto and later – when its area was diminished – passing near its walls, frequently delivered packages with food and arms or, by slowing down, made it possible for Poles and Jews to board the cars or to jump off in predetermined places. Some were caught by the Germans. One of them, conductor **Józef Podkański**, was shot to death on one of such occasions.

B.-R. p. 62. T.B. p. 73.

576. Warsaw (51). 1941-1943. After the decree of the German commandant, Fischer, dated Nov. 10, 1941, the issuing of "Aryan" identification cards to Jews became punishable by death. These activities in the municipal Department of Registration caused the arrest and subsequent death of many employees, among others: **Tadeusz Wopiński** – shot in Palmiry forest, **Edward Jaskółka** – killed in a concentration camp, **Stanisław Borzym**, **Jan Grabicki** and **Wiktor Sajdak** – in Aschwitz, **Tadeusz Młotek** – killed in Germany, **Łucjan Łucejko** – murdered in Pawiak prison, and **Tadeusz Chruszcz** – shot while escaping from a deportation train. Only one of them, Włodzimierz Ignaczak, survived the ordeal of a concentration camp. The witness who preserved this information himself was caught by the Germans while delivering false papers to Jola Tuwim, but managed to escape from a temporary confinement by sliding down a lightning conductor.

Testimony of Edward Chądzyński in the "Biuletyn" of the Jewish Historical Institute, nr 75 (1970) p. 130. Also Tadeusz Czarnowski in the same issue, p. 126-7.

577. Warsaw (52). 1941-1943. Municipal employee, **Leon Szeszko**, helped the Polish Council to Aid Jews in collecting the fingerprints of those who needed false identification cards. Caught on one of these dangerous missions, he paid for it with his life.

Testimony of Irena Sendler in B.-L. p. 141. S.L. p. 281, S.W. p. 70.

578. Warsaw (53). January 28, 1944. **Włodzimierz Siwek**, 33, was shot to death by the Germans, but the Jewish child he was sheltering was saved and was educated by his wife, who managed to escape.

B.-L. p. 1028.

579. Warsaw (54). February 2, 1944. Among the eighty Poles shot in a great wave of city executions, one of the victims was an educator and member of the editiorial staff of "Gazeta Rolnicza", **Mikołaj Łazęcki**, 68, arrested February 4, 1943 for giving shelter to Jewish escapees from the Ghetto.

W.B. p. 91.

580. Warsaw (55). Early Spring 1944. A street peddler by the name of **Marczak**, first name unknown, gave shelter to a group of 8 to 10 Jews who built a rather comfortable dug-out under the floor of his cellar, with two rooms, kitchen and even a telephone. One day a young Jewish girl came to this place demanding admission into the group and threatening otherwise to inform the Gestapo. This she did when Mr. Marczak was away. Warned about this incident, he did not return that evening and the Gestapo took 108 inhabitants of the building as hostages to be shot, if Marczak failed to come. He returned home and was promptly executed. His guests were executed too.

T.B. p. 147-8.

581. Warsaw (56). Early 1944. Member of the Polish Home Army, janitor **Jabłoński**, used to purchase arms for the

Jews and made his apartment at Próżna St. 14 available for Jewish refugees from the Ghetto, In an emergency, one could always spend a night with him. Once, during Jabłoński's absence, German military police raided his apartment, which, at this time, housed some armed members of Hashomer. They barricaded themselves and opened fire until their ammunition ran out. Jabłoński was caught and tortured, but betrayed no one.

B.G. p. 220.

582. Warsaw (57). March 7, 1944. On Grójecka St. no. 84, a "bunker" for 34 Jews was built under a greenhouse. Tender care for the quarrelsome crowd in the "Krysia" or kryjówka (a hideout) was described in detail by Emmanuel Ringelblum, who was sheltered there together with his wife and son. All involved in this activity, the entire family of the gardener, **Władysław Marczak**, including his **wife, two sisters** and a cousin named **Mariusz**, as well as **Mieczysław Wolski**, were executed in the ruins of the Ghetto when the Germans discovered the shelter.

B.-L. p. 120-4. S.D. p. 104, 114. I.O. p. 279. W.-Z. p. 294, 433. GKBZH WB VI 1366. L.S. p. 265, B.G. p. 229-30.

583. Warsaw (58). March 7, 1944. A **Catholic midwife** who had been called to the hide-out at Grójecka St. to deliver a Jewish baby, was arrested and executed in the ruins of the Ghetto.

R.S. p. 19.

584. Warsaw (59). March 1944. In the course of German raids on Poles sheltering Jews after the Ghetto Uprising, hundreds of them were liquidated. W. Bartoszewski testified that from the window of his apartment on Mickiewicz St. he witnessed **dozens of such culprits** conducted for execution together with Jews they were trying to protect.

W. Bartoszewski, stenogram in possession of T. Prekerowa, T.P. p. 163.

585. Warsaw (60). May 20, 1944. Assistant pastor of the Holy Cross parish, **Rev. Józef Leńko, C.M.**, 44, was arrested already for the second time and brought to the Pawiak jail on February 7, 1944, for helping Jews. Deported to the camp of Rogoźnica (Gross Rosen), he gave his life for his charitable works.

J.-W. v. 5, p. 639. Z.Z. p. 648.

586. Warsaw (61). May 1944. **Jan Woźniak** was executed with his companion from Mińsk Mazowiecki for giving shelter to Jewish refugees from the Ghetto.

GKBZH WB VI 897.

587. Warsaw (62). Spring 1944. On Nowogrodzka Street Gestapo entered an apartment at night, killing three Jews and **a Christian couple** who gave them shelter. The witness who let two Jews into the attic spent the whole night in fear that they may be discovered and lead the persecutors to him, as it happened frequently.

S. N. p. 89-90.

588. Warsaw (63). June 8, 1944. A laboratory worker of the Pharmaceutical Institute, **Edward Zaremba**, was executed for sheltering Jewish escapees in the spacious basement of the Institute.

B.-L. p. 366. B.-R. p. 45. GKBZH WB VI Z (Zaręba).

589. Warsaw (64). July 20, 1944. A member of the Polish Underground, **Jerzy Gosiewski**, who, according to a sentence passed by the Polish Underground authorities, executed a Polish doorkeeper for betraying some Jewish refugees to the Germans, was arrested and murdered in KL Stutthoff.

B.-L. p. 1024.

590. Warsaw (65). August 4, 1944. Another priest of St. Vincent's Congregation, stationed at the Holy Cross parish, **Rev. Leon Więckiewicz, C.M.**, 30, paid with his life not only for his aid to Jews and Poles, but also for his courageous stand against German atrocities. Arrested on December 3, 1943, taken to Pawiak jail and to Gross Rosen on March 30, 1944, he was murdered there shortly after Fr. Leńko.

J.-W. p. 377, Z.Z. p. 647.

591. Warsaw (66). August 1944. During the assault on the Wola district, **eight Sisters of Charity** were taken by the Germans to the Pfeffer Co. plant and shot to death there. Their "crime" was a refusal to give up Jewish children kept in their orphanage at Dzielna St. and at the convent of St. Mary in the New Town. The victims included: **Sister Zofia Dziewanowska**, 65, **Sister Helena Jezierska**, 68, **Sister Zofia Kowalczyk**, 77, **Sister Anna Apolonia Motz**, 69, **Sister Maria Nadolska**, 64, **Sister Józefa Ogrodowicz**, 57, **Sister Aurelia Pomierny**, 65, and **Sister Maria Florentyna Wilman**, 61. Their memory was not honored by the Yad Vashem, in spite of having been recorded by the prominent Jewish historian, Dr. Szymon Datner, in 1968.

S.D. p. 108, 144. GKBZH WB VI 108, 437, J, K, M, 113N, O, W. W.-J. v. 5, p. 580, 581, 582, 585, 586, 587, 590.

592. Warsaw (67). 1944. During the entire German occupation until the Warsaw insurrection of 1944, **Tytus Przybyszewski** kept a Jewish couple with a daughter in his apartment at Nowe Miasto. Discovered by the Germans, he was shot to death with his **wife** and his own **daughter**.

W.-Z. p. 437. GKBZH WB VI 493.

593. Warsaw (68). 1944. **Mr. Frąckowiak** died in Auschwitz where he was deported for sheltering a Jew in his apartment. When Germans entered the house, the frightened Jew ran to the attic and jumped to his death on the pavement of the street.

GKBZH WB VI 255.

594. Warsaw (69). 1944. Germans shot to death a **Catholic shoemaker** in the backyard of Świętojerska St. no. 10. He was sheltering three Jews.

T.B. p. 98-9.

595. Warsaw (70). 1944. Germans executed the **Polish manager** of the building at Próżna St. no. 14, for helping Jews from the Warsaw Ghetto to find a shelter on the Christian side.

Testimony of H. Merenholz in T.P. p. 271.

596. Warsaw (71) July 21, 1942. A professor of medicine at the University of Poznań, **Dr Franciszek Raszeja**, 46, while on an errand of mercy at 26 Chłodna St. inside the Warsaw Ghetto, was shot to death by the Germans. Together with him, they killed his former assistant, Dr. Kazimierz Polak, his nurse, the Jewish patient, Abe Gutmajer, and all members of the family who were there. After the German henchmen left, the whole building (we are told by the witnesses) smelt like a slaughter house and blood ran down the staircase.

Testimony of Dr. L. Hirszfeld in B.-L. p. 817. S.D. p. 88. M.K. p. 60. W.-Z. p. 407. GKBZH WB VI 1372.

597. Warsaw (72). A **Director** of an ink factory of M. Leszczyński Co., located at Ogrodowa St. no. 33, was shot for helping Jews.

T.B. p. 92.

598. Warsaw (73). **Jan Janiszek**, a bank official, was arrested and killed in KL Gross-Rosen for keeping a Jew named Grossman in his apartment.

GKBZH WB VI 39.

599. Warsaw (74). The best camouflage for a Jew with an "Aryan" appearance was the uniform of a streetcar conductor, driving Germans and Poles through the city streets. But the risk had to be taken by somebody else. A former employee,

Henryk Kański, thus described the situation: "Many of the tramway workers... well knew that there were Jews among their co-workers on the tracks. But they pretended not to have noticed this and refrained from speaking about it, lest the news of Jews being employed by the municipal transport should leak out to the provocateurs and Gestapo agents". There were, however, mishaps: Head of the Employment Office, **Kazimierz Wendt**, was arrested and executed for providing Jews with uniforms and fake identity cards of streetcar workers. Engineer **Zbigniew Grabiński** was sent to KL Oranieburg and killed there. **Józef Rutka** and another Catholic worker named **Chrobociński** were executed in Auschwitz.

W.P. p. 33-4.

600. Warsaw (75). **Marian Janosik** of Wolska St. was shot to death for furnishing Jews with "Aryan" identification papers prepared by Zygmunt Sekuła. His **wife** and **daughter** also died with him.

GKBZH WB VI 891.

601. Warsaw (76). **Dr. Zofia Garlicka** was arrested and deported to Auschwitz for providing shelter to her Jewish patients. She never returned.

B.-L. p. 420. GKBZH W.B. VI 91.

602. Warsaw (77). Arrested with several Jews in his apartment at Wileńska St. no. 15, **Wacław Kosek** was killed together with them by the Germans.

W.Z. p. 445. GKBZH WB VI K.

603. Warsaw (78). **Marian Kowalczyk** died in Auschwitz, because the Germans surprised him while he was at the house of his parents of Rybaki St. no. 3, where some Jews were sheltered.

Testimony of his brother, Stanisław Kowalczyk, in "Życie Warszawy" of March 23, 1968. B.-L. p. 1028.

604. Warsaw (79). A prominent psychologist, **Janina Kunicka**, was executed by the Germans for her aid to Jews.

B.-L. p. 88. S.D. p. 111, 114. W.-Z. p. 447. GKBZH WB VI 1363.

605. Warsaw (80). **Irena Próchnik**, wife of a well known historian, Adam Próchnik, was killed by the Germans for her work on behalf of Jews.

B.-L. p. 88. S.D. p. 110, 114. W.-Z. p. 447. GKBZH WB VI 1363.

606. Warsaw (81). For hiding Jews in his apartment on Koszykowa St., **Modest Sierant** was sent to KL Majdanek and murdered there. His wife, **Zofia Sierant**, went to the Ravensbrük concentration camp.

W.-Z. p. 443. GKBZH WB VI 1143.

607. Warsaw (82). **Stefan Prokopek**, who was engaged in bringing arms to the Ghetto, had a supply of them in his apartment of Washington St. In addition, he sheltered a Jewish boy there. When the German military police attempted to break in, Prokopek fought back until he was killed.

GKBZH WB VI 1364.

608. Warsaw (83). A commissioned officer of the Polish Army **Józef Pera**, was killed by the Germans for giving aid to Jews.

GKBZH WB VI P.

609. Warsaw (84). **Jan Bazyli Boreszko** was murdered in his apartment by the Germans for sheltering the Jewish family of Szymon Freiman, including his wife Luta and son, Michał. All the Jews managed to escape.

GKBZH WB VI 8.

610. Warsaw (85). A **Captain of the Polish Army**, unknown by name, was arrested by the Germans for preparing "Aryan" papers needed by the Jews. He was beaten in order to extort from him the names of his clients, and was finally shot to death by the Gestapo.

Testimony of Romana Dalborowa in B.-L. p. 570.

611. Warsaw (86). A **Catholic maid** of Dr. Rosental's family voluntarily went to her death in Treblinka, as did many Polish maids because of their attachment to their Jewish employers, especially when they were in bad health and needed their help.

B.-L. p. 570. W.-Z. p. 299.

612. Warsaw (87). A "navy blue" **police commissioner** of the 9th district in Warsaw was killed by the Germans, because he kept his Jewish wife. Policeman Siwek, who gave this information to the Germans, was executed by verdict of the Polish Underground court.

W.-Z. p. 445.

613. Warsaw (88). A **Polish lady** took a Jewish child into her family. In time, the Germans found out about this and decided to give her a cruel lesson: Gestapo agents in plain clothes entered her home and shot to death two of her own children, sparing for a while the life of the Jewish child. "And now", they said, "you can take care of this Jewish bastard".

Testimony of Gen. T. Bór-Komorowski in "Genocide of the National Character" by Joseph Modrzejewski, p. 6.

614. Warsaw (89). For hiding a Jewish couple in his apartment on Chmielna St., **Antoni Jasiński** was shot to death by the Germans. His Jewish tenants had the temerity to open a dental office there and this was their dowfall.

W.-Z. p. 443. GKBZH WB VI 1370. T.P. p. 176.

615. Warsaw (90). A little Jewish boy, Rachmil, wandered into the shop of a **Polish typesetter** on Prądzyńska St. trying to buy a compass in order to look for his gradfather after his mother was killed by the Germans. He was placed with the

Catholic priest in a small village. Shortly afterwards, **the type-setter, his wife** who took care of the boy, and their own **child** were killed by the Germans who probably were after the Jewish boy.

B.-L. p. 743. GKBZH WB VI 167-8.

616. Warsaw (91). **Józef Dąbrowski** was shot to death near the walls of the Warsaw Ghetto while delivering flour for its starving inmates. If not for such illegal deliveries of close to 250 tons daily, the Jewish community would have starved to death, as calculated by the German dieticians.

GKBZH WB VI 954.

617. Warsaw (92). Eventually, **Wiktoria Iwańska** herself paid with her life for the dedication of her entire family to the Jewish cause. While taking care of a Jewish lady with an open case of tuberculosis she contracted the disease and died. No monument, not even a modest plaque, was left to commemorate the heroism of Iwański's family. A piece of paper and a medal given by Yad Vashem withoust much publicity was all. One has lots of trouble trying to locate the modest grave of Henryk Iwański.

R.E. p. 666.

618. Wawer Nowy, voivodship of Warsaw. March 3, 1944. **Jan Pazur** and **Anna Pazur** were shot to death by the German military police along with two Jews, Herman Kaftel and Anna Wiącek, who were sheltered by them.

B.-L. p. 841. S.D. p. 104, 114. W.-Z. p. 433. GKBZH WB VI 1393 (Herman Kaftuka).

619. Werbkowice, Hrubieszów county, voivodship of Lublin. In a concentration camp for Poles, Ukrainians and Jews, **Józef Pomarański** died after being severely beaten for his refusal to whip a Jew.

W.-Z. p. 443. GKBZH WB V 184.

620. Węgrów, voivodship of Warsaw. German military police shot to death **Mrs. Piątkowska** together with Mr. Klein, a Jew who found refuge in her household.

T.Sz. p. 50.

621. Widły, Chełm county, voivodship of Lublin. May 26, 1942. German SS and Army units murdered **eleven Catholic farmers** and **some visitors** under suspicion of aiding "Jews and partisans". Those identified by name were: **Jan Cygan**, 30, **Jan Kijowski**, 38, **Adam Stadnik**, 56, and his two sons, **Klemens Stadnik**, 17, and **Stefan Stadnik**, 20, **Andrzej Stankowski**, 52, **Jan Wójcik**, 65, and his son, **Jan Wójcik**, 36, in addition to a game keeper, **Paweł Wawer**, 56. All were buried in one common grave at the site of the execution.

F.-R. p. 60. OKBZH in Lublin, Ds 30/67.

622. Wieliczka (1), Miechów county, voivodship of Kraków. **Stanisław Cekiera** was arrested and tortured by the Gestapo for helpig Jews. Finally, he was executed.

B.-L. p. 39, 78. W.-Z. p. 447.

623. Wieliczka (2), Miechów counnty, voivodship of Kraków. **Feliks Ciesielski**, 47, and his wife, Romualda, were aiding Jews of the town by providing them with "Aryan" papers. They also sheltered Dr. Edmund Fiszler and his wife, Leonora, as well as Zofia Rosenbaum and her mother. Denounced to the Germans, they were deported to Auschwitz. During a transfer of the inmates, Mrs. Cieślik-Ciesielska managed to escape, while her husband never came back alive. Mrs. Cieślik-Ciesielska was decorated with a medal by Yad Vashem in 1967.

S.D. in the "Biuletyn" of the Jewish Historical Institute, no. 76 (1970) p. 81-82.

624. Wieprzec, Zamość county, voivodship of Lublin. November 15, 1942. German military police shot to death **Jan**

Kudyk, Anna Kudyk, Michał Kudyk and **Zofia Kudyk**, all members of the same family which took the risk of giving shelter to Jews.

GKBZH ASG V 121/170/Zm.

Wierbka see **Pilica**.

625. Wierzbica (1), Miechów county, voivodship of Kraków. January 29, 1943. **Franciszek Książek**, 50, took the Jewish Wandelsman family into his house. Betrayed by Wandelsman's son-in-law, Naftul, the entire family of Książek was exterminated, including mother, **Julia Książek**, 40, with her two sons, **Jan Książek**, 21, and **Zygmunt Książek**, 18.

B.-L. p. 849. S.D. p. 91, 92, 113. W.-Z. p. 413. GKBZH WB II 109-11.

626. Wierzbica (2), Miechów county, voivodship of Kraków. January 29, 1943. A similar fate was suffered by the Kucharski family which gave shelter to the Naftul family of three. As a result of Naftul's betrayal, the mother, **Anna Kucharska**, was killed with her four sons: **Mieczysław Kucharski**, 15, **Bolesław Kucharski**, 9, **Józef Kucharski**, 7, and **Stefan Kucharski**, 7. Their father, Izydor Kucharski, lost one eye and his son, Bronisław Kucharski, lost both eyes as a result of a head wound. In addition, Germans shot to death their grandmother, **Julianna Ostrowska**.

B.-L. p. 849. S.D. p. 91-2, 113. W.-Z. p. 413. GKBZH WB II 109-12.

627. Wierzbica (3), Miechów county, voivodship of Kraków. January 29, 1943. The same tragedy, caused by Naftul's moment of weakness, engulfed the **Nowak family**, including their two-year old daughter. They were sheltering part of the Wandelsman family and were executed for this offense.

GKBZH WB II 116.

628. Wierzbica (4), Miechów county, voivodship of Kraków. January 29, 1943. Finally, **Stanisław Bielawski** and his wife, **Balbina Bielawska**, were killed by the Germans for sheltering a Jewish family of six persons.

GKBZH WB II 107 8.

629. Wierzbno, Proszowice county, voivodship of Kraków. February 18, 1943. Germans have shot to dath **Stanisław Wilk**, 45, his wife, **Katarzyna Wilk**, 52, and their son, **Mieczysław Wilk**, 20, for sheltering Jews.

B.-L. p. 850. S.D. p. 92, 115. I.O. p. 276. W.-Z. p. 415. GKBZH WB II 197, 198.

630. Wierzchowisko (1), Bochnia county, voivodship of Kraków. March 5, 1943. Two Catholic Poles died for sheltering a Jew: **Franciszek Paneczko** and **Jan Paneczko**.

B.-L. p. 850. S.D. p. 93, 114. I.O. p. 277. W.-Z. p. 415. GKBZH WB II 183-4.

631. Wierzchowisko (2), Bochnia county, voivodship of Kraków. A **Polish family of five** was executed for giving shelter and food to Jews.

Cz.M. v. 2, p. 350.

632. Wieś Komarowska, Tomaszów Lubelski county, voivodship of Lublin. The entire **Skowronek family** was wiped out for sheltering Jews. Taken by Gestapo to a nearby forest, they were forced to dig a common grave for themselves and then were shot to death.

Testimony of L. Monot in the Catholic weekly "WTK" June 16, 1968.

633. Wiewiórka (1), Dębica county, voivodship of Rzeszów. March 5, 1943. The Head of the Gestapo in Dębica, Julius Gabler, personally led several raids on neighboring villages in order to trap Catholic families sheltering Jews: first, on Wiewiórka, where **sixteen Poles** were murdered and two households were burned down. Then, on June 30, 1943, on Brzeźnica, where **fourteen Catholic Poles** were shot to death; on July 7, 1943 on the Róża hamlet with toll of **eighteen victims**, and on July 8, 1943, on Bobrowa with **eighteen** killed and thirty-six deported to the Reich. During the raid on Wiewiórka, a young girl, **Antonina Skwira**, 18, died pleading that she is not Jewish. Her father, **Wojciech Skwira**, 68, and mother, **Julia Skwira**, 70, her brothers, **Kazimierz Skwira**, 20, **Jan Skwira** and **Andrzej Skwira**, werre killed in bed along with her sister Władysława's fiancee **Piotr Wawrzonek**, 20, her niece, **Maria Dumanowska**, 11, and their servant named **Radzicki**. Władysława Skwira, managed to escape and join the partisans under a changed name. Skwira's neighbor, **Wojciech Wałęga**, 70, and his son, **Władysław Wałęga**, 20, were shot to death while standing in the door; then, their daughter, **Władysława Wałęga**, 18, and the youngest, **Stanisława Wałęga**, who ran frightened into the arms of her mother, **Maria Wałęga**, still lying in bed. Both were killed while embracing each other at the terrible sound of raging flames consuming their pigsties, cowsheds and stables and desperate cries of domestic animals, pigs, cows and horses locked up by the Germans before the slaughter began. Fire consumed entire householdss with their inhabitants inside.

S.Z. p. 171-4. OKBZH in Rzeszów, II Ds 12/69. F.-R. p. 422.

634. Wiewiórka (2), Dębica county, voivodship of Rzeszów. March 23, 1943. After the massacre of the Skwira and Wałęga families, Germans went on searching for another elderly couple, **Jan Grzyb**, 80, and **Jadwiga Grzyb**, 80, who were listed in Gabler's execution orders as having sheltered Jews. They were shot to death.

F.P. p. 442. S.Z. p. 174.

635. Wilkołaz, Kraśnik county, voivodship of Lublin. October 25, 1943. During a raid on Jewish shelters in the village, Germans killed **three Catholic farmers** and two Jews sheltered by them.

GKBZH V Ds 357/67.

636. Wilno (1). December 1942. **Ignacy Zagórski**, an attorney who provided Jews with the "Aryan" papers and sheltered some Jews in his house, was arrested and executed by the Germans. His wife, Dr. Maria Zagórska, managed to escape and find refuge in Warsaw.

Testimony of S. Dubrawska in W.S. p. 30, 34, 310.

637. Wilno (2). 1942. **Wacław Mickiewicz** and his wife, **Maria Mickiewicz**, were murdered for their aid to Jews. Their household was burned to the ground.

Archives of the Jewish Historical Institute in Warsaw. Their son, Władysław Mickiewicz, who managed to escape, was decorated by Yad Vashem on May 7, 1981. His parents were only mentioned on the list. As a rule, dead "martyrs of charity" don't receive Jewish decorations for their heroism.

638. Wilno (3). February 1943. The Catholic clergy formed **a secret group** to help Jews. The group sheltered many Jews and provided them with "Aryan" papers. It was discovered and all its members were deported to concentration camps. Nothing was heard of them any more.

Ph.F.R. p. 417.

639. Wilno (4). 1943. For a few months, **Grzegorz Turyłło** gave shelter to 49 Jews. They were hidden in his cellar and in the attic of his house. Surprised by the Germans, Turyłło lost his life with 41 Jews hiding in the cellar, while those in the attic survived; among others, Rebecca Feldman, who migrated to New York. Yad Vashem honored the heroic Christian family of Grzegorz Turyłło with a medal in 1979.

"Życie Warszawy", Dec. 11, 1979. GKBZH WB VIII 39.

640. Wilno (5). 1943. A Polish liaison officer named **Kozłowski** was caught by the Germans in the ghetto and execu-

ted. Polish underground press names several other Poles hung
for hiding Jews.

R.P. 122. B. Chrzanowski in Bull. of Jewish Hist. Inst. Jan. – June, 1985,
p. 99.

641. Wilno (6). July 16 er 17, 1944. A mathematics student
at Stefan Batory University, **Jadwiga Dudziec**, 32, sacrificed
her life on behalf of her fellow Jews, died of gangrene which
developed from a wound received. As a cover-up for her activities she became a manager of a German-owned shoe workshop where she employed young escapees from the local ghetto, held meetings for the Jewish underground in her own apartment, personally delivered to ghetto fighters supply of arms
which she received from J. Grzesiak, officer of the Polish
Home Army, placed Jewish children at the orphanage of Sisters of Charity, provided Jews with fake identity cards produced by Polish underground, carried messages for the ghettos
in Kaunas, Šiauliai, Panovežys, Trakai and other Lithuanian
towns – each of these exploits punishable by death. She was
buried at the highest point of Rossa cemetery in Wilno next to
Mrs. Grzesiak.

K.W. p. 556-61. Ph.F. p. 29. B.-L. p. 307-9.

642. Wilno (7). **Father Lipnianus** had to pay with his life
for sermons encouraging Lithuanian Catholics to forget the
old grievances against Jews and to help them during the German persecution. He paid for this with his life.

Ph. F.R. p. 417.

643. Wilno (8). **Two elderly clergymen** from the Uniate
monastery of the Basilian Fathers were arrested by the Gestapo for helping Jews and were heard from no more.

Ph.F.R. p. 417.

644. Wiśnicz Stary (1), Bochnia county, voivodship of
Kraków. 1942. Two German policemen, Rogusen and Litman,

shot to death **Wojciech Gicała** for helping Jews and giving a home to a 2-year old Jewish girl. The child was killed with him.

W.-Z. p. 413. GKBZH WB II 11.

645. Wiśnicz Stary (2), Bochnia county, voivodship of Kraków. Autumn 1942. In the last moment before being taken by a Gestapo man, a Jewish mother pushed her child into a ditch, thus separating it from a crowd of Jews driven along the road. A **local peasant** who found the child and was taking care of it, lost his life as a result of a denunciation by a certain Szmenda of the "navy blue" police.

Testimony of T. Seweryn in W.-Z. p. 292.

646. Włodzimierz (1), voivodship of Wołyń, April 1944. **Maria Dąbrowska**, a teacher often resented by Jews and called an "anti-Semite" for encouraging Polish and Ukrainian youth from the overcrowded countryside to seek a carter in commerce, an area traditionally dominated by the Jews, took into her house eighteen Jews, among them a paralyzed woman, a crippled man with one leg and a blind girl, all who needed to be taken care of, the rest being mostly small children. She personally washed the laundry and cleaned the woman. She begged for food in the nearby farms. She prevailed upon her cook to take into her house a Jewish family of three. One day the inevitable happened. The Gestapo walked in, murdered all the Jews and took their host for torture to discover the whereabouts of the Jewish family of Jakub Rajski, sheltered with the cook. Though promised immunity, she refused to cooperate and had to be carried out for execution because she could not walk by herself any more on account of broken limbs as a result of beating she received.

B.-L. p. 456. W.-Z. p. 435. Also author's interview with Mrs. Maria Janiak.

Regina Zajączkowska (left) with her children: Iza Stasiuk, Maria Janiak and Ryszard Zajączkowski, were awarded a medal and a tree at the Alley of the Righteous, but **Ludwik Janiak** (right) who took the risk of harboung Jews in his house and ultimately paid for it with life – was omitted in a petty act of vengeance.

647. Włodzimierz (2), voivodship of Wołyń. 1944. **Ludwik Janiak**, who permitted his mother-in-law, **Regina Zajączkowska**, to shelter a Jewish mother, Irena Franziak, with a baby in his house, found an unexpected new hazard in hiding Jews, when Irena turned out to be a spy for the Soviet secret police. Taking advantage of the trust she enjoyed in Zajączkowski's family, she betrayed one unit of the Polish Home Army to the returning Soviets. Ludwik Janiak, with four of his colleagues in the Army, was deported to Siberia. After three years of forced labor there, he came home swollen from malnutrition and died shortly afterwards. Similar fate overtook a yo-

תעודה

ATTESTATION

Regina Zajaczkowska et ses enfants Ryszard, Maria et Izabela

שמו נפשם בכפם להצלת יהודים בתקופת השואה.

AU PERIL DE *leur* VIE ONT SAUVE DES JUIFS PENDANT
L'HOLOCAUSTE

נטעו עץ בשדרת חסידי אומות העולם

ONT PLANTE UN ARBRE DANS L'ALLEE DES JUSTES

LE 27 Juin 1985   ביום ח תמוז תשמ׳׳ה

ung Jesuit cleric, **Jan Zajączkowski, S.J.**, stranded from his religious community and desiring to return. Apprehended while crossing the border, he was also deported to Siberia where he contracted tuberculosis in the inhuman working conditions. Brought with General Anders' army to Lebanon he attempted to finish his theological studies in Beirut, but never recovered from his illness. He returned, after the war ended, only to die on his native soil. His mother died of a heart attack after remaining the Soviet Union for many years just for the purpose of educating Irena's young daughter, Ania, and bringing her to Poland. The Franziaks found their way to Tel-Aviv and for 30 years didn't bother to express their gratitude to the Zajączkowski family; finally when, the Yad Vashem Committee on the Righteous decided to grant customary distinction of the Just among the Nations in the form of a medal and a tree in the Alley of the Just, none of the Franziaks showed up at the ceremony. There are tens of thousands of similar cases in which the Jews saved by the sacrifices of their Christian brothers in Poland, respond with contempt and denigration. The number of grateful Jews may be compared to the ten lepers cured by Christ in Luke 17, 15-16, where only one of them, after finding himself cured, turned back praising God aloud. And he was a Samaritan. At this Jesus said "Were not all ten cleansed? The other nine, where are they? Could none be found to come back and give praise to God except this foreigner?"

Evewitness account of Mrs. M. Janiak in Washington, D.C. An interview of the author with Irena Franziak in Tel – Aviv (her daughter couldn'ts be located in Israel under the address given by her mother). Maria died on the day her brother (the Author) planted a tree to her honor at Yad Vashem. Sister Rittner falled to invite her to a State Dept. conference on the Rescuers just 3 blocks away from her apartment.

648. Włodzimierz (3), voivodship of Wołyń. One Catholic family was seen being executed for sheltering Jews.

Testimony of Józef Szwed in Author's possession.

649. Włodzimierz (county), voivodship of Wołyń, Bielin. Andrzej Szwed was killed while transfering the Wapniarski family along with some other Jewish refugees, from one hideout to another shelter in Bielin, where they were protected by the Polish Home Army from the Ukrainian assassins.

Testimony of Janina Zajączkowska, daughter of A. Szwed. Also, J. Szwed. The detailed account of the case was given by Anrzej's son in the daily Żołnierz Wolności in 1968.

His children were supposed to be decorated by General Yitzhak Arad, director of Yad Vashem during the large convention of Jews to honor the 40-th anniversary of the Warsaw Ghetto revolt, but only 48 out of 170 designated for this honor received medals, because the Israeli delegation didn't bring them in April 1983 to Warsaw. Eventually, they were decorated at a later date.

Wodzisław see **Skwaryszów**.

650. Wojciechów, Krasnystaw county, voivodship of Lublin. October 17, 1942. German military police from Niedrzwica arrested and, on the next day, executed **Wojciech Szczepan Tomczyk** together with ten Jews, among them women and children, sheltered in the household of **Jan Wójcik**, whose fate remains unknown.

GKBZH Ds 8/650/71/W 889.

651. Wojciechówka, Garwolin county, voivodship of Warsaw. April 1943. German military police shot to death **Stanisław Marciniak**, 40, and his wife, **Zofia Marciniak**, 40, together with five Jews, sheltered by them.

B.-L. p. 835, 839. S.D. p. 103, 113. W.-Z. p. 419. GKBZH WB VI 1390 (Feb. 15).

652. Wola Gościeradzka, Kraśnik county, voivodship of Lublin. August 1943. **Bronisław Kędra** was arrested and executed in a nearby forest for sheltering Jews.

GKBZH WB V 104.

653. Wola Komborska, Krosno county, voivodship of Rzeszów. October 19, 1943. German SS men shot to death **Zofia Inglot, Janina Kwolek, Józef Prejznow, Katarzyna Prejznow**, and two Jews sheltered by them.

B.-L. p. 834, 841. S.D. p. 103, 113. W.-Z. p. 427. GKBZH WB IV 312.

654. Wola Przybysławska (1), Łuków county, voivodship of Lublin. December 10, 1942. Having spotted two Jews sneaking out of the forest to the farm of the Aftyka family, the Germans and their Vlassovian henchmen surrounded the farmhouse, tossing grenades through the windows. Ignoring the cires for mercy in Polish and Yidish, they put the house on fire and burned alive: **Józef Aftyka**, 54, his wife, **Aniela Aftyka**, 52, their children, **Zofia Aftyka**, 17, and **Marianna Aftyka**, 14, as well as **Czesław Gawron**, 20, **Leonard Gawron**, 21, and **Stanisław Kamiński**, 21, along with their cousin **Władysław Abramek**, 2.

B.-L. p. 707, 833, 837, account of F. Wremiej. S.D. p. 91, 112. W.-Z. p. 411. GKBZH WB V 145.

655. Wola Przybysławska (2), Łuków county, voivodship of Lublin. December 10, 1942. **Józef Ochmiński** was burned alive in his house with **four members of his family** for sheltering Jews. Also murdered were: **Jan Deć** 18, **Andrzej Woźniak** and **Kacper Matras**.

B.-L. p. 703, 833, 838. W.-Z. p. 411. GKBZH WB V 144 (Ochniński).

656. Wola Przybysławska (3), Łuków county, voivodship of Lublin. December 10, 1942. **Aniela Kamińska**, suspected of contacts with Jews, was burned alive in her house.

B.-L. p. 703. GKBZH WB V 144.

657. Wola Przybysławska (4), Łuków county, voivodship of Lublin. December 22, 1942. German military police put to death four Catholic peasants for sheltering Jews. Thus perished: **Łucja Filipiak**, 55, **Katarzyna Janczak**, 42, **Natalia Smolak**, 40, and **Marianna Suska**, 50. They all were buried in the field, and after their exhumation when the war ended, transferred to the cemetery in Garbów.

L.S. p. 176, 191. GKBZH – ASG 16 p. 797.

658. Wola Przybysławka (5), Łuków county, voivodship of Lublin. December 1942. German military police burned alive **Jan Nalewajko**, 48, his wife, **Julia Nalewajko**, and their **three children**, for sheltering Jews. Their farm was burned to the ground.

Account of F. Wremiej in B.-L. p. 703. GKBZH ASG 16, K 797 (Nalewajek, Dec. 22, 1943). GKBZH WB V 149-53 (Nalewajka).

659. Wola Rafałowska (1), Rzeszów county, voivodship of Rzeszów. October 1943. German military police shot to death **Rozalia Paczka**, 50, for sheltering Jews in her house.

B.-L. p. 834, 840. S.D. p. 101, 114. W.-Z. p. 292. GKBZH WB IV 365.

660. Wola Rafałowska (2), Rzeszów county, voivodship of Rzeszów. December 1943. **Rozalia Socha** gave shelter in her attic to seven Jews from Albigowa and Zabratówka, among them three children from the Szal family. She was discovered by the Gestapo, but succeeded in escaping and hiding for three months. Finally, she was caught and executed with one of the Jews. Two Jewish women were saved and later emigrated to Canada.

Account of A. Kusz in W.-Z. p. 360, also 425. S.Z. p. 190. GKBZH WB IV 310.

661. Wola Skrzydlańska, Limamowa county, voivodship of Kraków. **Franciszek Zając** was arrested and sent to Dachau concentration camp for sheltering Jews. He never returned.

B.-L. p. 848. S.D. p. 101, 115. W.-Z. p. 292. GKBZH WB II 205.

662. Wolica, Dębica county, voivodship of Rzeszów. November 11, 1943. **Antoni Kępa** was shot by the German military police for his part in sheltering Jews.

S.D. p. 101, 114. W.-Z. p. 427. GKBZH WB IV 317.

663. Wołkowysk, Lida county, voivodship of Wilno. 1941. **Sister Jadwiga Assadowska**, Superior of the local convent of nuns of the Family of Mary, was repeatedly arrested and kept in jail under conditions which ruined her health. Her crime was aiding the Jews.

T.F. p. 411.

Wróblówka see **Czarny Dunajec**.

664. Wrzosy, Kowel county, voivodship of Wołyń. February 9, 1943. **Roman Kociubowski**, 47, and his wife, **Józefa**

Kociubowska, 49, were shot to death by the Germans along with their son, **Stanisław Kociubowski**, 20, for sheltering a Jew from Zamość named Bergman. The Jew was killed together with them.

Testimony of S. Janowski in W.-Z. p. 360, also 413. GKBZH WB VI 618-20.

665. Wsielub, Nowogródek county, voivodship of Nowogródek. July 31, 1942. **Rev. Józef Kuczyński**, 63, Pastor of Wsielub, was executed in a forest behind the army barracks in Nowogródek for sheltering Jewish children. During the Spring of 1944, his body was transferred to the old cemetery in Wsielub.

J.-W. v. 4, p. 276.

666. Wysoka, Łańcut county, voivodship of Rzeszów. **Zofia Wilczek** and her **father-in-law**, unknown by name, were executed by the Germans for sheltering Jews.

S.Z. p. 193.

667. Zabratówka, Rzeszów county, voivodship of Rzeszów. June 1943. **Józef Bażan** was murdered by the Germans for sheltering Abraham Lejba, a Jew.

Report of A. Kusz in W.-Z. p. 360, also 423. GKBZH WB IV 309.

668. Zagościniec, voivodship of Warsaw. 1943. German military police found out that a **Polish forester**, his name being unknown today, was sheltering Jews in his house. He and his entire family were executed together with the Jews.

L.Sch. p. 174.

669. Zagórzany, Gorlice county, voivodship of Rzeszów. November 16, 1943. **Władysław Sterkowicz** was shot to death in his barn together with six Jews he was sheltering there.

L.D. p. 198.

670. Zagórze (1), Sanok county, voivodship of Rzeszów. 1942. Mr. and **Mrs. Józef Balewski,** who were caught sheltering in their house the Jewish Rott family, paid dearly for this offense. Mrs. Balewska died in Auschwitz while her husband barely managed to escape the death.

T.K. p. 186.

671. Zagórze (2), Sanok county, voivodship of Rzeszów. Spring 1943. **Mikołaj Hanas** and **Paraska Hanas,** a Catholic Ukrainian couple, were arrested by the Germans for hiding three Jews in the cellar of their house Mr. Hanas was shot to death on the spot and his wife was sent to a concentration camp, from which she never returned.

A court deposition, taken March 22, 1971 in Sanok, in W.-Z. p. 443. GKBZH Ds 2/70. GKBZH WB IV 150 (Chanas, Paraska H.).

672. Zagórze (3), Sanok county, voivodship of Rzeszów. A member of the Polish Home Army, **Józef Organ** was taken to Auschwitz for providing the Jews, confined to the local ghetto, with flour. He did not return.

W.-Z. p. 445. GKBZH WB IV 445.

673. Zagórze (4), Sanok county, voivodship of Rzeszów. **Lipiński, Jr.,** son of the village bailiff, was deported to Auschwitz for helping Jews. He was killed there.

W.-Z. p. 445.

674. Zagórze, Sucha Beskidzka county, voivodship of Kraków. April 4, 1944. Under suspicion of "aiding the Jews and partisans", German military police and Gestapo from Maków Podhalański detained **twenty-two Catholic peasants.** Thirteen of them were brought to the nearby hamlet of Juszczyn and executed there. They were: **Agnieszka Bania,** 45, **Anna Biela,** 40, **Michał Gierat,** 54, **Emil Jurek,** 41, **Józef Maczuga,** 55, **Michał Maczuga,** 60, **Michał Pieronek,** 59, **Helena Pieronek,** 55, **Rozalia Solecka,** 66, **Jan Solecki,** 55, **Antonina Zajda,** 44, **Helena Zajda,** 17, and **Józef Zajda.** The rest were killed in Zakopane: **Bolesław Jurek**, 20, **Edward Jurek**, 22, **Józef Jurek**, 57, **Edward Gierat**, 20, **Jan Macko**, 20, **Antoni Piątek**, 26, **Roman Piątek**, 34, **Stanisław Solecki**, 30, and **Józef Zajda**, 54.

OKBZH in Kraków, Ds. 6/70. F.R. p. 52-3.

675. Zagórzyce (1), Ropczyce county, voivodship of Rzeszów. 1943. For sheltering Jews, one by the name of Simcha and one from the village Szkodna, unknown by name, a Catholic farmer, **Józef Kubik**, was shot to death in Góra Ropczycka.

Court deposition of F. Siwiec in W.-Z. p. 397, also 441. GKBZH WB IV 252.

676. Zagórzyce (2), Ropczyce county, voivodship of Rzeszów. 1943. **Józef Mech** and **Józef Ochał**, who were suspected of giving shelter to Jews coming from the forest, died from German hands.

W.-Z. p. 398. GKBZH WB IV 253-4.

677. Zagórzyce (3), Ropczyce county, voivodship of Rzeszów. 1942/43. For hiding Jews, Germans murdered **Franciszka Żuraw** and her son, **Jan Żuraw**, who was tortured before his death, because he refused to indicate their hiding place. One of the Germans noticed another farmer, **Walenty Sroka**, observing the scene from close vicinity. He ran after him and shot him to death.

Testimony of F. Siwiec in W.-Z. p. 398, also 441. GKBZH WB VII 427-8.

678. Zajączków (1), Lipsko county, voivodship of Kielce. Winter 1942/43. For sheltering Jews, Germans burned alive three Catholic farmers: **Lelunek**, **Grzeszczyk** and **Rutkowski**. Flames also consumed their houses.

Court deposition of J. Mirowski in W.-Z. p. 372, also 413. GKBZH WB I 170-1.

679. Zajączków (2), Lipsko county, voivodship of Kielce. January 1943. For taking Jewish children into their house, the German military police from Ciepielów arrested **Gabriel Wołowiec**, 53, executed at a later time, then murdered his wife, **Stanisława Wołowiec**, and all their daughters: **Bronisława Wołowiec**, 3, **Janina Wołowiec**, 12, **Leokadia Wołowiec**, 10, and **Kazimiera Wołowiec**, a baby 6-month old. To complete this frightening lesson, the Germans also executed **Józef Jelonek** because he failed to inform them of this offense.

GKBZH WB I 100, 126. OKBZH in Kielce, Ds. 18/64. F.-R. p. 306. W.-Z. p. 415. E.F. p. 397.

680. Zajączków (3), Lipsko county, voivodship of Kielce. January 1943. **Franciszek Zaporowski**, 40, a farmhand, was executed for failing to inform German authorities about Jews being sheltered in the village.

F.-R. p. 306. W.-Z. p. 415. OKBZH in Kielce, Ds 58/69. GKBZH WB I 127.

681. Zalesie, Węgrów county, voivodship of Warsaw. March 16, 1943. Germans tortured and then killed a Catholic woman named **Wierzbicka** accused of sheltering Jews.

W.W. p. 129.

682. Zarzew, Krasnystaw county, voivodship of Lublin. August 1943. The German *Wehrmacht* (armed forces) murdered **Aleksandra Rachwalska**, 35, together with two Jews sheltered by her. The murder occurred in a cemetery close to the forest.

GKBZH Egz. Ds 12/70 K.

683. Zarzetka, Węgrów county, voivodship of Warsaw. March 16 to 31, 1943. In the local school building, Germans initiated inquiries aimed at forcing the Catholic peasants to disclose details of aid given to Jewish escapees from Treblinka by the local Polish population. In the course of cruel beatings and other tortures, the following Christians gave their lives:

Stanisław Bula, Jan Ćwiek, Cyran, Gajewski (bailiff from Brzoza), whose **wife** and **three daughters** were also murdered by the Germans, **Jan Gałązka, Kic, Stanisław Kobyliński, Jan Kolbarczyk** and **Jadwiga Kozioł** from Czaplowizna, **Czesław Krawczyk** from Rożny, **Józef Leśniewski** and **Zygmunt Siatkowski** from Szymbarzyna and **Stefan Zadrożny**.

W.W. p. 129.

684. Zassów, Dębica county, voivodship of Rzeszów. April 8, 1943. German Gestapo, under the command of Julius Gabler, killed **four Catholic peasants** and burned down three households as a punishment for sheltering Jews.

S.Z. p. 171.

685. Zawadka, Kałusz county, voivodship of Stanisławów. Night of February 23/24, 1944. The principal of the local school, **Aleksander Sosnowski**, was sheltering two Jewish women in his attic, Ucia Fuchs and Cunia Fuchs, for one and half years. In spite of repeated warnings from friends, he didn't abandon them and was joined in this heroic decision by his daughter, **Antonina Sosnowska**, 17. One frightful night, the Germans entered and murdered all four of them.

Court deposition of W. Wojtynkiewicz in B.-L. p. 872. GKBZH WB IV 455-6.

686. Zawiercie, voivodship of Katowice. Two Catholics, **Piotr Kuchta** and his son, **Tadeusz Kuchta**, died for sheltering Jews. The father was executed on the spot and the son was deported to Auschwitz to be killed there.

W.-Z. p. 443. GKBZH WB VII 256.

687. Zawoja (1), Sucha Beskidzka county, voivodship of Kraków. October 1943. **Piotr Wiecheć** and his wife, **Regina Wiecheć**, were arrested for sheltering Jews. They were taken to the Gestapo office in Maków Podhalański and murdered there in Villa Marysin.

Testimony of S. Chowaniak in GKBZH Kp 31/10. GKBZH WB II C.

688. Zawoja (2), Sucha Beskidzka county, voivodship of Kraków. December 1943. **Karol Chowaniak** and his wife, **Tekla Chowaniak**, were arrested with their foster child, **Karolina Marek**, for giving aid to Jews. They were deported to Auschwitz and killed there by the end of January 1944.

Court deposition of S. Chowaniak in Sucha Beskidzka, GKBZH Kp. 31/1. GKCBZH WB II 24-5.

689. Zawóz (1), Lesko county, voivodship of Rzeszów. **Franciszek Wronowski** and his wife, **Rozalia Wronowska**, were noticed by the Germans as they brought food to Mr. Nusbauam, a Jew sheltered on their farm. Both were apprehended and disappeared without trace.

B.-L. p. 861. W.-Z. p. 445.

690. Zawóz (2), Lesko county, voivodship of Rzeszów. **Leon Ferenc** gave shelter to his Jewish neighbor, Mr. Majer. Denounced to the German authorities, both were taken to an extermination camp from which neither returned.

B.-L. p. 861. GKBZH WB VI 370 (Zawozie).

691. Zawóz (3), Lesko county, voivodship of Rzeszów. Germans arrested **Michał Fenczak** under the suspicion of bringing food to a Jewish family which remained in hiding. He was deported to a concentration camp and murdered there.

W.-Z. p. 344, 448. GKBZH WB IV 371.

692. Zazamcze, Dąbrowa Tarnowska county, voivodoship of Kraków. 1943. **Józefa Kogut** was discovered hiding six Jews in her household. She was shot to death together with them.

W.-Z. p. 344, 448. GKBZH WB II 173 (Anna Jozefa K).

693. Zdziary, Dąbrowa Tarnowska county, voivodship of Kraków. Autumn 1943. **Józef Szkotak** and his wife, **Teresa Szkotak**, were shot to death for giving refuge to four Jews in their house, contrary to the German law.

Court deposition of W. Juras in W.-Z. p. 376, also 344, 427. GKBZH
WB II 4-5.

694. Zemborzyce, Lublin county, voivodship of Lublin.
Stefan Chabros, 28, was murdered by the Germans for helping Jews.

GKBZH WB V ch. GKBZH Ds 20/70.

695. Zienki, Biała Podlaska county, voivodship of Lublin.
A Catholic farmer, **Mieczysław Izdebski,** 26, lost his life together with the Jewish family of six he was sheltering in his
household. Neighbors, risking their own lives, saved his 5-
year old daughter from certain death.

GKBZH WB V 49.

696. Ziomaki, Biała Podlaska county, voivodship of Warsaw. November 20, 1943. Germans burned to the ground the
farm of **Wiktor Ratyński** for giving shelter to a group of twelve Jews. Eventually, he was caught and deported. Nobody
knows what happened to him.

S.L. p. 252.

697. Złotki, Węgrów county, voivodship of Warsaw.
1943. Germans killed **nine Catholics** for helping Jews.

T.Sz. p. 51.

698. Zwierzyniec, Zamość county, voivodship of Lublin.
October 24, 1942. **Janina Sedlakowska** was murdered by the
Germans for giving aid to Jews.

Testimony of Bishop Edmund Ilcewicz in "Tygodnik Powszechny" weekly, April 13, 1980.

699. Zwięczyce, Rzeszów county, voivodship of Rzeszów. June 8, 1943. The German Gestapo, with the aid of the
Ukrainian SS Galizin, killed **ten Polish farmers** during a man-
hunt and arrested **another nine** under suspicion of "belonging
to the Communist party or aiding the Jews". Arrested persons

were executed with a shot through the head. Thus perished: **Andrzej Bednarski**, 22, **Edward Czyż**, 33, **Tadeusz Dander**, 2, **Wojciech Deręgowski**, 41, **Ignacy Kłaczak**, 42, **Andrzej Kocur**, 41, **Andrzej Kozioł**, 35, **Andrzej Kubicz**, 53, **Stanisław Mięsik**, 28, **Tomasz Pięta**, 31, **Jan Płonka**, 23, **Stanisław Płonka**, 21, **Bronisław Popek**, 21, **Władysław Rak**, 2, **Marcin Smyrzeń**, 24, **Henryk Sołtys**, 21, **Jan Szalacha**, 45, **Paweł Szalacha**, 36, and **Andrzej Ząbczyk**, 33. After the execution another twenty-four persons were deported to Pustków concentration camp, from which many never returned.

F.-R. p. 326. OKBZH in Rzeszów, Ds II 19/67.

700. Zwola Stara, Zwoleń county, voivodship of Kielce. September 6, 1944. **Józef Suchecki** and **Jan Wolski** were deported to a prison camp in Radom and killed there for their aid to Jews. The Jews they had helped, Ida Korman along with her family, and a man named Tanenbaum from Gniewoszów, also lost their lives.

Testimony of S. Paciorek in E.F. p. 436-7.

701. Żurawicze – Zaborka, Łuck county, voivodship of Wołyń. Germans murdered **fourteen Polish families** here for sheltering Jews.

Court deposition of H. Kownacka in W.-Z. 389.

702. Żyrowice, Słonim county, voivodship of Wołyń. December 2, 1942. Rector of a Jesuit church in Słonim and, since September 1939, also Pastor of the Roman Catholic parish in Żyrowice, **Rev. Adam Sztark, S.J.**, 35, exposed himself to continuous danger, gathering Jewish orphans who escaped from the holocaust, taking them to his residence and delivering them to Catholic orphanages. One night, a German car stopped in front of his house. The Germans didn't permit the Jesuit take even a piece of bread with him. "Where you are going", said one of them, "there is plenty of bread". His face became white, but resolved: „It's my martyrdom", were his last words upon departure. The next day, he was loaded on a truck, along with a group of similar "offenders", and taken to Górki Pantalowickie, the usual execution place. Everybody had to undress. He wanted to die in the black robe he received in the novitiate. His desire was granted. When shots were fired into a pit, bullets hit his left side. He still managed to lift himself and say with a faint voice: "All for Christ, the King. Long live Poland".

W.-J. v. 5, p. 92. Bogdan Nowak in the Jewish "Folks-Sztyme", Feb. 20, 1982, art. "Father Adam Saves Jewish Children".

703. *Some place in Poland.* Renia Kukielke, in her book **Escape from the Pit**, N.Y. 1947, related the story of a Catholic **Polish woman**, hung by the Germans together with her **two children**, for hiding a former Jewish employer of hers. In numerous Jewish accounts from the first years after the war, there are many similar stories of heroic Christians who gave their lives to save the Jews. However, with the sacral version of the Jewish tragedy in Europe in the form of the "holocaust", such stories are gradually being replaced by a torrent of vituperations directed at the Catholic Church.

Ph.F. p. 185.

SCOTLAND

704. Miss Hannig of the Scotch Mission in Budapest was deported to KL Auschwitz for having sheltered seventeen Jewish children and forty adults in the headquarters of the Baptized Jews. She didn't come back.

Ph.F. p. 89.

SWEDEN

705. A Swedish diplomat in Budapest, **Raoul Wallenberg**, carried out fantastic activity on behalf of Jews with the aid of

powerful financial resources. He was taken by the Soviet authorities to Lubianka prison in Moscow and probably died there.

Ph. F. p. 159-60.

UKRAINE

706. Blagodatnoye, oblast Dnepropetrovsk. 1941. The activity of German squads which killed Ukrainians who dared to
shelter Jews was known to the collective farm bookkeeper, **Pa-
vel S. Zirchenko**. However, he didn't betray to the Germans
seven Jewish families from Ordzhonikidze who were seeking
refuge there. Protected by him, the Jews worked on the farm
until they were liberated on Nov. 22, 1943. That is how the families of Trayberg, Nukhimovich, Babsky, Gontov, Pereseds-
ky and Shabis were saved – thirty people in all.

E.-G. p. 366-7.

707. Kiev. An **Ukrainian** lady married a Jew. When he
was being led to the cemetery to be shot, she did not permit
him go without her. "We were together in the days of joy",
she said, "and I won't abandon you now". They perished together.

E.-G. p. 6.

708. Odessa, Crimea (1). October 1941. An Ukrainian engineer, **Leonid Suvorovskyi**, not only warned his Jewish ac-
quaintances not to register as Jews, but took them into his
apartment, gave them false passports and, with the help of his
friends, concealed and fed 22 Jewish families. To cover this expense, he distributed newspapers and even sold his own clothes. On the eve of his arrest by the German-Rumanian authorities, he managed to provide a fresh refuge for Jewish families.

E.-G. p. 90.

709. Odessa, Crimea (2). October 1941. "**Andrey Iwano-vich Lapin** and **Varvara**, his wife, were an old couple who hid Jewish children in their rooms. When the danger of detection became too obvious, Mrs. Lapin sent the children to a safe place in the countryside. Arrested, Varvara refused to reveal their location and was shot".

E.-G. p. 90.

II. JEWISH RESPONSE
TO THE HOLOCAUST

ENGLAND

710. London. May 13, 1943. Thirteen days after the futile Bermuda Conference, when it became clear that all the appeals of the Polish and Jewish Underground for aid to Jews were doomed because of the indifference of the free world, including the international Jewry, **Szmul Zygielbojm**, a member of the Polish National Council-in-exile, committed suicide as a protest against man's inhumanity towards other human beings. The memoirs of Prof. Hirszfeld show that the remaining Polish Jewry had the same grievance against their coreligionists in free countries and the same objections were expressed in the last three telegrams Zygielbojm received from his constituency in Warsaw on April 20, April 28, and May 11, 1943.

W.-Z. p. 196-8.

GREECE

711. On June 30, 1944, a group of four hundred and six young Jews from Salonica, selected by the SS to serve as a Sonderkommando in undressing the other Jews and pushing them into the gas chambers, decided to disobey German orders and were burned in the furnaces of Auschwitz.

Report of Raoul Saporta in the Tel Aviv Museum of Combatants and Partisans "Bulletin", September 1980, p. 55.

LITHUANIA

712. Kaunas. During the liquidation of the Kaunas ghetto, Germans set fire to the Jewish hospital for communicable diseases. **Dr. Dawidowicz** voluntarily remained with his patients and, together with them, was consumed by fire.

R.P. p. 27.

PALESTINE

713. Four years before its formal birth, Israel, with a Jewish population of 550,000, supplied a total of **thirty-two volunteers** willing to risk their lives in order to arouse the spirit of resistance among 250,000 Hungarian Jews, still awaiting deportation to KL Auschwitz. The aircraft carrying the Jewish parachutists, was piloted by a Polish airman over the enemy territory. **Eight** of the Jewish volunteers were killed; among them, **Hannah Senesh**, 23, executed November 6, 1944, **Reuben Dafni** and **Joel Nussbecker**. Thousands of Jews, who had enrolled in Gen. Anders' Army in order to leave the Soviet Union, preferred to remain in Palestine, including the Premier of Israel, Menachem Begin, who requested and obtained permission from Gen. Leopold Okulicki to stay away from the German front.

R.H. p. 543.

POLAND

714. Będzin (1), Sosnowiec county, voivodship of Katowice. To counteract the lies of Moses Merin which were designed to bring the Jewish community into submission to German orders, **Rabbi Bunin** alerted the Jews of the town that the alleged "resettlement scheme" proposed by Merin in fact meant extermination in a death camp. For that, he and his sons were denounced to the Gestapo. On his way to death, Rabbi Bunin put on his "gartel", mindful of the old Maimonides maxim: "Let all be killed, they shouldn't deliver one Jewish soul".

M.S. p. 121.

715. Będzin (2), Sosnowiec county, voivodship of Katowice. When the sisters of **Rabbi Yosef Kanel** were arrested by the order of the Jewish Council and the Rabbi received a proposal that two other girls be substituted in their place, if only he would join the infamous Jewish Council and its treacherous leader Moldetsky, the proposal was rejected. The Rabbi went to death with his sisters. Criminal Moldetsky was later killed in Israel by some of the surviovors for his part in making Będzin "Judenfrei".

P.W. Płowa bestia (The Blonde Beast) München, 1948. M.S. p. 122.

716. Kalisz, voivodship of Poznań. A community leader, **Rabbi Yosef Haber,** appointed by the Gestapo to the post of a "Kapo" (foreman) in a forced labor camp, refused to strike his exhausted workers. For this disobedience, he had his hands nailed to a table. He died in terrible pain.

M.S. p. 81.

717. Kielce. In a Jewish educational institution, the German SS-men tried to force a **Jewish educator** to undress the children before they were to be pushed into a ditch full of hot quicklime. She refused and was shot to death before being pushed into the ditch herself.

R.P. p. 44.

718. Przemyśl. Three Jewish freedom fighters, **Krebs, Grund** and **Grum,** voluntarily surrendered themselves into

German hands in order to save the lives of fifty hostages who were to be killed if they were not found. All three were murdered.

R.P. p. 55.

719. Równe, voivodship of Wołyń. During the extermination of Jews, **Rabbi Majufes** was offered a chance of rescue, but declined, saying: "A shephard should die with his sheep".

R.P. p. 46.

720. Stanisławów. February 1943. **Artur Safrin**, who was providing Jews with false identification cards, was denounced to the Gestapo by one of his clients and arrested. After he escaped and was hiding with his Christian friends, a Gestapo man named Mauser arrested the family of his fiancee, Elza Kostman, in his place. Arrested again and tortured, he refused to point out his Christian friends who furnished him with materials needed for false identification cards. He was shot to death.

S.D.T. p. 147. Also, M. Lieberman in "Yad Vashem Studies" March 1964, p. 64.

721. Warsaw (1) July 23, 1942. President of the Jewish Council, **Dr. Adam Czerniakow**, who initially disregarded warnings from the Polish Underground and issued orders to the Jewish Police that 6,000 Ghetto dwellers be delivered into German hands, took his own life when the daily quota was raised to 7,000. His last message to Mrs. Czerniakow was: "I couldn't kill my people with my own hands". His successor, M. Lichtenbaum, didn't entertain such scruples. On July 25, 1942 the Jewish Police caught and delivered 7,000 and on July 25, 1942 started to deliver them at a rate of 10,000 a day, sometimes even exceeding this number. An average Jewish policeman sent to their death two thousand Jews, just to save his own life.

W.-Z. p. 93, 98, 101, etc.

722. Warsaw (2). April 20, 1943. To save a group of his compatriots from being mowed down by a German machine gun while running across the street, **Michał Klepfisz** stepped in front of its nozzle and took the entire burst of bullets into his body. The Supreme Polish Commander, Gen. Sikorski, in recognition of this act of heroism awarded him the Virtuti Militari Cross (Poland's highest military honor) and both events were broadcast immediately by radio from London, in order to lift the spirits of Warsaw Ghetto defenders. This decision was officially confirmed by Sikorski's successor, **Gen. Sosnkowski**, in the order no. 159/GWN of February 2, 1944, registered in the Official Journal on May 15, 1944.

Testimony of Dr. Edelman in H. K. p. 85. B.-L. p. 1017.

723. Warsaw (3). May 31, 1943. **David Hochberg** was so young that his mother had strictly forbidden him to join the fighting organization. But in the ghetto he was a group commander in charge of a bunker. When Germans approached one of the narrow passages while pursuing his group, he stripped himself of his weapons and wedged himself between the walls in order to stop the Germans with his dead body. By the time they managed to pry his body riddled with bullets from their path, the Jewish fighters escaped.

B.G. p. 199.

724. Warsaw (4). Three Rabbis, **Manachem** Zemba, **Shimson Stockhamer** and **D. Shapiro**, refused to accept the generous offer from the Catholic Archbishop's Chancery in Warsaw to be smuggled out into a safe hiding place at a time when thousands of priests and bishops were dying in German concentration camps. The offer was accepted by one, while the others contemptuously rejected brotherly aid from the Catholic side preferring to die with their flock.

M.S. p. 34.

725. Warsaw (5). **Dr. Helena Rabinowicz** voluntarily went to death with her nurses when their hospial was liquidated, although she could claim immunity as an employee of the Jewish Council.

L.H. p. 287.

726. Warsaw (6). **Dr. Józef Stein** and **Dr. Hellerowa** refused to seek refuge on the "Aryan" side and died together with their patients.

L.H. p. 325.

727. Warsaw (7), Among thousands of helpless Jewish victims driven by their own police to death trains destined for Treblinka, one group of neatly dressed children was headed by **Dr. Janusz Korczak**, 64, in his Polish Major's uniform. He refused to be spirited away by the Polish underground. His closest co-worker, **Stefania Wilczyńska**, and some other associates made the same decison. Wilczyńska woke up all the children in the morning and prepared them, as if they were going on a picnic. The educators were seen carrying small orphans in their arms and leading the others, to save them horrors of being beaten and pushed into the cars by force.

W.-Z. p. 108, 356-7. M.J. p. 207.

728. Warsaw (8). **Mrs. Grynberg** obtained a shelter with a Catholic family for her child, but, as a nurse, remained and perished with her patients.

L.H. p. 297.

729. Wilno. July 16, 1943. "The most tragic chapter in the annals of the Holocaust" occurred when the Jewish UPO (United Partisan Organization) convinced their own commander, **Ichok Wittenberg**, that the majority of the ghetto population wanted his surrender to the Gestapo. Surrounded by Jewish Polise, he was delivered ino German hands, but succee-

Icchak Wittenberg, commander of Wilno Ghetto resistance unit, agreed to be extradited into the hands of Gestapo under the pressure of frightened ghetto population, thus preventing severe reprisals. (See case no. 729).

Michał Klepfisz, trained by Polish underground in making explosives, jumped in front of a machine gun to save his companiona, decorated by Gen. Sikorski with the *Virtuti Military* cross. (See case no. 722).

Adam Czerniaków, Chairman of the Warsaw Judenrat, gave his life to avoid dispatching his fellow Jews to Treblinka at a rate of ten thousand a day. (See case no. 721).

Szmul Zygielbojm, member of the Polish National Council-in-exile, offered his life to awake conscience of the West, including Western Jewry, to the tragedy of Shoah. (See case no. 710).

ded in putting an end to his life by swallowing poison, in order not to betray his companions under the stress of tortures.

Dr. Mark Dworzecki in "They Fought Back" by Yuri Suhr, p. 169-72. R.P. p. 122.

RUMANIA

730. Braila (1). Febuar 12, 1942. After being brought to the execution place with **his wife, Barbara**, an Elderly of the Jewish community, **Joseph Kulik** suddenly received permission to go home. His wife wanted him to take advantage of this unexpected lease on live, but her husband made his own decision. Turning to the Germans he said: "You already killed two thousand of my people and there is nothing left for me as the Elderly of my community". He was shot together with his wife.

E.-G. p. 47.

731. Braila (2). February 12, 1942. **Yakov Vladimir** refused to be exempted from a general execution of the Jewish population on account of his skill as a tailor. He died with his daughter and his grandchildren, rejecting the notion that individual life is the value to be preserved at all costs.

E.-G. p. 41, 48.

732. Braila (3). February 12, 1942. Eighty-year old **Chaim Arn** successfully evaded a search by German police by hiding in a cellar for half a day. When he saw the street full of Jews who were taken for execution, he went to get a scroll of the Torah and with the Holy Script in his arms, he begged the German executioners to be permitted to take it to his grave. He was shot in the open pit embracing the Torah.

E.-G. p. 48.

UKRAINE

733. Niemirov. February 2, 1943. During the deportation of Jews to a place of execution, an **eighteen–year old girl** begged to die with her mother. Her request was granted and she boarded the sleigh which was taking persons selected for execution by the Germans. Gripped, however, with a sudden fear, she wanted to change her mind, but was not permitted and was driven to her death.

E.G. p. 105.

734. Rostov-on-Don. August 11, 1942. A Jewish lady, **Yekatierina Leontyeva**, 82, stayed with two former nuns who loved her and took care of her. „I will not go anywhere", she said, „let the Germans come here and kill me". When, however, she heard that, if discovered, both nuns would be killed too, she left her shelter and surrendered herself into German hands.

E.G. p. 259.

Addenda to
CHRISTIAN RESPONSE TO THE HOLOCAUST

BYELORUSSIA

735. Mińsk. July 21, 1941. The German SS-men ordered 30 Byelorussians to cover with earth a pit with Jewish bodies, some of them still alive. After they refused, all were machinegunned by the German soldiers.

M.G. p. 172.

FRANCE
736. Ville-La-Grande, between Paris and Lyons. **Marianne Cohn** caught while accompanying a group of Jewish children, refused to be freed as an "Aryan" and was executed.

M. G. p. 700.

POLAND

737. Kobryń (3) Brześć nad Bugiem county, voivodship of Białystok. October 21, 1942. **Two peasant families** were massacred by the Germans for "maintaining contacts with Jewish partisans."

M. G. p. 481.

738. Lwów, May 1942. For organizing aid to persecuted Jews, **Regina Barbara Wilczur** was arrested by the Germans and executed together with 9 other Polish women in the forest near Lesienice.

Testimony of Jacek E. Wilczur in Polityka, Oct. 25, 1986.

739. Wola Przemykowska, Brzesko county, voivodsship of Kraków. **Tadeusz Jeż** was shot to death for sheltering a lewish child. The father of the child survived and settled in Kraków under the name of J. Długowiejski.

W.-Z. p. 447.

740. Raduń, Lida county, voivodship of Nowogródek. May 8, 1942. Rebellious **grave-diggers** who refused to dig pits for Jews who were still alive, were killed on the spot.

M. G. p. 335.

UKRAINE

741. Kremenchug, near Poltava. Jan. 16, 1942. The Einsatz Kommando shot to death a Red Army officer, **Major Senitsa Vershovsky**, because "he tried to protect the Jews."

M.G. p. 290.

Addenda to JEWISH RESPONSE TO THE HOLOCAUST

742. Baranowicze, voivodship of Nowogródek. 1942. Chairman of the Jewish Council, **Joshnua Izykson**, and his secretary, Genia Men, refused to draw a list of sick and old Jews and to deliver it for the feat of Purim to the Gestapo, and were shot by the Germans.

M. G. p. 298.

743. Białystok (1) June, 1943. A Jewish clandestine agent, **Lonka Kozibrodzka**, was caught by the Germans disguised as a Polish girl, but didn't disclose anybody's identity; sent to Auschwitz, she shared the fate of Polish inmates marked for the labor camps, prison, ill-treatment and death.

M. G. p. 552.

744. Białystok (2) 1943. **Yitzhack Malmed** managed to escape from German hands, but when the Gestapo threatened to kill 5 thousand Jews for him, surrendered himself and was hung at the gate to the ghetto suspended there for three days.

M. G. p. 535.

745. Biłgoraj, voivodship of Lublin. May 3, 1942. Vice-chairman of the Jewish Council, **Hillel Janower** and three other members of the Council, **Szymon Bin, Shmuel Leib,** and **Ephraim Waksschul**, were shot to death by the Germans for a refusal to compile a list of Jews for deportation fo KL Bełżec.

M. G. p. 331.

746. Dąbrowa Górnicza, voivodship of Katowice. May 5, 1942. Chairman of the Jewish Council, **Adolf Weinberg**, who refused to issue a list of candidates for "resettlement" was himself deported with his entire family.

M. G. p. 331.

747. Hrubieszów, voivodship of Lublin. Dec. 3, 1939. Young Jewish boy, named **Loewenberg** while seeing his father led for execution approached the German guards with words: Leave my father alone, I will take his place. Both were taken away and shot to death.

M. G. p. 104.

748. Iwie, Jasło county, voivodship of Rzeszów. Two Jewish Council members, **Shalom Żak** and **Bezalel Mil-**

kowski, took off their Council member armbands and joined other deportees to their death.

M. G. p. 331.

749. Kałuszyn, Mińsk Mazowiecki county, voivodship of Warsaw. Sept. 25, 1942. Chairman of the Jewish Council, **Abraham Gamz**, refused to supply the Germans with a list of Jews for deportation from the ghetto and was shot in his own house.

M. G. p. 467.

750. Kamień Koszyrski, Pińsk county, voivodship of Polesie. August 1941. Chairman of the Jewish Council, **Shmuel Werble**, delivered to Germans the list of 80 Jews, but when he realized that its purpose was to have them killed, joined them and was shot as the 81st.

M. G. p. 181.

751. Lwów (1) June 1941. Editor of a Jewish newspaper "Opinia", **Yekeskel Lewin**, while returning from the palace of Metropolitan Szeptycki, was warned by his Christian friends not to enter his home, ignored the warning and was promptly arrested and shot in jail.

M. G. p. 164.

752. Lwów (2) Four members of the Jewish Council, **Eberson** – the chairman, **Marclei Buber, Oswald Kimmelman** and **Jakub Chigier**, were murdered for not complying with the German wishes.

M. G. p. 532.

753. Łachwa, Pińsk county, voivodship of Polesie. September 4, 1942. A member of the Jewish Council, **Yisrael Dubski**, refused to cooperate with the preparation of Jewish lists, and was shot by the Germans.

M. G. p. 446.

754. Łomża, voivodship of Białystok. November 1942. A member of the Jewish Council, **Dr. Joseph Hepner**, committed suicide "rather than cooperate with the Nazis in the extermination of Jews".

M. G. p. 489.

755. Łuck, voivodship of Wołyń. June 26, 1941. **Dr. Benjamin From** 47 was shot by the Germans for disobeying order to discontinue an operation on a Christian woman which was already in progress. His entire family was killed with him.

M. G. p. 157.

756. Międzyrzec, Radzyń Podlaski county, voivodship of Lublin. Chairman of the Jewish Council, **Abraham Schwetz**, committed suicide after the Germans ordered him to deliver 100 Jews for deportation.

M. G. p. 181.

757. Mołczadz, Słonim county, voivodship of Polesie. July 15, 1942. Chairman of the Jewish Council, **Ehrlich**, and a Council member, **Leib Gilerowicz**, urged German authority not to embark on the "resetlement" scheme which served only to cover extermination of Jews. Both were beaten and killed for that.

M. G. p. 380.

758. Ozorków Łęczyca county, voivodship of Łódź. May 22, 1942. **Mania Rzepkowicz** rejected the offer of being exempt from deportation as a secratary of the Jewish Council and joined the transport of some 300 Jewish children sent to the death camp of Chełmno.

M. G. p. 350.

759. Piotrków Trybunalski, (1) voivodship of Łódź. Sept. 13, 1941. After all Jewish Council members were arrested for cooperation with the Jewish undergroung, **Jakub Berliner**

who accidentally was not arrested surrendered himself "out of loyalty to his comrades".

M. G. p. 193.

760. Piotrków Trybunalski, (2) voivodship of Łódź. October 14, 1942. A Jewish baker, **Yehuda Russak,** was shot because he refused to abandon his paralysed wife.

M. G. p. 482.

761. Równe, voivodship of Wołyń. **August 1941. A** member of the Jewish Council, **Jakub Sucharczyk** appealed to his colleagues not to submit to the Germans any lists of Jews. When overruled, he committed suicide. So did the chairman, **Dr. Bergman**.

M. G. p. 181.

762. Szczebrzeszyn, Zamość county, voivodship of Lublin. May 1942. A Jewish Council member, **Hersz Getzel Eichbaum,** on learning that none of those listed for "resettlement" survived, told his colleagues that he will not serve as a dispatcher of Jewish people to their death and himself in his attic.

M. G. p. 331.

763. Warsaw (1) October 1939. Among the four Polish citizens executed by the Germans for possession of arms one was listed as "a Jew, **Samson Litsenberg**".

M. G. p. 95.

764. Warsaw (2) April 17, 1941. Ringelblum recorded in his notes that a Jewish policemen from Łódź, named Ginsberg, who asked a German guard to give back potatoes taken from a Jew, was knocked to the ground, stabbed and shot.

M. G. p. 148.

765. Warsaw (3) April 17, 1942. A Jewish baker, **Dawid Blajwas** was shot by the Germans together with his wife who ran after him.

M. G. p. 324.

766. Wilno (1) December 21, 1941. Sister of Reuben Ainsztein, Mania Liffe, saw **a Jewish woman** giving a piece of bread to a Soviet prisoner of war being shot, together with him, by a German soldier.

M. G. p. 246.

767. Wilno (2) September 14, 1943. Chairman of the Jewish Council, **Jakub Gens**, who sent to their deaths thousands of Jews in hope to save the others, refused to flee from the Ghetto saying that "thousands of Jews would pay for this with their lives". He made a visit to the Gestapo and never returned.

M. G. p. 608.

768. Wilno (3) For his refusal to coperate in the extermination of Jews, **Dr. J. Wygodzki** was killed by the Germans.

C. Ma. p. 386.

769. Włodawa, voivodship of Lublin. June 7, 1942. A **Jewish young man**, in order to save a local Rabbi from arrest, pretended that he is the rabbi. Germans, however, saw through the deception, found the real Rabbi and shot them both.

M. G. p. 362.

770. Włodzimierz, voivodship of Wołyń. September 1942. A member of the Jewish Council, **Jakub Kogen**, after realizing that seven thousand Jews demanded by the Germans, would be killed, committed suicide together with his wife and a 13-years old son. He didn't want to cooperate in the extermination of Jews.

M. G. p. 440.

771. Zduńska Wola (1), voivodship of Łódź. Feast of Purim 1942. Chairman of the Jewish Council, **Dr. Jakub Lemberg**, when ordered by the Germans to deliver 10 Jews to be hung in memory of biblical Haman's ten sons hung by Mordecai's orders replied that the only Jews he will deliver will be four: himself, his wife and his two children. All were killed at the order of Hans Biebow in Łódź.

M. G. p. 299.

772. Zduńska Wola (2), voivodship of Łódź. Feast of Purim 1942. **Shlomo Żelechowski** when brought with other Jews to be hung in memory of Haman's sons, lifted his arms to heaven and cried that "Jehovah is God".

M. G. p. 350.

UKRAINE

773. Dubosary, near Poltava. September 1941. Three **Berenboim** brothers, **Itzhok, Idel** and **Moshe**, together with **Dr. Fain, Peisakh, Glimberg** and **Sara Skolnik**, were hung in the market, because they refused to serve in the Jewish Council.

M. G. p. 188. C. Ma. T. 2, 735.

READERS' LETTERS

POLISH RIGHTEOUS GENTILES

To the Editor of The Jerusalem Post

Sir, – Having come to Israel for the Tel Aviv celebration of the Righteous Gentiles, I read with interest Ernie Meyer's article "The making of a Righteous Gentile" in your magazine of January 16. Especially interesting for me were the remarks of Dr. Paldiel about the liberal interpretation of the clause contained in the Knesset law of 1953 in awarding Yad Vashem medals to those German, Dutch or Danish rescuers who didn't exactly "risk their lives" – the death penalty for aiding Jews in any form being promulgated and mercilessly enforced only in Poland.

In my book, *Martyrs of Charity*, to be published in Washington, D.C. on June 1, 1987, I have assembled 749 cases of executions involving over 3,000 Christians, some of them described in the Yad Vashem bulletin and Szymon Datner's *Forest of the Just* in 1968, more than 90 per cent of them concerning Polish Catholics, 22 of them priests.

Dr. Paldiel is right in stating that Poland was "slower" than other countries, especially the Netherlands, in getting the awards. Thousands of Polish rescuers were killed, burned alive and executed together with the Jews they were trying to save, and there was nobody left alive to testify at Yad Vashem about their noble deeds.

However, it is hard to explain the delay in actual delivery of the medals after they were awarded. The last batch of over 100 have been awaiting delivery to Poland since June 1985, while many persons involved, among them my sister Mary Janiak, have died in the meantime, either on account of injuries received, or old age. Even the rescuers of such well-known personalities as Zivia Lubetkin, "Antek" Cukierman and Abba Kovner had to wait until almost their last days for official recognition.

W. ZAJACZKOWSKI
Jerusalem (Washington, D.C.)

THE JERUSALEM

POST

PUBLISHED DAILY IN JERUSALEM

Feb. 1, 1987

Dear Dr. Zajaczkowski

Here is a brief note to restore your faith in mankind and in the integrity of The Jerusalem Post. I'm enclosing some copies of your letter as it appeared today. As I explained to you, I have no control over whether – and when – a letter appears.

But your letter made a valid and interesting point – and here it is.

I'm looking forward to receiving your book and welcome you on your next visit here.

With kindest regards

yours

Ernie Meyer

Head Office: The Jerusalem Post Building, Romema, Jerusalem 91000
P.O.B. 81 / Tel. 551616 / Telex 26121/2
Tel Aviv 61201 / 11 Rehov Carlebach / P.O.B. 20126 / Tel. 294222 / Telex 341767
Haifa 31047 / 16 Rehov 'Nordau / P.O.B. 4810 / Tel. 645444 / Telex 46838

BIBLIOGRAPHICAL REFERENCES

Abbrev.

J.A.   Aleksandrowicz, Julian. *Kartki z dziennika doktora Twardego*, Kraków: Wydawnictwo Literackie, 1967; p. 236.

A.-B.   Arczyński, Marek and Wiesław Balcarek, *Kryptonim "Żegota"*, Warszawa: Czytelnik, 1979, 257 p. illus.

L.B.   Bartelski, Lesław M. *Pamięć żywa*, Warszawa: Wyd. Szkolne i Pedagogiczne, 1977, 302 p.

W.B.   Bartoszewski, Władysław. *Straceni na ulicach miasta*, Warszawa: Książka i Wiedza, 1970, 173 p.

B.-L.   Bartoszewski, Władysław and Zofia Lewin, eds. *Ten jest z Ojczyzny mojej: Wspomnienia z lat 1939-1945*, 2nd ed. Kraków: Znak, 1969. 1109 p. maps.

T.B.   Bednarczyk, Tadeusz, *Obowiązek silniejszy od śmierci: Wspomnienia z lat 1939-1945; O polskiej pomocy dla Żydów*, Warszawa: Krajowa Agencja Wydawnicza, 1982, 161 p. maps.

T.Bi.   Bida, Tadeusz, *Assistance to Jewish Population in South-Eastern Poland*, 13 p. (Paper read at the scientific session of GKBZH in Warsaw, April 14 - 17, 1983).

B.-R.   Berenstein, Tatiana and Adam Rutkowski, *Pomoc Żydom w Polsce, 1939-1945*, Warszawa: Polonia, 1963, 151 p. illus.

C.-G.   Cynarski, Stanisław and Józef Garbacik, *Jasło oskarża*, Warszawa: Książka i Wiedza, 1973, 342 p. illus.

J.Cz.   Czerwiński, Józef. *Z wołyńskich lasów na berliński trakt*, Warszawa: MON, 1972, 301 p.

S.D.   Datner, Szymon. *Las sprawiedliwych*, Warszawa: Książka i Wiedza, 1968, 117 p.

S.D.T. Datner, Szymon. *Tragedia w Doessel*, Warszawa: Książka Wiedza, 1970, 329 p.

L.D.   Dusza, Ludwik. *Kryptonim "Nadleśnictwo 14"*, Warszawa: Ludowa Spółdzielnia Wydawnicza, 1981, 306 p.

L.S.D. Dawidowicz, Lucy S. *The War against the Jews: 1933-1945*, N.Y.: Bantam Books, 1976, 610 p.

E.-G.   Ehrenburg, Ilya and Vasily Grosman. *The Black Book*, New York: Holocaust Library, 1983.

R.E.   Einsztein, Reuben. *Jewish Resistance*, New York: Barnes and Noble, 1974.

J.F.   Fajkowski, Józef. *Wieś w ogniu,* Warszawa: Ludowa Spółdzielnia Wydawnicza, 1972, 512 p.

F.-R.   Fajkowski, Józef and Jan Religa. *Zbrodnie hitlerowskie na wsi polskiej, 1939-1945.* Warszawa: Książka i Wiedza, 1981, 656 p. illus.

E.F.   Fąfara, Eugeniusz. *Gehenna ludności żydowskiej,* Warszawa: Ludowa Spółdzielnia Wydawnicza, 1983, 671 p.

T.F.   Frącek, Teresa. *Zgromadzenie Sióstr Franciszkanek Rodziny Marii w latach 1939-1945,* Warszawa: Akademia Teologii Katolickiej, 1978 (Dissert.).

Ph.F.   Friedman, Philip. *Their Brother's Keepers,* New York: Crown, 1957, 224 p.

R.G.   Gicewicz, Ryszard. *Obóz pracy w Poniatowej, 1941-1943,* in *Zeszyty Majdanka,* t. 10. Lublin; Wydawnictwo Lubelskie, 1980, 224 p.

M.G.   Gilbert, Martin. *The Holocaust.* New York: Holt, Rinehard and Winston, 1985, 959 p.

B.G.   Goldstein, Bernard. *The Stars Bear Witness,* N.Y.: Viking, 1949, 265 p.

GKBZH   Główna Komisja Badania Zbrodni Hitlerowskich. Bielawski,
WB.   Wacław and Czesław Pilichowski. *Zbrodnie dokonane na Polakach przez hitlerowców za pomoc udzielaną Żydom,* Warszawa: 1981, 78 p. facsims.

S.G.   Goszczurny, Stanisław. *Mord w lesie Kociewskim,* Warszawa: Książka i Wiedza, 1973.

Ph.H.   Hallie, Philip. *Lest Innocent Blood Be Shed,* New York: Harper and Row, 1979, 352 p.

F.H.   Heer, Friedrich. *God's First Love: Christians and Jews Over Two Thousand Years,* Tr. from the German by G. Skelton, New York: Weybright and Talley, 1970, 530 p.

R.H.   Hilberg, Raoul. *The Destruction of the European Jews,* Chicago: Quadrangle Books, 1967, 610 p.

L.H.   Hirszfeld, Ludwik. *Historia jednego życia,* Warszawa: PAX, 1967, 387 p.

R.Hr.   Hrabar, Roman. *Na rozkaz i bez rozkazu,* Katowice: Śląsk, 1968, 275 p.

I.J.A.   Institute of Jewish Affairs. *Hitler's Ten-year War on the Jews,* New York: 1943, 311 p.

I.O.   Iranek-Osmecki, Kazimierz. *Kto ratuje jedno życie. Polacy i Żydzi, 1939-1945,* London: Orbis, 1968, 323 p. maps, tables.

J.-W.   Jacewicz, Wiktor and Jan Woś. *Martyrologium polskiego duchowieństwa rzymsko-katolickiego, 1933-1945,* Warszawa: Akademia Teologii Katolickiej, 1977-81, 5 vols.

A.J.   Jankowski, Andrzej. *Pacification of Villages in Kielce-Radom. Religion as a form of extermination of the Polish population.* International Scientific Session on Nazi Genocide, Warsaw, April 14-17, 1981. 13 p.

M.J.   Jaworski, M. *Janusz Korczak*, Warsaw: Interpress, 1977, 204 p.

A.J.   Jedynak, Rev. Andrzej, Master's thesis for the Academy of Catholic Theology (typescript).

L.K.   Kaczanowski, Longin. *Zagłada Michniowa*, Warszawa: Ludowa Spółdzielnia Wydawnicza, 1980, 211 p.

L.K.H.   Kaczanowski, Longin. *Hitlerowskie fabryki śmierci na kielecczyznie*, Warszawa: Książka i Wiedza, 1984, 230 p.

A.M.K.   Kaim, Anton-Maria. *Die Judenretter aus Deutschland*, Mainz: Matthias Grünewald Verlag, 1983, 160 p.

M.K.   Kann, Maria. *Niebo nieznane*, Warszawa: MON, 1964, 217 p.

J.K.   Kazimierski, Józef. *Dzieje Sokołowa Podlaskiego i jego regionu*, Warszawa: Państwowe Wydawnictwo Naukowe, 1982, 349 p. illus.

A.K.   Korsak, Andrzej. *Akcja Żegota na terenie powiatu nowosądeckiego*, in *WTK*, 1972, no. 47.

K.-M.   Kowalczyk, Józef and Waldemar Monkiewicz. *Die Bevölkerung des Raums von Białystok angesichts der hitlerfaschistischen Ausrottung der jüdischen Bevölkerung, 1939-1944*, 13 p. (Paper read at the scientific session of GKBZH in Warsaw, April 14 – 17, 1983).

T.K.   Kowalski, Tadeusz. *Obozy hitlerowskie w Polsce Południowo-Wschodniej, 1939-1945*, Warszawa: Książka i Wiedza, 1973, 256 p.

H.K.   Krall, Hanna. *Zdążyć przed Panem Bogiem*, Kraków: Wydawnictwo Literackie, 1979, 111 p.

Ch.L.   Lazar, Chaim. *Muranowska 7*, Tel-Aviv: Massada, 1966, 341 p. illus.

S.L.   Lewandowska, Stanisława. *Ruch oporu na Podlasiu, 1939-45*, Warszawa: MON, 1982, 478 p.

M.L.   Libermann, M. and Arthur Safrin in *Yad Vashem Studies*, no. 14 (March 1964)

P.L.   Lapide, Pinchas E. *Three Popes and Jes.* New York: Hawthorn, 1967, 384 p.

S.Ł.   Łukasiewicz, Stanisław. *Okupacja*, Warszawa: Państwowe Wydawnictwo Naukowe, 1958, 431 p.

C.Ma.   Madejczyk, Czesław. *Faszyzm i okupacja, 1938-1945.* Wyd. Poznańskie, 1965.

Cz.M.   Madajczyk, Czesław. *Polityka III Rzeszy w okupowanej Polsce*, Warszawa, 1970, 2 vols.

Z.M.   Mańkowski, Zygmunt. *Między Wisłą a Bugiem, 1939-1945*, Lublin: Wydawnictwo Lubelskie, 1978, 471 p.

306   *Bibliographical references*

J.M.   Mirewicz, Rev. Jerzy, S.J., *Emigracyjne sprawy i spory*, Londyn, 1975, 288 p.
H.M.O.   Mortkowicz-Olczakowa, Hanna. *Janusz Korczak*, Warszawa: Czytelnik, 1978, 278 p. illus.
S.N.   Neszamit, Sarah. "Rescue in Lithuania during the Nazi Occupation" in *Rescue attempts during the Holocaust, Proceedings of the Second Yad Vashem International Conference, April 1974*, Jerusalem, 1977, p. 289-331.
A.P.   Paczkowski, Alfred. *Lekarz nie przyjmuje*, Warszawa: PAX, 1981, 271 p.
T.Pa.   Pankiewicz, Tadeusz. *Apteka w getcie krakowskim*, Kraków: Wydawnictwo Literackie, 1982.
J.P.   Pietrzykowski, Jan. *Walka i męczeństwo*. Warszawa: PAX, 1981, 159 p.
J.Pi.   Pietrzykowski, Jan. *Cień swastyki nad Jasną Górą*, Katowice: Śląski Instytut Naukowy, 1985, 244 p.
C.P.   Pilichowski, Czesław. *Dzieci i młodzież w latach drugiej wojny światowej*, Warszawa: Państwowe Wydawnictwo Naukowe, 1982, 611 p.
P.A.G.B.   Polish Association in Great Britain. *Jews in Poland, Yesterday and Today*, London: White Eagle, 1968, 88 p.
W.P.   Poterański, Władysław. *Getto warszawskie*, Warszawa: Książka i Wiedza, 1983, 91 p.
T.P.   Prekerowa, Teresa. *Konspiracyjna Rada Pomocy Żydom w Warszawie, 1942-1945*, Warszawa: Państwowy Instytut Wydawniczy, 1982, 483 p. illus.
H.R.   Rechowicz, Henryk. *Polska Partia Robotnicza w Śląsko-Dąbrowskim obwodzie*, Katowice: Śląski Instytut Naukowy, 1972.
E.R.   Ringelblum, Emanuel. *Kronika getta warszawskiego, 1939-1944*. Warszawa: Czytelnik, 1983, 641 p. illus.
R.-F.   Röhm, Eberhard and Jörg Fierfelder. *Evangelische Kirche zwischen Kreuz und Hakenkreuz*, Stuttgart: Calwer Verlag, 1981, 160 p. illus.
R.P.   *Ruch podziemny w ghettach i obozach*, Warszawa: Centralna Żydowska Komisja Historyczna, 1946, 213 p.
F.R.   Ryszka, Franciszek, *Sprawa polska i sprawy Polaków*, Warszawa, 1966.
R.S.   Sakowska, Ruta, ed. Archiwum Ringelbluma. *Ghetto warszawskie, lipiec 1942 – styczeń 1943*, Warszawa: Państwowe Wydawnictwo Naukowe – Żydowski Instytut Historyczny w Polsce, 1980, 411 p.
L.SCH.   Schmidt, Leokadia. *Cudem przeżyliśmy czas zagłady*, Kraków: Wydawnictwo Literackie, 1983, 33 p.

L.S.   Siemion, L. "Egzekucje na lubelszczyźnie" in *Zeszyty Majdanka,*
            Lublin, 1972.

W.S.   Smólski, Władysław. *Za to groziła śmierć,* Warszawa: Pax, 1981,
            326 p.

W. Sm.   Smólski, Władysław. *Zaklęte lata.* Warszawa , 1964.

M.S.   Shonfeld, Rabbi Moshe. *The Holocaust Victims Accuse,* New
            York: B'nei Yeshivos, 1977, 134 p. illus,.facsims.

A.S.   Stanisławski, Andrzej. *Pole śmierci,* Lublin: Wydawnictwo Lubel-
            skie, 1969, 276 p.

J.Sz.   Szczawiej, Jan. *Ciosy z lat walki, 1939-1945,* Warszawa: Ludowa
            Spółdzielnia Wydawnicza, 1975

T.Sz.   Szczechura, Tomasz. „Życie i zagłada Żydów w powiecie węgrow-
            skim", in *Biuletyn ŻIH,* nr. 105/Jan. – March 1978.

C.T.   Tomczyk, C. "Diecezja częstochowska w latach okupacji hit-
            lerowskiej, 1939-1945" in *Studia z historii Kościoła w Polsce,*
            T. 4, Warszawa: ATK 1978, 374 p.

J.T.   Tenenbaum, Joseph. *Race and Reich: The story of an epoch,* New
            York: Twayne, 1958, 554 p.

W.W.   Ważniewski, Władysław. *Na przedpolach stolicy,* Warszawa:
            MON, 1974, 557 p. illus.

S.W.   Wiesenthal, Simon. *The Murderers Among Us,* New York: Ban-
            tam Books, 1968, 346 p.

W.J.   Wilbik–Jagusztynowa, W. *Bataliony chłopskie na rzeszowszczy-
            źnie,* Warszawa: MON, 1973, p. 516. illus. maps.

J.W.   Wilczur, Jacek. *Do nieba nie można od razu,* Warszawa: Książka
            i Wiedza, 1961.

T.W.   Wroński, Tadeusz, *Kronika okupowanego Krakowa,* Kraków:
            Wydawnictwo Literackie, 1974, 562 p.

W.-Z.   Wroński, Stanisław and Maria Zwolak. *Polacy-Żydzi, 1939-1945;*
            Warszawa: Książka i Wiedza, 1971, 433 p. illus. maps. facsims.

K.W.   Wyczańska, Krystyna ed. *Harcerki, 1939-1945. Relacje i pamięt-
            niki,* Warszawa: PWN, 1985, 813 p. illus.

S.Z.   Zabierowski, Stanisław. *Rzeszowskie pod okupacją hitlerowską,*
            Warszawa: Książka i Wiedza, 1975, 440 p.

F.Z.W.   Ząbecki, Franciszek, in *Więź,* no. 4, 1972, p. 124 ss.

F.Z.   Ząbecki, Franciszek. *Wspomnienia dawne i nowe,* Warszawa:
            PAX, 1977.

W.Z.   Zajdler–Żarski, Władysław. *Martyrologia ludności żydowskiej
            i pomoc społeczeństwa polskiego.* Warszawa: Związek Bojowników
            o Wolność i Demokrację, 1968, 63 p.

Z.Z.   Zieliński, Zygmunt, ed. *Życie religijne w Polsce pod okupacją
            hitlerowską 1939-1945,* Warszawa: Ośrodek Dokumentacji i Stu-
            diów Społecznych, Warszawa, 1982, 1016 p.

PERSONAL INDEX
to the "Martyrs of Charity",
(with numbers indicating individual cases)